Q

Thomas
Reader

Q
Thomas
Reader

John S. Kloppenborg

Marvin W. Meyer

Stephen J. Patterson

Michael G. Steinhauser

SONOMA, CALIFORNIA

POLEBRIDGE PRESS

Library of Congress Cataloging-in-Publication Data
Q-Thomas reader by John S. Kloppenborg . . . [et al.].
    p.   cm.
  Includes English translations of the Gospel of Thomas and of the Q
passages in the Gospels of Matthew and Luke, as presented in: Q
parallels John S. Kloppenborg.   1988.
  Includes bibliographical references.
  ISBN 0-944344-11-9 : $14.95
  1. Q hypothesis (Synoptics criticism) 2. Gospel of Thomas-
Criticism, interpretation, etc. I. Kloppenborg, John S., 1951–
  II. Kloppenborg, John S., 1951–   Q parallels. III. Gospel of
Thomas. English
BS2555.2.Q2   1990
226'.066–dc20   90-30774
                                                     CIP

Printed in the United States of America

10   9   8   7   6   5   4

Contents

The Sayings Gospel Q

The Gospel of Thomas

Preface

The proposal to create the *Q–Thomas Reader* originated with the Board of Regents of Polebridge Press.

Inasmuch as translations of Q and Thomas were already being prepared for inclusion in the new edition of the New Testament Apocrypha, it was decided to make use of those translations as the basis for the *Reader*. John S. Kloppenborg, St. Michael's College, University of Toronto, had prepared the translation of Q, and Marvin W. Meyer, Chapman College, had finished work on a fresh translation of Thomas. Their translations form the body of the present work.

It was decided to print only a translation of Q, since the original language texts are readily available in John Kloppenborg's *Q Parallels*. But Thomas was a different matter. At the instigation of Marvin Meyer, the editors decided to include the Coptic text of Thomas for the benefit of those who wished to have the Coptic text at hand for comparison with the translation. The publisher and Prof. Meyer would like to thank Gawdat Gabra, Girgis Daoud Girgis, and Samiha Abd El Shaheed of the Coptic Museum in Cairo for kindly providing access to the Coptic manuscript of the Gospel of Thomas.

The Greek text of the three fragments of Thomas, Papyrus Oxyrhynchus 1, 654, and 655, is not printed because the Greek is so fragmentary. A reconstructed version of the Greek fragments is available in *Nag Hammadi Studies, XX,* edited by Bentley Layton (Leiden: Brill, 1989) 96–128; the texts were edited by Harry W. Attridge.

Stephen J. Patterson, Eden Theological Seminary, is responsible for the introduction to Thomas. He has also assisted Marvin Meyer with certain translation problems.

The introduction to Q was written by Michael G. Steinhauser, Toronto School of Theology.

The suggestions for reading were prepared by John Kloppenborg and Stephen Patterson, as was the glossary. The table of Q–Thomas parallels was taken from Patterson's forthcoming book: *The Gospel of Thomas and the Jesus Tradition.*

Robert W. Funk, Publisher
Polebridge Press

vi

Foreword

Q and the Gospel of Thomas are two examples of sayings gospels that have survived. And even they were lost until modern times.

Copies of Q must have existed in the last half of the first century c.e., long enough to have been used by the authors of Matthew and Luke, after which time these canonical gospels supplanted Q, and Q was lost from sight. The fact that there had once been such a text was first rediscovered in 1838, when it was sensed to lie imbedded in the New Testament itself by a scholar trying to explain the striking agreements between Matthew and Luke.

The Gospel of Thomas was apparently rather widely known in early Christianity. Like many other early Christian gospels, however, it was not included in the group that was eventually included in the New Testament. Almost a century ago Greek fragments of three copies of the Gospel of Thomas emerged from the dry sands of Egypt, and almost a half century ago a complete copy, though translated from Greek into Coptic, also came to light there. Hence the Gospel of Thomas has really been available for study for only a single generation.

The four canonical gospels are all narrative in cast; they are quasi-biographical, in story form. The sayings gospel, on the other hand, is limited to collections of sayings, much like the book of Proverbs, with only an occasional brief narrative that provides a setting for a saying that would otherwise lose its point.

The sayings gospel imbedded in the New Testament is quite appropriately called a gospel, in that the verb "evangelize," from which the noun "gospel" is derived, actually occurs at Q 7:22: "the poor are given good news" (the "good news" is another way to way to express the term "gospel"). Matthew seems already to have recognized "gospel" as an appropriate designation for Q, in that in Matt 4:23 and 9:35, just before and after the most prominent part of Q (what we call the Sermon on the Mount), Jesus' activity is summarized as "teaching in their synagogues and preaching the 'gospel' of the kingdom and healing every disease and infirmity." Similarly, the verb used here in Matthew, "preaching," echoes the noun "kergyma," from the same stem, which is used in Q 11:32 to refer to what Jesus was doing as greater than "the 'preaching' of

Jonah." It would hence be inappropriate to continue referring to Q as just a sayings source behind the canonical gospels, in that Q understood itself and was understood by Matthew to be a gospel in its own right.

Texts in antiquity were often composed without titles. They were referred to simply by allusion to the opening lines. The opening line in the original form of Q was probably the first beatitude, which initiates Jesus' inaugural sermon in Q. Q's reference to "the poor" in Q 7:22 ("the poor are given the good news") echoes this initial beatitude, just as Matthew's reference to "the kingdom" points to that same opening line: "Blessed are you poor, for yours is the reign of God."

The Coptic version of Thomas has an appended title, "The Gospel according to Thomas." Since the term gospel occurs nowhere in the text itself, this title was probably secondarily added, to validate this text as worthy of the status of a gospel. The opening lines of the text itself describe the text as consisting of "secret sayings." Q uses this same term, logoi, to describe its own contents, when the inaugural sermon concludes (6:46–49) with the parable of a house being built on rock or sand, depending on whether or not one hears Jesus' "words" and practices them. Thus it is appropriate to designate these gospels that consist primarily of sayings as sayings gospels.

When the complete Gospel of Thomas became available a generation ago, scholars tended at first to view it as having excerpted sayings from the more familiar narrative gospels, whether from canonical or non-canonical gospels—an occasional saying from the latter has also found its way into the Gospel of Thomas. The assumption was that the gnostics peeled away almost all the narrative framework of the gospels because they were not interested in Jesus' action but focussed rather on his word. For the Gnostic myth had a redeemer who saved by revealing esoteric truths rather than by performing saving works or dying a saving death. But the gnostic myth is not explicit in the Gospel of Thomas. And then other texts from the same Nag Hammadi discovery indicate that gnostics could very well use the narrative traditions about Jesus for their own purposes. Hence, they would not have needed to eliminate the narrative portions as completely as they are absent from the Gospel of Thomas, whose gnostic tendencies are not sufficiently dominant in any case to make such a procedure seem probable.

A large number of sayings in the Gospel of Thomas are not found in the canonical gospels at all, and to derive them from lost non-canonical narrative gospels would be pure speculation. In fact, there are very few instances in the Gospel of Thomas where dependence on the canonical gospels seems actually a reasonable assumption. This suggests that the Gospel of Thomas derives primarily from oral tradition, with only a secondary overlay from the canonical gospels: this overlay would have been a kind of 'contamination' which could have taken place in the oral tradition itself, in the process of copying the Greek text repeatedly, in the translation from Greek into Coptic, and then in the ongoing process of copying the Coptic text. Thus one can conclude that the Gospel of Thomas, like Q, is a sayings gospel rooted in oral tradition, and hence of major importance, rather than being a secondary and rather irrelevant excerpt from the canonical gospels.

Some have resisted the close association of a collection of sayings located in the canonical gospels—the Q gospel—with a similar collection of sayings found among the tractates in the gnostic library discovered at Nag Hammadi—the Gospel of Thomas. Those who resist argue that, whereas the Gosepl of Thomas is indeed a collection of sayings with no apparent train of thought connecting one saying with another, and with hardly any indication that individual sayings had been collected into small clusters prior to their inclusion in Thomas, by contrast Q is a collection of small clusters, and thus is a completely different literary genre. This difference is reflected in a difference in nomenclature: Q is no longer a "sayings source," it is a "discourses source." However, this distinction is not rigid, for, apart from there being in Q a number of individual sayings not previously brought into clusters, there are often sayings in the Gospel of Thomas that actually are a mosaic, made up of fragments from a series of sayings, a kind of fused cluster or compressed discourse.

The Gospel of Thomas rather consistently, even mechanically, introduces each saying anew with "Jesus said," or "He said," whereas such quotation formulae seem to be largely absent from Q. For example, the inaugural sermon, Q 6:20–49, is interrupted only once with such a formula, since 6:39a is a Lukan addition. The single instance in the Q sermon, at 6:27, is put on Jesus' tongue in the first person. Thus it does not in effect interrupt the flow of the sermon, which of course was not actually a sermon, but rather a collection of sayings and clusters that move directly from one to the other.

Such formal distinctions that can be drawn between Q and the Gospel of Thomas are no greater than those among the various narrative gospels in the New Testament. Mark and John begin with the preaching of John, but Matthew and Luke preface this with lengthy birth narratives. Mark has no resurrection appearance, whereas Matthew, Luke, and John have more than one each. Mark has remarkably little by way of sayings, whereas Matthew and Luke, by interpolating Q into the Markan text, produce gospels with a much stronger balance between stories and sayings, but each in a different way, Matthew by collecting the sayings into five thematic discourses, Luke by scattering the sayings largely through the first half of the gospel, with most of the sayings clustered into a non-Markan trip through Samaria on the way from Galilee to Jerusalem.

To miracle stories the Gospel of John appends lengthy discourses composed to spiritualize such stories, and to present Johannine theology. Constitutive for the form of Mark and John is their use of a then-current distinction of two levels of text, one coded and the other uncoded (Mark 4:33–34/8:32; John 16:25/16:29). Mark and John employ this device to claim that the higher, uncoded level applies even prior to Easter, in spite of the prime emphasis put on Easter by the early Christian gospel, the kerygma. Matthew and Luke, on the other hand, seem to overlook this shift of levels that was so decisive for Mark and John in constituting their gospel form. Thus a rigorous definition of narrative gospel would fit only the one or two gospels used as a model and would tend to exclude the others.

It is best suited to the evidence to recognize a broad distinction between narrative and sayings gospels, while acknowledging that the genre is fluid and comes to expression differently in individual cases.

The main surviving examples of narrative gospels are readily available in the New Testament. The present volume presents two extant examples of the sayings gospel. Since Jesus' sayings, transmitted, shaped and augmented by his immediate followers in Galilee and Syria, provide most of what can be said about him and about apostolic Christianity (the first generation of his followers), the value of a *Q–Thomas Reader* is apparent: it puts the reader in touch with invaluable sources for understanding how Christianity really began.

James M. Robinson
Claremont Graduate School

The Sayings
Gospel Q

ΙC ΙC ΙC

The Sayings Gospel Q

INTRODUCTION

The Sayings Gospel Q dates from the earliest Christian times, prior to the composition of the Synoptic gospels (Matthew, Mark and Luke). It is a written source of sayings and discourses attributed to Jesus used by the authors of the gospels of Matthew and Luke. Matthew and Luke used Q to supplement the material they both inherited from the Gospel of Mark (more will be said about this later). The name "Q" has nothing to do with the original name of this document, which did not survive antiquity. It is simply a scholarly convention, coming from the first letter of the German word *Quelle*, which means "source." It is believed that Johannes Weiss was the first to use "Q" to designate the sayings source used by Matthew and Luke. In an essay written in 1890 he refers to the verses in Luke 11:14–26 as coming partly "from the sayings source (*Redenquelle*), which is to be reconstructed from Matthew and Luke (Q)."[1] Throughout the rest of the essay Weiss uses the symbol Q to refer to this document. Through Weiss' writings it became the recognized symbol for the non-Markan material shared by Matthew and Luke. Why Weiss used "Q" and not "R" to designate the term "*Redenquelle*" is not known. In 1876, Julius Wellhausen had used the symbol "Q," from the Latin word "four" (*quattuor*), to designate a source document in the Old Testament. Weiss was familiar with Wellhausen's work and perhaps simply adopted the symbol.

Although scholars now refer to "Q" as a gospel, it is not a *narrative gospel* like the Synoptics. Matthew, Mark and Luke all present a continuous narrative from the birth or baptism of Jesus to his resurrection. Q

3

by contrast is not a continuous narrative. It is a collection of sayings and speeches of Jesus organized thematically. For example, Luke 9:57–62, a passage from Q, is a collection of sayings dealing with discipleship. Also the sayings found in the Sermon on the Mount (Matt 5–7), the Sermon on the Plain (Luke 6:20–49) and the missionary discourse (Matt 10:26–33 par. Luke 12:2–9) come from Q. Such sayings, or discourse materials are characteristic of Q. Accordingly, Q should be called a *discourse* or a *sayings gospel*. In this respect it is much closer to the Gospel of Thomas, a collection of Jesus' sayings, than it is to the canonical gospels, Matthew, Mark, Luke and John, all of which present one with a narrative purporting to tell the story of Jesus' life. For both Q and Thomas, the emphasis lies not so much on Jesus' life, but on his teaching, his words.

Although early Christians are thought to have passed down many of their traditions orally, there is broad scholarly consensus that Q was a written document. The often extensive verbatim agreement found between Matthew and Luke are inexplicable if the evangelists were independently recording oral sayings. Sometimes they copy Q almost word for word, for example Matt 3:7b–10 par. Luke 3:7b–9 and Matt 11:21–23 par. Luke 10:13–15.

Matt 3:7–10	Luke 3:7–9
[7] . . . "You brood of vipers! Who warned you to flee from the coming wrath? [8] Bear fruit worthy of repentance, [9] and do not presume to say to yourselves, 'We have Abraham as our father'; for I tell you, God is able from these stones to raise up children to Abraham. [10] Even now is the axe laid to the root of the trees; every tree therefore that does not bear good fruit is cut down and thrown into the fire."	[7] . . . "You brood of vipers! Who warned you to flee from the coming wrath? [8] Bear fruits worthy of repentance, and do not begin to say to yourselves, 'We have Abraham as our father'; for I tell you, God is able from these stones to raise up children to Abraham. [9] Even now is the axe laid to the root of the trees; every tree therefore that does not bear good fruit is cut down and thrown into the fire."

At other times either Matthew or Luke has changed the wording of a Q saying. If one knows the editorial habits of Matthew and Luke, such as their literary style, vocabulary and theological intention, it is possible to recover the original wording of Q by a careful comparison of the Matthean and Lukan versions of the saying. For example, Matthew and Luke have taken the following saying from Q:

Matt 5:6	Luke 6:21
6 "Blessed are they that hunger **and thirst for righteousness,** for they shall be filled."	21 "Blessed are you that hunger **now,** for you shall be filled."

In the Matthean version, Matthew's typical concern for righteousness may be seen in the words written in bold type, which do not occur in Luke. Matthew has probably added them to the original saying drawn from Q. Likewise, Luke may have added the word "now," as a way of emphasizing the immediacy of the problem of hunger, and the promise that it will be assuaged. The Q version of the beatitude probably read something like: "Blessed are you that hunger, for you shall be filled."

Since no copies of Q survived antiquity, what we know of it must be derived from the Q material incorporated into Matthew and Luke, both of whom used Q independently of one another. Using the process illustrated above, scholars must "reconstruct" Q from this material, generally identified as the passages shared by Matthew and Luke which do not occur in Mark. By paying close attention to the wording of such passages in Matthew and Luke, the reader can get a very good idea of the content of the Sayings Gospel Q. In citing Q scholars usually make use of the Lukan versification of Q texts, rather than the Matthean chapter and verse notations, since it is thought that, generally speaking, Luke preserves the original order of Q better than Matthew. For example, Q 4:1–13 refers to the Q text Luke 4:1–13 (parallel to Matt 4:1–11).

Date and Provenance

Since Q was used as a source by Matthew and Luke, it must have been composed before these gospels, both of which were edited in the last decades of the first century. Matthew and Luke indicate that they are aware of the destruction of Jerusalem in 70 C.E. Q, by contrast, displays no such knowledge. Therefore, one may conclude that it predates that event. It also predates the Gospel of Mark, since Mark was probably written either during the Jewish War (66–70 C.E.) or shortly thereafter. Thus, Q is normally dated sometime in the period between 50 C.E. and 70 C.E.

Although the disciples of Jesus are sent to all the towns of Israel (cf. Luke 10:1; Matt 10:5, 6, 23), Q and the synoptic gospels set much of Jesus' activity in northern Galilee. The present form of Q indicates that one might also expect to find the Q community there. Most place names cited in Q are from northern Galilee or western Syria. Jerusalem is mentioned only twice (cf. Q 4:9 and 13:34), and the region around the Jordan but once (Q 3:3). The mention of the Galilean towns of Chorazin and Bethsaida (cf. Q 10:13), which play no special role in the Synoptic gospels, suggests a familiarity with that area. Capernaum, also a Galilean town, is named twice (cf. Q 7:1; 10:15) and the Gentile cities of Tyre and Sidon, located in western Syria, are also mentioned (cf. Q 10:13). This indicates that Q may have been composed in or near Galilee.[2]

The "Discovery" of Q

Before reading and studying the Sayings Gospel Q, it is helpful to ask the question, "How did we come to learn about Q, its literary genre and its reconstruction?" Since scholarly opinions concerning Q were not formed overnight, we must understand the *history of the research* that led to our present knowledge of it. In the following pages we will trace the high points of synoptic study and of the recent developments in the study of Q. As usual, the best way to begin is to read the New Testament itself.

A careful reading of Paul's letters reveals that the Apostle is aware of sayings of the resurrected Lord and credal formulae that have been handed down to him. Striking examples can be found in 1 Corinthians. In 1 Cor 15:3–4 Paul informs his readers:

> [3] I delivered to you as of first importance what I also received, that Christ died for our sins in accordance with the scriptures, [4] that he was buried, that he was raised on the third day according to the scriptures . . .

The words "to deliver" ($\pi\alpha\rho\alpha\delta\acute{\iota}\delta\omega\mu\iota$) and "to receive" ($\pi\alpha\rho\alpha\lambda\alpha\mu\beta\acute{\alpha}\nu\omega$) are technical terms used to denote the passing on or handing down of a tradition. The same technical terms are found in 1 Cor 11:23 where Paul narrates the tradition of the Lord's supper that he "received" and "delivered" to the Corinthians. Early Christianity valued traditions that were passed down and Paul praised the Corinthians for holding fast to the traditions that he delivered to them (1 Cor 11:2).

Paul is aware not only of credal formulae but he also knows of sayings of Jesus. Making reference to "the Lord" (by which he apparently means Jesus) in 1 Cor 7:10 he writes:

[10] To the married I give charge, not I but the Lord, that the wife should not separate from her husband [11] (but if she does, let her remain single or else be reconciled to her husband)—and that the husband should not divorce his wife.

A similar Jesus tradition is found in Mark 10:11–12, Matt 19:9, Luke 16:18 and Matt 5:31–32. These latter two versions probably derive from Q:

Matt 5:32	Luke 16:18
[32] "But I tell you that everyone who divorces his wife, except on the grounds of unchastity, forces her to commit adultery, and whoever marries a divorcée commits adultery."	[18] "Everyone who divorces his wife and marries another commits adultery and he who marries a divorcée is an adulterer."

Paul is not alone in his concern for traditions and in his use of material passed down to him. The author of Luke's gospel reveals that he used sources that were "delivered" to him when compiling his gospel. He writes:

[1] Inasmuch as many have undertaken to compile a narrative of the things which have been accomplished among us, [2] just as they were delivered to us by those who from the beginning were eyewitnesses and ministers of the word, [3] it seemed good to me also, having followed all things closely for some time past, to write an orderly account . . . —Luke 1:1–3

Although by the time Luke writes his gospel "many have undertaken to compile a narrative," we do not know how many sources, such as other gospels, collections of Jesus' sayings, miracle stories and parables were available to the evangelist. We do know, however, that many scholars over the years have observed clusters or collections of sayings, parables, or miracle stories in the gospels. For example, there appears to be a collection of parables in Mark 4. There is also a collection of material in Mark 13 (and the parallel passages in Matthew and Luke) that speaks about the end of time and the signs that will accompany the coming of the end. Scholars have also observed the close textual relationship of the first three gospels. They have a great deal in common, including very close verbal parallels. Scholars have attempted to explain this problem of the relation of the first three gospels, which became known as the "synoptic problem," in different ways. Nevertheless, one fundamental explanation widely shared by specialists is that Matthew and Luke are dependent on a written source that has come to be known as Q.

The Synoptic Fact and the Synoptic Problem[3]

As we have seen, the first three gospels of Matthew, Mark and Luke, which appear in that order in most early collections or Canons, are called synoptic gospels. J. J. Griesbach first used the term *synoptic* (from συν-όψομαι, "to see together") in his *Synopse* published in 1774. The work printed the three gospels parallel to each other and showed the agreements and disagreements among them. Thus it allowed the reader to observe the threefold synoptic fact:

1. Virtually all the material in Mark appears in Matthew and/or Luke. Of the 661 verses in Mark over 600 of them are substantially found in Matthew and over 300 of them in Luke. Furthermore, apart from that material they share with Mark, Matthew and Luke also share in common about 240 verses not found in Mark. These verses consist almost exclusively of sayings of Jesus and discourses.

2. A close comparison of the three synoptic gospels reveals a high degree of similarity in vocabulary, in word order and sentence structure, as well as in the particularities of style.

3. The sequence of the narrative units (or pericopes) is similar in each of the three synoptic gospels. It is unlikely that three different authors working entirely independently would have followed narrative sequences so strikingly alike.

The question of the literary relationship of the first three gospels or, more specifically, the question of how the agreements and disagreements in wording and content, and the order of events, are to be explained became a central question in New Testament scholarship and remains an important question to this day. This issue constitutes the synoptic problem.

Yet even before the publication of Griesbach's gospel synopsis, early Christian and medieval authors were aware of these facts, as can be seen from Eusebius' "Canon Tables" and Augustine's *De consensu evangelistarum* (*On the Harmony of the Gospels*), both of which set out tables comparing and contrasting the canonical gospels. But neither Eusebius nor Augustine considered the agreements and disagreements to be a problem. They simply believed that the gospels originated in the order in which they appeared in the New Testament and that each evangelist was aware of his predecessor(s)' work.

By the end of the 18th century, however, scholars were becoming aware of the synoptic problem and began to put forward solutions. G. E.

Lessing (1778) and J. G. Eichorn (1794), for example, attempted to explain the similarities between Matthew, Mark, and Luke on the basis of historical reminiscence codified in a single, original document, which all three would have used. They thus posited the existence of an *Urevangelium*, that is, an original or primal gospel, which, they surmised, would have been written in Hebrew or Aramaic. Similarly, F. Schleiermacher (1817) proposed a Fragment Hypothesis. According to his view, various story tellers in the earliest period related vignettes or short literary sketches about Jesus, which were eventually gathered into collections. These in turn would have become the basis of the written gospels as we know them. On the other hand, J. G. von Herder (1796) and J. K. L. Gieseler (1818) held that the synoptic gospels are independent and that the similarities among them could be explained by a common oral tradition. This solution is known as the Oral Transmission Hypothesis. All of these attempts to solve the synoptic problem were ultimately rejected because of the detailed verbal agreement among the Synoptics. The degree to which Matthew, Mark, and Luke exhibit verbatim agreement is difficult to reconcile with the hypothesis of a mere shared oral tradition, or even simultaneous translation of a primitive Aramaic or Hebrew gospel source, but points rather to the conclusion that the Synoptics are dependent on a written source or sources, one or more of which could be present in the Synoptic gospels themselves. The prevailing solution to the synoptic problem—the one accepted by most scholars—has been some variation of the Two Source Hypothesis. The Two Source Hypothesis holds that Matthew and Luke are dependent on Mark and one other written source, now lost, which contained a collection of Jesus' sayings. This second source is the hypothetical document Q.

The Two Source Hypothesis

It was H. J. Holtzmann who first stated in a formal way the rudiments of the Two Source Hypothesis. Holtzmann proposed that Matthew and Luke, independently of one another, made use of an early form of the Gospel of Mark (he called this *Urmarkus*, or "original Mark") as the basis for their narrative outline of the life of Jesus. The additional material shared by Matthew and Luke, but absent from Mark, was drawn from a second source composed primarily of Jesus' sayings.

What Holtzmann and others after him have noticed about the relationships between the three synoptic gospels is quite compelling. First,

Matthew and Luke incorporate almost all of Mark into their gospels, while large sections of Matthew are omitted from Mark and Luke, and much of Luke is omitted from Mark and Matthew. Second, when Matthew and Luke parallel Mark, they seem to follow the Markan order of events. In fact, Matthew and Luke agree chronologically only when they both agree with the Markan chronology. These two facts, more than any others, suggest that Mark was written first (an hypothesis scholars refer to as "Markan priority"), and that Matthew and Luke used Mark as a source. But there is a third observation to be made: Matthew and Luke share much material in common that does not occur in Mark. These Matthew-Luke parallels often exhibit a high degree of verbatim agreement. Furthermore, these parallels show a good deal of formal uniformity: they consist primarily of saying and discourses. Finally, though Matthew and Luke tend to insert this material at differing points in the Markan order of events, the order in which its sayings are used by the two different authors is remarkably consistent. That is, though Matthew may insert sayings a, b, and c into one Markan context, while Luke places them in another, in both texts the sayings themselves occur in the same sequence relative to one another![4] The existence of this material, and the patterns to be observed in it, has led most scholars to conclude that Matthew and Luke must have shared one other source, a sayings source, besides Mark. This source today is commonly referred to as the Sayings Gospel Q.

The Two Source Hypothesis

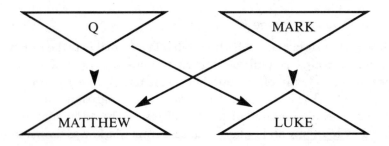

Over the years not all scholars have accepted the Two Source Hypothesis. The negative implications of Markan priority for the time-honored assumption of the gospels' historical reliability, for example, made it difficult for some to accept this hypothesis. Others, however, offered more empirical evidence against the thesis. For example, there are a handful of passages, such as the metaphor of the "divided kingdom" (Mark 3:24–26 par. Matt 12:25b–26; Luke 11:17b–18) in which Matthew and Luke agree against Mark, whose version is slightly different.

Matt 12:25–26	Mark 3:24–26	Luke 11:17–18
[25] But knowing their designs, he said to them, "Every kingdom divided against itself is laid waste, and a city or household divided against itself will not survive. [26] And if Satan exorcises Satan, he is divided against himself; how then will his kingdom endure?"	[24] "Now if an empire is divided against itself, that empire cannot stand. [25] And if a house is divided against itself, that house will not be able to stand. [26] So if Satan rebels against himself and is divided, he cannot last but is finished."	[17] But knowing their thoughts, he said to them, "Every kingdom divided against itself is laid waste, and a house that is against itself collapses. [18] And if Satan is divided against himself, how will his kingdom endure? For you say that I exorcise demons by Beelzebul."

Such passages are called "minor agreements," and they raise a number of interesting questions. Since it is highly unlikely that Matthew and Luke would have, independently of one another, made the same editorial changes to a common Markan source, one cannot easily assume that both Matthew and Luke are indebted to Mark for these sayings. For this reason, some have found in them evidence against the two source hypothesis.

But the minor agreements are not decisive for this question. One way to account for them would be to suppose that Matthew and Luke drew their version of the saying from an earlier version of Mark, an *Urmarkus*, which was edited later, thus creating a new Markan version out of step with the older one used by Matthew and Luke. As we have seen, this was in fact how Holtzmann initially framed the Two Source Hypothesis. Another way to account for them would be to suppose that Matthew and Luke took their version of the saying from another source altogether, supplanting the Markan version with a competing version from Q. For this reason, many of these minor agreements are regarded as points of Mark-Q overlap, and not necessarily as evidence for the existence of an *Urmarkus*. Today most scholars are more apt to regard Mark-Q overlap as the solution to this problem rather than appealing to the hypothesis of an *Urmarkus* to account for them.

There are two other observations that periodically have led scholars to question the Two Source Hypothesis. The first is that Luke contains a large amount of special material, that is, material unique to Luke, and often disagrees with Mark in sections that they otherwise have in common. This phenomenon, seen especially in the passion narrative, could suggest that Luke did not use Mark, but relied upon his own sources. But few have seen this as adequate grounds for dismissing the Two Source Hypothesis. F. Rehkopf, H. Schürmann and J. B. Tyson,[5] for example, contend that Luke used, besides Mark and Q, another narrative source or, at least, a different version of the passion narrative than Mark, but do not reject the basic position of Markan priority. Others such as B. H. Streeter and V. Taylor[6] hold that Luke incorporated material from Mark and Q into an early gospel of his own, a proto-Luke, so to speak. Streeter proposed a Four Source (or Document) Hypothesis, a variation of the Two Source Hypothesis more widely accepted among British scholars. In his scheme, in addition to Q and Mark, the authors of Matthew and Luke each had a source peculiar to him. Thus, the material particular to Matthew on the one hand and Luke on the other is attributed to two ancient documents "M" and "L" (so-called because they represent special sources used by Matthew and Luke, respectively). In the case of Luke, he suggested the existence of a proto-Luke compiled from Q and the Lukan "L." Markan material was then added to the Lukan sequence later to form the present Gospel of Luke.

The second observation is this: The fourth century historian Eusebius of Caesarea cites Papias, bishop of Hierapolis: "Now Matthew collected the oracles (τὰ λόγια) in Hebrew language, and each one interpreted them as he was able."[7] From this statement some scholars have concluded that an original apostolic Aramaic Gospel existed. They contend that the same sequence and common Old Testament citations in long passages of Matthew, Mark and Luke, as well as the agreements between Matthew and Luke against Mark, point to an Aramaic Matthew, which was subsequently translated into Greek and served as the common source for all three synoptic gospels.[8] But the hypothesis of an original Aramaic Matthew or of an oral Aramaic source for the synoptic gospels is not widely accepted. Most scholars contend that it is methodologically incorrect to explain the literary relationship of the synoptic gospels by appealing to Papias because he himself had no first hand knowledge about the composition of the gospels, and thus cannot give us more certain knowledge concerning the origin of the synoptics than we can gain from the study of the texts themselves. Furthermore, it is likely that Papias' reference to the "oracles" collected by Matthew refers to the Gospel of Matthew itself, and not to some earlier primitive gospel that could have been used by later authors.[9]

Although in the past some scholars were cautious about the collection of Jesus' sayings and attempts to reconstruct this document were considered unsuccessful, in the last two decades research into the literary genre, reconstruction and theology of Q has advanced beyond previous expectations. The literary evidence provided by a Q extracted from Matthew and Luke requires one to postulate that Matthew and Luke used a "Q" document, with its own integrity and its own theological view; they could not have used disconnected oral or written material and produced the result they did. Today few would speak as M. Dibelius did and call "Q" an amorphous layer or "stratum" of tradition. Nor do many regard Q as a mere supplement to the narrative gospels to be used in the instructional activity of the early church, as Streeter once maintained. Rather, today most have come to think of Q as a carefully conceived document in its own right, with its own theological message, or kerygma, independent of the passion kerygma characteristic of the canonical gospels.

Literary Genre of Q[10]

Modern literary criticism has made scholars of the New Testament aware of the importance of genre in the interpretation of a text. A genre is a type or category of literary composition, such as the categories "novel," "short story" or "sonnet." The determination of the genre of a text is not simply a method or procedure of classification. It is necessary to know the genre in which an author is writing if one is to understand the meaning of a text. For example, one would not read a novel about Napoleon in order to pass a history examination because the author's intention was to write a fictitious novel, not a factual book about history. If one does not know the genre of a text, its meaning will be easily misunderstood. Jokes, for example, may be painfully misunderstood if the hearer is unaware of the fact that it is a joke that is being told, and not a tragic story, or a tale of some other more serious genre. If the teller does not successfully communicate irony, or facetiousness, or other characteristics appropriate to the genre, the result may be misunderstanding or even embarrassment for the hearer and the teller. The importance of the assumption that the meaning of a text, such as Q, is connected with genre, is not always immediately apparent until one examines the understanding with which authors approached the study of early Christian literature.

Until recently, scholars neglected considering the genre of biblical works because of their understanding of the nature of early Christian literature. During the nineteenth century, for example, most scholars came to understand Christian literature as growing out of oral tradition. Therefore, it was not considered to be real literature, and thus comparable to the high literary products (*Hochliteratur*) of classical culture. Karl Ludwig Schmidt summed up this attitude writing: "The gospel is fundamentally not high literature but folk literature, not the production of an individual but a folk book, not a bibliography but a cult legend."[11] The basis for this presupposition can be found in the work of Franz Overbeck,[12] who observed that there seemed to be no continuity in literary forms between New Testament writing and later patristic literature. Early Christian literature contained either non-literary forms, such as letters, or literary forms that were not typical of patristic and contemporary Hellenistic literature. One therefore posited for early Christian literature a unique form of pre-literature (*Urliteratur*) that grew out of the interest of the Christian community. This community was apocalyptically oriented, that is, preoccupied with the end of the world, and not at all concerned to create a literary legacy for later generations. Therefore, its literary production could only be classified as folk literature (*Kleinliteratur*).

This way of regarding early Christian literature was not altered with the rise of form criticism, a method developed to classify the various oral forms of primitive Christian literature, and then also to categorize the written genres utilized by the emerging church. Early Christian literature was viewed simply by the form critics as a surrogate for oral tradition. The gospels, for example, were collections of oral units. Perhaps Martin Dibelius, an early New Testament form critic, typified this understanding of the gospels, considering the gospel text to be little more than "collections of material."[13] Even Rudolf Bultmann expressed a similar understanding when he wrote:

[The literary composition of the gospels] involves nothing new in principle, but only completes what was begun in the oral tradition . . . it can only be considered in organic connection with the history of the material as it lay before the evangelists.[14]

With the rise of redaction criticism, however, this view began to change. Redaction criticism gave more careful consideration to the specific way in which each of the gospels was assembled from traditional materials. It was discovered that the gospel writers did not simply collect stories, sayings, parables, etc. at random, but rather carefully selected and edited materials, weaving them together in a very intentional way. The redaction critics argued that the gospels are the result of each author's own theological intention, and not just random collections. Furthermore, the assumption that the early church was an apocalyptic community incapable of refined literary activity, because it was preoccupied with the coming of the end and the coming of the resurrected Lord, was shown to be false by the literary production of other groups that also had apocalyptic expectations. For example, apocalypticists and the members of the Qumran community produced a high quality of literature in spite of their convictions about the imminent end of the world. And other fields of research began to turn up results significant to the resolution of this problem. For example, research into folklore has shown that there is a distinction between oral tradition and written text. Since a written text is read and an oral tradition performed, there is a significant shift in form and function when a tradition moves from oral form into written form. These studies convinced scholars that it was necessary to give more attention to the question of form and genre, even in regard to Q, a *written* collection of Jesus' sayings. The study of Q has shown that the proverbs and parables of Jesus, once thought to have been collected according to no particular literary genre, do indeed constitute a genre.

Since the terms sayings source (*Logienquelle, Spruchquelle*), speech source (*Redenquelle*), or simply the sayings ("the Logia") used by early authors, presumably described the nature of Q, there appears to have been little effort to define its genre. There are notable exceptions. Friedrich Schleiermacher, for example, referred to the Sermon on the Mount section of Q as a gnomologium,[15] that is, an anthology of wisdom sayings. H. J. Holtzmann compared Q with the *Aphorisms* of Hippocrates, presumably because both were thematically organized.[16]

Other scholars, however, were less inclined to see Q as a simple sayings collection. For one thing, they found it difficult to conceive of a document like Q, which appears to show little interest in the life of Jesus. Bernard Weiss,[17] for example, argued that, although it did not contain a passion narrative and was biographically incomplete, many of the sayings do have "historical introductions." In view of this, he maintained that Q was at least the "beginning of a biography."[18] His conclusion, however, was based upon a reconstruction of Q that included not only the non-Markan passages common to Matthew and Luke, but also the speech material found in Mark 2:24–28; 3:31–35; 10:28–34; and 13:5–31, and "such pieces of Mark's narrative as have a simpler and more original form in the first Gospel."[19] Weiss believed that Mark had also used Q, editing it and adding narrative to it. Since both Matthew and Luke used Q, they often preserved simpler and more original forms of the sayings and narratives which they had in common with Mark. In such cases Weiss believed that Matthew and Luke had preserved the simpler version of Q, which Mark had embellished. By including so much of this Markan material in his reconstruction of Q, Weiss created a document that was much more biographical than most would consider Q to be.

B. W. Bacon also held that Q was intended as a presentation of Jesus' ministry. In his view, it portrayed Jesus as "the redeeming 'Wisdom' of God, the Suffering Servant of Isaian prophecy" who was to be highly exalted.[20] Bacon based this theological reading of Q upon Matt 12:18–21, the quotation from Isa 42:1–4. This text, however, has no parallel in Luke. It is therefore questionable whether precisely the most important text for Bacon's interpretation was ever part of the Q document at all.

F. C. Burkitt, W. E. Bundy and Emanuel Hirsch also went beyond viewing Q simply as a sayings source, and thought of Q in more biographical terms. Most puzzling for them was the fact that if Q was reconstructed solely on the basis of material shared by Matthew and Luke, it would have no passion narrative, and no word about Jesus' resurrection. Could Q have been silent on such important matters as these? They therefore attempted to reconstruct a passion narrative for Q by attributing to Q sections of Luke's special material and the "minor agreements" in the passion narrative.[21] In spite of the number of questionable texts that they assigned to Q, the alleged passion account of Q was still not a continuous narrative and the reconstructed text could not be convincingly viewed as comparable to the later "biographical" gospels.

There were also those, such as Adolf Jülicher, Paul Wernle and Adolf von Harnack, who saw in Q the gospel of Jesus himself. They argued that the collection of Jesus' sayings would have served a catechetical, or teaching purpose. In Harnack's view, Q was simply a collection of sayings spoken by Jesus during the Galilean ministry. It was compiled by a collector who did not inject into the document any particular bias of his/her own.[22] Jülicher even went so far as to say that the collection handed down the sayings of Jesus "in an authentic form,"[23] just as Jesus himself had spoken them.

But such views were not long-lived. They were supplanted by the ideas of those who began to consider Q subordinate to the theology expressed in Mark. This shift in emphasis can be seen even in Jülicher, who in his 1906 *Introduction* changed his position with regard to the relation of Q to Mark. Q was not prior to Mark, as he had previously held, but reached its final form later than and under the influence of Mark. Beginning with lists of Jesus' words, it developed as a catechetical supplement to Mark.[24] An important figure in the development of this shift of opinion was Julius Wellhausen, who also held Q to be a collection compiled to supplement the Gospel of Mark with materials suitable for instruction. The author of Q, he believed, intentionally omitted narrative material, such as the passion and resurrection accounts, since Q presupposed and attempted to elaborate on Mark. Although for many scholars at this time Q was not historically secondary to Mark, it certainly was "theologically and hermeneutically dependent upon the Second Gospel."[25] They believed that Q presupposed the theology of Mark and should be interpreted in the light of Mark's gospel. Wellhausen, examining the Mark-Q overlaps, went so far as to propose that Q was also literarily dependent upon Mark. This thesis proved untenable because it was impossible to show that Q relied upon the structure or plan of Mark.

Later scholars, such as B. H. Streeter[26] and T. W. Manson[27] in England and M. Dibelius in Germany, adopted the idea that Q was theologically dependent upon the early Christian preaching, or kerygma, of Jesus Christ as the crucified and risen Lord. Therefore, Q was not interpreted on its own terms, but in light of the Gospel of Mark, with its emphasis on the passion and resurrection. Streeter believed that Q was a handbook for missionaries and provided answers to problems encountered by early missionaries. For example, Q 3:7–9, 16–17 and 7:18–35 dealt with the relation of John the Baptist and his disciples to Jesus. For Streeter, as well as for Dibelius, Q was parenesis. It was a hortatory composition, containing material that admonished the reader to attain to a certain ethical standard. As such it formed an ethical supplement to the keryg-ma. Though these judgments were eventually eclipsed, Streeter did make some valuable observations from a literary perspective. He noted, for example, that Q was "a collection of the 'Wise Sayings' of Christ comparable to a book like Proverbs or the *Pirke Aboth*, with very little attempt at arrangement"[28] and that, similar to the *Didache*, Q ended with an apocalyptic section.[29] As will be seen below, these observations would turn out to be proleptic of the solution to the problem of Q's genre that would emerge years later.

Rudolf Bultmann also characterized Q as concerned primarily with ethical instruction, but believed that the early church had expanded the collection of Jesus' sayings, creating its own sayings of Jesus and coopting proverbs from popular culture, which were then attributed to Jesus. A similar process could be seen in Sirach, where ancient collec-tions of sayings were enlarged and combined with other proverbial material. Therefore, Q was not a source of the teachings of Jesus, as Harnack believed, but a source for the teachings of the early church.[30] According to Bultmann, originally Q may have contained collections of Jesus' sayings, arranged thematically, according to form or catchword association. However, in a long process of editing, beginning with an Aramaic version and continuing in the Greek translation of Q, material for edification of the community, such as apocalyptic and prophetic words, and material for parenesis were added and transmitted. Bult-mann insisted on the central position of the Christian kerygma and, in his *History of the Synoptic Tradition*, viewed Q as a supplement to it. The assertion that the theological center of the Christian faith was the kerygma proclaiming Jesus Christ, the crucified and risen one, to be God's eschatological act of salvation[31] was to have important conse-quences for the interpretation of Q.

In his *Theology of the New Testament* Bultmann's position in regard to Q changed. He began with the assertion that the message of the historical Jesus was "among the presuppositions for the theology of the New Testament rather than part of that theology itself."[32] The church did not pass on the message of Jesus unchanged. For them, Jesus was not simply a prophet or teacher or critic of the law or the coming Son of Man. If he was, the church would still be a Jewish sect and not the

Christian church. Likewise, if the early Christian community proclaimed Jesus as the crucified and risen one whom God exalted to the Son of Man, this would not properly distinguish the Christian church from a Jewish sect. What was decisive was that the Church understood the person and fate of Jesus as an eschatological event that "breaks the frame of Jewish eschatology."[33] Implicitly Q manifested this by beginning with the eschatological preaching of John the Baptist, continuing with the beatitudes and ending with sayings concerning the return of Christ. Therefore, in his *Theology of the New Testament* Bultmann introduced into the discussion of Q a dimension that was not present in the *History of the Synoptic Tradition.* Q was not simply a hortatory or didactic supplement to the kerygma, as Dibelius, Manson and Streeter held, but it has an independent, although undeveloped, theological understanding of the eschatological significance of Jesus' person and fate. Q represented a "transitional stage between the non-messianic preaching of Jesus and the fully self-conscious kerygma of the Hellenistic churches."[34]

This understanding of the interpretation of Q raised some important questions. If Q was the proclamation of the eschatological event, that is, the death and resurrection of Jesus (in Bultmann's terms), and not simply parenesis supplementing the kerygma, did two different versions of the kerygma exist in the early churches? This question is pertinent because the message of Q is clearly different from the message of the canonical gospels. A second question was this: Did Q's "kerygma" originate in a community different from the one which began preaching Jesus as the "crucified and risen Lord"? In that case, a difference in the message embodied in Q would be understandable. Certainly Streeter, while still insisting that Q presupposed the Passion and its redemptive significance and asserting that Q was an ethical supplement to this kerygma, pointed out that for Q the message of the parousia that the risen Lord would come, not the passion, was the center of the gospel.[35] Therefore, Q contained a doctrine of salvation that was different from that of the passion kerygma. These problems raised by Bultmann's treatment of Q were addressed more directly by H. E. Tödt.

Tödt pointed out that many segments or pericopes in Q express no real parenetic interest at all. For example, the Beelzebul accusation in Q 11:14–26, which contains the words, "If it is by the finger of God that I exorcise demons, then the reign of God has come upon you," deals with Jesus' preaching of the kingdom and by what authority he performs his mighty works. Likewise, the prophetic sayings in Q 11:29–32 show no apparent interest in ethical instruction, but simply pronounce judgment on "this generation," a theme typical of Q. The thanksgiving in Q 10:21–22 praises God the Father for Jesus' revelation, but offers nothing of parenetic interest. Therefore, Tödt argued that Q was not intended as a parenetic, or ethical supplement to other more kerygmatically oriented documents, such as the Gospel of Mark. Rather, in preserving the words of Jesus Q sought to continue the preaching of Jesus himself. The subject of the preaching was not the resurrection of Jesus (that is, the kerygma) but the kingdom preached by Jesus. In naming Jesus as the future Son of Man, however, Q presupposes the authority which the proclamation of the resurrection imparts to the original preacher and the content of his preaching. If one assumed that the life of Jesus was initially regarded as non-messianic, the reason why sayings of Jesus were transmitted at all was that "Jesus was recognized as having the future task of acting as the Son of Man."[36] Jesus had, therefore, also to be recognized as having authority while on earth. His "pointing to the coming of God's kingdom had not lost meaning in the post Easter situation, but must be proclaimed anew."[37] Tödt thus provided the reason for collecting the sayings of Jesus in Q and the theological understanding of the document based on a christology that was sufficiently different from the "crucified and risen Lord" kerygma.

A new point of departure is represented by the work of Siegfried Schulz. Unlike Tödt, Bultmann, and their predecessors, Schulz tried to understand Q on its own terms, that is, without reference to a passion story at all. He believed that Q reflects a more "pharisaic-nomistic and apocalyptic structure of thought," meaning that Q was written in relation to a pharisaic legalism and an expectation that the world would end soon. In Schulz's view, Q presents the legal instruction (the Torah) of the messiah and the interpretation of that instruction (halakah) in the style of a tractate of the Mishnah known as the *Pirke Aboth*, a collection of sayings of sages in the Jewish tradition.[38] The salvific action of Jesus is found not in Jesus' death and resurrection but in his "messianic Torah, his prophetic-apocalyptic proclamation and his priestly instruction."[39] In other words, Schulz interprets Jesus' redeeming work as vested in his instruction and in his proclamation of the coming cosmic catastrophe.

But none of these attempts at solving the question of how one is to interpret Q really came to grips with the question of the literary genre of Q. The first major step in determining the literary nature of Q was taken by James M. Robinson.[40] Robinson began with the basic observation that

Q is a collection of sayings, and then attempted to locate Q generally within the genre of ancient collections of sayings, such as Proverbs, *Pirke Aboth*, and the Gospel of Thomas. Robinson noticed that such collections commonly bear the designation *logoi* ("words" or "sayings") such as one finds, for example, in *Did.* 1:3–2:1, and the sayings clusters in *1 Clem.* 13:1–2; 46:7–8. The term *logoi* is also used in Matthew's gospel to designate the sermons of Jesus (7:28; 19:1; 26:1). But the convention of referring to such collections as *logoi* is to be found already in Jewish wisdom collections (Prov 30:31 and 22:17–24:22) and extends to collections such as Ahikar and Amenemope. In this genre, which Robinson called *logoi sophōn*, there is a tendency to associate the sayings with a sage. Although Q is not composed entirely of wisdom sayings, but contains a variety of material, including chriae (that is, brief stories or anecdotes which climax with a pronouncement or saying), prophetic and apocalyptic sayings and the temptation story, the prominence of wisdom sayings among Jesus' *logoi*, and Q's association of Jesus with the heavenly Sophia (Wisdom personified: Q 7:35; 11:49) suggests that the collection of the sayings used by Matthew and Luke also be considered within the parameters of the genre *logoi sophōn*. In this way Robinson both identified Q's genre, and provided the hermeneutical principle by which Q should be read, that is, as words of divine Wisdom or her envoys.

Building upon Robinson's idea that Q belongs to the genre *logoi sophōn* or "sayings of the sages," Helmut Koester proposed the term "wisdom gospel" for Q and the other early Christian sayings collection, the Gospel of Thomas. This term best denotes the literary and theological nature of the two documents. They are sapiential sayings collections and they make a kerygmatic statement apart from the passion kerygma. The teacher, "Jesus, the Living One," is present in the words he has spoken. "Faith is understood as belief in Jesus' words, a belief which makes what Jesus proclaimed present and real for the believer."[41] Therefore, the internal principle of the genre which motivated the collection is the authority of the sapiential words in which Jesus is present and alive to the listener or reader.

Important for the later development of the study of Q is Koester's observation that there are in the genre "wisdom gospel" or *logoi sophōn* a multitude of diverse forms, some of which are more typical of the genre and others which are less so. Wisdom sayings, legal pronouncements, prophetic sayings, such as "I"-words, blessings and woes, and parables are more evident, whereas apocalyptic sayings and apocalyptic Son of Man sayings are least evident. On the basis of this observation Koester argues that the introduction of apocalyptic eschatology would have come relatively late in the history of the Q document, representing perhaps a secondary redaction of an earlier wisdom book.[42] As such, it moved Q in a new direction, and tended to moderate the radical eschatology and gnosticizing tendencies present in the earlier forms of Q.[43] This observation offers a way to disentangle and stratify the diverse forms present in Q, by viewing the wisdom sayings as more primitive, and the apocalyptic sayings as late.

Still, the number of different forms in Q presents a continuing problem in understanding this document, to which several solutions have been proposed. M. Eugene Boring[44] argues that a large number of Q sayings are the product of Christian prophets, and that many others have at least been reformulated by such prophets. Although the text contains other sayings besides oracles, Q is a collection of oracles of Christian prophets speaking on Jesus' behalf. It should be understood as the address of the risen Lord to his community. In a similar manner Werner Kelber,[45] who believes that Q represents an oral genre, imagines Q as a collection of sayings to be performed, by which act the community was able to evoke the presence of their exalted Lord. This prophetic and contemporizing tendency of Q can be seen in a Christology centered on the present and the future, not upon the past and crucified Messiah as in Mark.

As might be guessed from this brief summary of the discussion of Q's genre, there is disagreement between those who consider Q as sapiential and those who see it as prophetic. This is due in part to the lack of clarity in regard to what constitutes "prophecy" and "wisdom," and in part to the diversity of the Q material itself. Recent studies have shown that the sage's counsel presupposes an appeal to divine authority as well as the prophet's pronouncements. But it is also clear that, once one has isolated the formative element of Q and identified its genre as *logoi sophōn*, certain types of sayings and theological tendencies may be considered typical of this genre. These may be considered primary and belong to the earliest stratum of the text. Other sayings and theological tendencies, such as apocalyptic Son of Man sayings and future-oriented eschatological sayings, are further removed from the tendency of the genre and may be considered secondary and belonging to later strata of the text.

Reconstruction of Q

There is a long tradition of reconstructing the text of Q based upon Matthew and Luke's use of it. By comparing those passages which they share in common, and taking into account the various known editorial tendencies of these authors, it is often possible to gain a fairly accurate picture of how the Q text Matthew and Luke had before them actually read. Using this procedure A. von Harnack, J. Schmid and T. W. Manson all produced reconstructions of Q.[46] More recently their efforts have been renewed by the more up-to-date work of the German scholar, Athanasius Polag.[47] In addition, John Kloppenborg has produced a new collection of Q parallels that will help to facilitate future reconstructive work.[48]

Though it seems inevitable that no two reconstructions of Q will be exactly alike, a broad scholarly consensus has been reached on some points. It is generally accepted, for example, that Luke has better preserved the sequence of the Q-material, whereas Matthew has tended to distribute it throughout his gospel. For that reason, references to the Q text are regularly given as chapter and verse corresponding to the versification found in the Gospel of Luke. Currently a number of scholars are collaborating on a project under the auspices of the Society of Biblical Literature and Claremont's Institute for Antiquity and Christianity that will eventually produce a Greek text of Q representing something of a current scholarly consensus. Many outstanding issues are still under discussion, such as how to recover Q in places where both Matthew and Luke may be suspected of having thoroughly reworked the original Q text, or to account for those inevitable places where either Matthew or Luke has omitted a sizeable portion of Q, thus leaving the mistaken impression that a Q text belongs to either Lukan or Matthean special material. Nonetheless, in recent years the patient work of many scholars has led to an increased confidence that it is indeed possible to reconstruct a plausible text of Q.

Still, even with the general understanding of Q derived from reconstructions currently available it is possible already to say much about the literary history of this text. For example, most recent Q scholarship has come to the conclusion that the "Q" document has undergone editing or, as New Testament scholars term it, redaction. It has also become clear that Q contains different types of sayings. These two conclusions together suggest that Q has undergone multiple stages of development. The work of Arland Jacobson in the United States[49] and John Kloppenborg in Canada[50] especially has contributed to the view that Q is made up of two, possibly three, layers of material.

However that may be, in Q one finds prophetical sayings, which announce the impending judgment of this generation.[51] They share a deuteronomistic understanding of history, in which the prophets experience Israel's impenitence in the form of hostility to them and their message.[52] Examples of this material may be found in Q 11:19–20, 30, 31–32; 17:23–37; and Q 7:31–35:

> [31] To what shall I compare the people of this generation, and what are they like? [32] They are like children seated in the agora and addressing one another, "We piped to you, and you did not dance; we sang a dirge, and you did not mourn." [33] For John came neither eating bread nor drinking wine and they say, "He has a demon." [34] The Son of man came eating and drinking; and they say, "Behold, a glutton and a drunk, a friend of tax collectors and sinners!" [35] Yet Wisdom is vindicated by her children.   —Q 7:31–35

Typical of this material is a certain hostility toward "this generation" as those who have not accepted the Q proclamation of Jesus and shall thus be liable to the judgment that is to come. Its focus is on "outsiders," those who have not joined the Jesus movement, but rejected its claims.

A second type of saying or cluster of material consists of sayings or community-directed "speeches" that are not formulated with outsiders in view. They are concerned with self-definition: attitude toward the world, discipleship, mission and the prospect of persecution and death. Examples of such speeches are found in Q 6:20–49; 9:57–60; 11:2–4, 9–13. These latter "speeches" are characterized by a predominance of wisdom sayings, and thus are more "native" to the genre of Q, "logoi sophōn." For this reason many have come to regard them as belonging to the earliest formative level of Q. The prophetic sayings which pronounce judgment upon outsiders are likely a later addition to this formative layer of Q, formulated after it became evident to the Q folk that they would encounter resistance to their claims among other Jews. Also belonging to this layer would be passages such as Q 7:1–10, which contrast the negative Jewish response to the positive response of an outsider. Whether the Q folk were in fact engaged in a Gentile mission, however, is still a matter of dispute.[53]

As we have seen, recent research has not reached a consensus concerning the theology of Q, although there is general agreement concerning some aspects of Q. The formative stratum of Q is sapiential and the community believes that Jesus, the Living One, is present in the word which he has spoken. Other elements stand within the prophetic tradition, and indicate that the community eventually came to see itself as the successors to the persecuted prophets of the past (Q 6:23). The deuteronomistic tradition provided the theological framework for the addition of later material, which included apocalyptic parenesis (Q 3:7–9, 16–17) and the imminent expectation of the Son of Man (Q 17:24).

Notes

1. Johannes Weiss, "Die Verteidigung Jesu gegen den Vorwurf des Bündnisses mit Beelzebul," *Theologische Studien und Kritiken* 63 (1890) 557. For a discussion of the letter "Q" as a designation for the sayings source, see Ivan Havener, *Q The Sayings of Jesus* (Wilmington, Delaware: Michael Glazier, 1987) 28–29.

2. Ivan Havener (ibid., 42–45), whose work is summarized here, presents more details on the date and place of the composition of Q.

3. For a detailed explanation of the synoptic fact, the synoptic problem and the Two Source Theory see W. G. Kümmel, *Introduction to the New Testament*; trans. H. C. Kee; rev. ed. (New York/Nashville: Abingdon, 1975).

4. This was an insight provided relatively late in the discussion by Vincent Taylor, "The Order of Q," *Journal of Theological Studies*, n.s. 4 (1953) 27–31.

5. See F. Rehkopf, *Die lukanische Sonderquelle: Ihr Umfang und Sprachgebrauch* (Tübingen: J. C. B. Mohr [Paul Siebeck], 1959); Heinz Schürmann, "Protolukanische Spracheigentümlichkeiten?," *Traditionsgeschichtliche Untersuchungen zu den synoptischen Evangelien* (Düsseldorf: Patmos, 1968); J. B. Tyson, "Sequential Parallelism in the Synoptic Gospels," *New Testament Studies* (1976) 276–308.

6. Burnett Hillman Streeter, *The Four Gospels* (London: Macmillan, 1924); Vincent Taylor, *Behind the Third Gospel: A Study of the Proto-Luke Hypothesis* (Oxford: Clarendon, 1926).

7. *Ecclesiastical History* III.xxxix.15–16.

8. L. Vaganay, *Le problème synoptique* (Tournai: Desclée, 1954).

9. See Alfred Wikenhauser, *Einleitung in das Neue Testament* (Freiburg: Herder, 1963).

10. For a detailed presentation of the question of the literary genre of Q and the opinions surrounding it see John S. Kloppenborg, *The Formation of Q: Trajectories in Ancient Wisdom Collections* (Philadelphia: Fortress, 1987) 1–40; the following section summarizes his work.

11. Karl Ludwig Schmidt, "Die Stellung der Evangelien in der allgemeinen Literaturgeschichte," EYXAPIΣTHPION: *Festschrift Herman Gunkel*, FRLANT 36 (Göttingen: Vandenhoeck & Ruprecht, 1923) 76.

12. Franz Overbeck, "Über die Anfang der patristischen Literatur," *Historische Zeitschrift* n.f. 12 (=48) (1882) 417–72.

13. Martin Dibelius, *From Tradition to Gospel*, trans. B. L. Woolf (New York: Charles Scribner's Sons, 1935).

14. Rudolf Bultmann, *The History of the Synoptic Tradition*, trans. John Marsh (Oxford: Basil Blackwell, 1963) 321.

15. Friedrich Schleiermacher, "Über die Zeugnisse des Papias von unsern beiden ersten Evangelien," *Theologische Studien und Kritiken* 5 (1832) 373.

16. H. J. Holtzmann, *Lehrbuch der historisch-kritischen Einleitung in das Neue Testament* (Leipzig/Tübingen: J. C. B. Mohr [Paul Siebeck], 1892) 364.

17. Bernard Weiss, *A Manual of Introduction to the New Testament;* trans. A. J. K. Davidson, 2 vols. (New York: Funk & Wagnalls, 1887–89) 2:224–27.

18. See Kloppenborg, *Formation*, 10.

19. B. Weiss, *Introduction*, 2:224–25.

20. B. W. Bacon, "The Nature and Design of Q, the Second Synoptic Source," *Hibbert Journal* 22 (1923–24) 680–86.

21. See F. C. Burkitt, *The Earliest Sources of the Life of Jesus* (Boston: Houghton Mifflin, 1910) 134–45; Walter E. Bundy, *Jesus and the First Three Gospels* (Cambridge: Harvard University Press, 1972) 481, 499; Emanuel Hirsch, "Fragestellung und Verfahren meiner Frühgeschichte des Evangeliums," *Zeitschrift für die neutestamentliche Wissenschaft* 41 (1942) 106–24.

22. Adolf von Harnack, *The Sayings of Jesus;* trans. J. R. Wilkinson (New York: Putnam's Sons/London: Williams & Norgate, 1908) 171.

23. Adolf Jülicher, *An Introduction to the New Testament;* trans. J. P. Ward (London: Smith, Elder, 1904) 358.

24. See Kloppenborg, *Formation*, 14.

25. Ibid.

26. B. H. Streeter, "The Literary Evolution of the Gospels," *Oxford Studies in the Synoptic Problem* (Oxford: Clarendon, 1911) 209–27.

27. T. W. Manson, *The Sayings of Jesus* (London: SCM, 1949) 9.

28. Streeter, *Four Gospels*, 286.

29. Ibid., 287–88.

30. See Kloppenborg, *Formation*, 19.

31. Bultmann, *Tradition*, 368.

32. R. Bultmann, *Theology of the New Testament;* trans. K. Grobel. 2 vols. (New York: Charles Scribner's Sons, 1951–55) 1:3.

33. Ibid., 37.

34. Kloppenborg, *Formation*, 21.

35. Streeter, *Four Gospels*, 292.

36. Heinz E. Tödt, *The Son of Man in the Synoptic Tradition* (London: SCM, 1965) 253.

37. Ibid., 249.

38. Siegfried Schulz, "Die Bedeutung des Markus für die Theologiegeschichte des Urchristentums," *Studia Evangelica* 2; Texte und Untersuchungen 87 (Berlin: Akademie Verlag, 1964) 138.

39. Ibid., 139.

40. See James M. Robinson, "LOGOI SOPHON: On the Gattung of Q," in idem. and Helmut Koester, *Trajectories Through Early Christianity* (Philadelphia: Fortress, 1971) 71–113.

41. Helmut Koester, "One Jesus and Four Primitive Gospels," *Trajectories,* 186.

42. Koester, "Apocryphal and Canonical Gospels," *Harvard Theological Review* 73 (1980) 113.

43. See Kloppenborg, *Formation,* 33.

44. *Sayings of the Risen Jesus,* Society for New Testament Studies Monograph Series 46 (Cambridge: Cambridge University Press, 1982).

45. *The Oral and the Written Gospel* (Philadelphia: Fortress, 1983).

46. See Harnack, *Sayings;* Josef Schmid, *Matthäus und Lukas: Eine Untersuchung des Verhältnisses ihrer Evangelien,* Biblische Studien 23/4–4 (Freiburg: Herder, 1930); T. W. Manson, *The Sayings of Jesus* (London: SCM, 1949).

47. Athanasius Polag, *Fragmenta Q: Textheft zur Logienquelle* (Neukirchen-Vluyn: Neukirchener Verlag, 1979).

48. *Q Parallels: Synopsis, Critical Notes & Concordance* (Sonoma, CA: Polebridge, 1988).

49. Arland Jacobson, "Wisdom Christology in Q" (Diss., Claremont Graduate School, 1978: to appear in revised form under the title, *The First Gospel: Introduction to Q* [Polebridge, 1990]) and "Literary Unity in Q," *Journal of Biblical Literature* 101 (1982) 365–89.

50. John Kloppenborg, *Formation* (see n. 10).

51. See Dieter Lührmann, *Die Redaktion der Logienquelle,* WMANT 33 (Neukirchen-Vluyn: Neukirchener Verlag, 1969).

52. See O. H. Steck, *Israel und das gewaltsame Geschick der Propheten;* WMANT 23 (Neukirchen-Vluyn: Neukirchener Verlag, 1967). Also Arland D. Jacobson, "Wisdom Christology in Q" and "The Literary Unity of Q," *Journal of Biblical Literature* 101 (1982) 365–89.

53. P. Meyer, "The Gentile Mission in Q," *Journal of Biblical Literature* 89 (1970) 405–17; S. Schulz, *Q: Die Spruchquelle der Evangelisten* (Zurich: Theologische Verlag, 1972).

The Sayings Gospel Q

SUGGESTED READING

The Text of the Sayings Gospel Q

John S. Kloppenborg. *Q Parallels: Synopsis. Critical Notes & Concordance.* Foundations and Facets: New Testament. Sonoma: Polebridge, 1988.

> *Q Parallels* presents the Greek text of the Sayings Gospel Q along with an English translation, brief commentary on each passage, a selection of parallels drawn from the Old Testament, early Christian literature and apocryphal writings, and a concordance of the Greek vocabulary of Q.

Other Literature on Q

M. Eugene Boring. "Christian Prophecy in Q." Pp. 137–82 in *Sayings of the Risen Jesus: Christian Prophecy in the Synoptic Tradition.* Society for New Testament Studies Monograph Series 46. Cambridge and New York: Cambridge University Press, 1982.

> Boring's classic study is the most detailed and convincing examination of the phenomenon of Christian prophecy and prophets to date. He argues that some of the sayings found in Q were either the product of prophets speaking in the name of the Risen Jesus, or influenced by the speech patterns of Christian prophecy.

J. Dominic Crossan. *In Fragments: The Aphorisms of Jesus.* San Francisco: Harper and Row, 1983.

> Although not a book devoted exclusively to Q, this volume is one of the fundamental studies of the use of proverbs and aphorisms in the Jesus tradition. Crossan looks at the way in which aphorisms have been gathered

into compounds and clusters, and describes the compositional effect of the combination of wisdom sayings. Since Q contains several lengthy aphoristic units, this book offers a good orientation into the composition of Q's wisdom speeches.

Ivan Havener. *Q: The Sayings of Jesus.* Good News Studies 19. Wilmington, Delaware: Michael Glazier, 1986.

In addition to providing an English translation of Athanasius Polag's Greek reconstruction of Q, Havener provides a succinct introduction to the "synoptic problem" and to the main features of the Q document.

John S. Kloppenborg. *The Formation of Q: Trajectories in Ancient Wisdom Collections.* Studies in Antiquity and Christianity. Philadelphia: Fortress, 1987.

After summarizing the history of scholarship on Q, Kloppenborg analyses the compositional layers in Q, showing that Q began as a collection of wisdom instructions and was later expanded through the addition of prophetic and apocalyptic sayings. The book also established the place of Q among ancient Near Eastern, Greek and Latin wisdom collections.

Helmut Koester. "Apocryphal and Canonical Gospels." *Harvard Theological Review* 73 (1980) 105–30.

_____. "One Jesus and Four Primitive Gospels" and "The Structure and Criteria of Early Christian Beliefs." Pp. 158–204 and 205–31 in Helmut Koester and James M. Robinson, *Trajectories through Early Christianity.* Philadelphia: Fortress, 1971.

These germinal articles explore the earliest literary genres used for the presentation of traditions about Jesus and the theology implicit in each genre. Koester develops his views on the relationship between Q and the Gospel of Thomas and shows that the Gospel of Thomas is largely untouched by apocalypticism and that in Q the apocalyptic material is secondary to the wisdom materials.

Burton L. Mack. *A Myth of Innocence: Mark and Christian Origins.* Philadelphia: Fortress, 1988 (chaps. 2–3).

In this ground-breaking reconstruction of the place of Mark in Christian origins, Mack sketches developments prior to Mark, including the Q material, the parables of Jesus and the pronouncement stories.

Ronald A. Piper. *Wisdom in the Q-Tradition: The Aphoristic Teaching of Jesus.* Society for New Testament Studies Monograph Series, 61. Cambridge and New York: Cambridge University Press, 1989.

Piper's somewhat technical discussion focuses on aphoristic clusters and isolated wisdom sayings in Q. He shows the literary art that has gone into the composition of Q sayings and concludes with a chapter on the Christians responsible for the composition and transmission of Q.

James M. Robinson. "Jesus as Sophos and Sophia." Pp. 1–16 in R. L. Wilken, ed., *Aspects of Wisdom in Judaism and Early Christianity*. Notre Dame: University of Notre Dame Press, 1975. And "LOGOI SOPHON: On the Gattung of Q." Pp. 71–113 in Helmut Koester and James M. Robinson, *Trajectories through Early Christianity*. Philadelphia: Fortress, 1971.

In the epochal article "LOGOI SOPHON" ('sayings of the sages') Robinson traces the development of the literary genre of 'sayings of the sages' from its roots in Near Eastern and Old Testament literature to its use in early Gnostic literature. In "Jesus as Sophos and Sophia" Robinson sketches the Old Testament figure of "Lady Wisdom" found in Proverbs, Sirach and Wisdom of Solomon, and argues that the early Christians represented by Q used the notion of Heavenly Wisdom to account for the significance of Jesus and John the Baptist in the history of salvation.

The Sayings Gospel Q

CONTENTS

Contents   33

Sigla Used for the Q Translation

Bold face
This represents verbatim or near verbatim agreements between Matthew and Luke (in Greek). In most cases, the translation reflects agreements in the original language.

Underscoring
In three pericopae (Q 6:43–45; 11:14–15; 11:16,29) there are two Matthean versions and one Lukan version. Agreements between the first Matthean version and the Lukan version are registered with bold face, while underscoring indicates the agreements of Matthew's second version with Luke.

Behold
Italic font is used for quotations from the Jewish scriptures. The source of the quotation is indicated in a note.

a
Where there is sufficient agreement between Matthew and Luke to permit the printing of a single text, the wording which, in the editor's view, is closer to Q is printed as the text and the variants from the other gospel appears in the apparatus. A raised letter indicates points in the text where either Matthew or Luke offers a different reading. This siglum is also used to identify obvious redactional additions in the text of Matthew or Luke in double column presentations.

fruit[a]
A superscript letter *attached* to a word in the text indicates a variant for that word.

hunger [d]
A superscript letter *preceded and followed by a space* indicates the presence of additional words or phrases in another gospel at this point.

(. . .)
Parentheses enclose verses or whole pericopes which are attested in only one gospel but which have a strong probability of deriving from Q.

[. . .]
Square brackets designate texts or verses that occur in a single gospel and which some scholars have included in Q. The likelihood of these coming from Q is, however, relatively small (e.g., Q 12:35–38).

⟨. . .⟩
In a few instances Q seems to presuppose introductory or transitional phrases, but Matthean and Lukan activity is so strong that only conjectural readings are possible. These readings are enclosed in angle brackets.

The Sayings Gospel Q

TRANSLATION & NOTES

Incipit

⟨These are the words of Jesus and John⟩

Introduction   ⟨Q 3:2⟩

(Matt 3:1–6 // Luke 3:1–6)

⟨**John** came into **all the region about the Jordan** . . .⟩

⟨Q 3:2⟩ ⇨ Mark 1:2–6

John's Preaching of Repentance   Q 3:7–9

Matt 3:7–10	Luke 3:7–9
[7] But when he saw many of the Phari-sees and Sadducees coming to his baptism, he said to them,	[7] He said therefore to the crowds that were coming out to be baptized by him,

"You brood of vipers! Who warned you to flee from the coming wrath? [8/8] Bear fruit[a] worthy of repentance, [9/]and do not presume[b] to say to yourselves, 'We have Abraham as our father'; for I tell you, God is able from these stones to raise up children to Abraham. [10/9] Even now is the axe laid to the root of the trees; every tree therefore that does not bear good fruit is cut down and thrown into the fire."

a   Matt; Luke: fruits
b   Matt; Luke: begin

35

John's Proclamation of the Coming One   Q 3:16b–17

Matt 3:11–12   Luke 3:16b–17

[11/16] [a] **"To be sure, I am baptizing you with water** [b]**; but the One who is** coming after me[c] **is stronger than I,** [d] **whose sandals I am not worthy to carry**[e]**; he will baptize you with the Holy Spirit and fire.** [12/17] **His winnowing fork is in his hand, to clear his threshing floor, and to gather the wheat**[f] **into his granary**[g]**, but the chaff he will burn with unquenchable fire."**

Q 3:16b–17 ⇨ Mark 1:7–8
a Luke + v. 15–16a: Since the people were in expectation and everyone was wondering in their hearts concerning John, whether perhaps he were the Christ, John anwered them all,
b Matt + for repentance
c Matt: Luke: **but the One who is stronger than I is coming**
d Matt: Luke + the thong of
e Matt: Luke: untie
f Luke; Matt: his wheat
g Luke; Matt: the granary

The Temptations of Jesus   Q 4:1–13

Matt 4:1–11	Luke 4:1–13

[1] Then **Jesus was led** up into **the wilderness** by **the Spirit** to be **tempted by the devil.** [2] **And** since he had fasted **forty days** and forty nights, afterward **he was hungry.** [3] And approaching, the tempter **said to him,**

"**If you are the Son of God, tell these stones to become loaves of bread."** [4] But he **answered, "It is written, 'No one can live by bread alone** [a]**.'"** [5] Then the devil took **him to** the holy city, **and set** him **on the pinnacle of the temple,** [6] **and said to him, "If you are the Son of God, throw yourself down; for it is written, 'He will give his angels charge of you,' and 'On**

[1] **Jesus,** full of the Holy Spirit, returned from the Jordan, and **was led** in **the Spirit** [2] for **forty days** in **the wilderness, tempted by the devil. And** he ate nothing in those days; and when they were completed, **he was hungry.** [3] The devil **said to him,** "**If you are the Son of God, tell this stone to become a loaf of bread."** [4] And Jesus **answered** him, "**It is written, 'No one can live by bread alone.'"** [9] And he led **him to** Jerusalem, **and set** (him) **on the pinnacle of the temple, and said to him, "If you are the Son of God, throw yourself down** from here; [10] **for it is written, 'He will give his angels charge of you,** to guard

*their hands they will bear you up,
lest you strike your foot against a
stone."'*
[7] **Jesus** said **to him,** *"Again it is written, 'You shall not tempt the Lord
your God.'"*
[8] Again, the devil took **him** to a very
high mountain, and **showed him all
the kingdoms of the** world **and their
glory;** [9] **and** he **said to him,** *"All these
I will give you, if you* will fall down
and **worship me."**

[10] Then **Jesus** said to **him,** *"Depart
Satan! for* **it is written,** *'You shall
worship the Lord your God and him
alone shall you serve.'"*
[11] Then **the devil** left him, and behold, angels came and were serving
him.

you,' [11] **and,** *'On their hands they will
bear you up, lest you strike your foot
against a stone.'"*
[12] And **Jesus** responded **to him,** *'It is
said,* *'You shall not tempt the Lord
your God.'"*
[5] And he led **him** up, and **showed
him all the kingdoms of the** earth in
a moment of time, [6] **and** the devil **said
to him, "To you I will give** all this authority **and their glory;** for it has been
delivered to me, and I give it to whom
I wish. [7] **If you,** therefore, will **worship** before **me,** it shall all be yours."
[8] And **Jesus** answered **him, "It is
written,** *'You shall worship the Lord
your God and him alone shall you
serve.'"*
[13] And having completed every temptation, **the devil** departed from him
until an opportune time.

Q 4:1–2a, 13 ⇨ Mark 1:12–13
Q 4:4: Deut 8:3b LXX
Q 4:8: Deut 5:9; 6:13 LXX
Q 4:10–11: Ps 90:11–12 LXX
Q 4:12: Deut 6:16
a Matt + but by every word that proceeds from the mouth of
   God. (=Deut 8:3c)

Jesus' Inaugural Sermon   ⟨Q 6:20a⟩

Matt 5:1–2

[1] **Now** when he saw the **crowds,** he
went **up the mountain,** and when he
sat down **his disciples** came to him.
[2] And he opened his mouth and
taught them, **saying,**

Luke 6:12, 17, 20a

[12] **Now** in these days, he went **up the
mountain** to pray; and he spent all
night in prayer to God. [17] And when
he came down with them, he stood on
a level place with a great **crowd** of his
disciples and a great multitude of
people... [20] And he raised his eyes to
his disciples, and **said,**

Blessings and Woes   Q 6:20b–23 (24–26)

Matt 5:3,6,4,11–12   Luke 6:20b–26

3/20b **"Blessed are** you[a] **poor, for** yours[a] **is the reign of**
God.[b]
6/21 **Blessed are** you[c] **that hunger** [d,e], **for** you[c] **shall
be filled.**
4/ **Blessed are** you that weep [f,d], **for** you shall laugh[g].

[11] **Blessed are you when** they
reproach you and persecute **you and**
say every **evil** against you falsely **on
my account.**
[12] **Rejoice and** be glad, for **your
reward is great in heaven, for** so they
persecuted **the prophets** who came
before you."

[22] **Blessed are you when** people hate
you, and when they exclude you and
reproach you, and cast out your name
as **evil, on account of** the Son of man!
[23] **Rejoice** in that day, **and** leap for
joy, for behold, **your reward is great
in heaven; for** so their fathers did to
the prophets."

a Luke; Matt: the, theirs
b Luke; Matt: the heavens
c Luke; Matt: they
d Luke + now
e Matt + and thirst for righteousness
f Luke; Matt: those who mourn
g Luke; Matt: they shall be comforted

Luke 6:24–26

([24] "But woe to you rich, for you have
received your consolation. [25] Woe to
you who are full now, for you shall be
hungry, Woe to you who laugh now,
for you shall mourn and weep. [26] Woe
to you, when all people speak well of
you, for so their fathers did to the false
prophets.")[a]

a Possibly in Q and omitted by Matthew.

On Retaliation   Q 6:27–35

Matt 5:43–44, 38–42   Luke 6:27–35

[44] [a] "Now **I tell you, Love** your enemies and **pray** for **those who** persecute **you**.

[27] "But **I tell you** who listen, **Love
your enemies,** do good to those who
hate you, [28] bless those who curse you,
pray for **those who** mistreat **you.**

³⁹ ᵇ If any one strikes **you** on **the** right **cheek**, turn to him **the other also;**

⁴⁰ **and** if any one wants to sue you and take **your tunic,** let him have **even the cloak**;

(⁴¹ and if any one presses you into service for one mile, go with him two miles.)ᶜ

⁴² **Give to one who begs from you, and** do **not** refuse one who wants to borrow **from** you."

²⁹ When someone hits **you** on **the cheek**, offer **the other also; and** when someone takes away **your cloak** do not withhold **even the tunic.**

³⁰ **Give to** every **one who begs from you; and from** someone who takes away your belongings do **not** ask for them back again.

Matt 7:12

¹² "So whatever **you wish that people would do to you, do** so also **to them;**ᵈ"

³¹ And as **you wish that people would do to you, do** so to them.

Matt 5:46–47, 45

⁴⁶ "For if **you love those who love you,** what reward have you? Do not **even the** tax collectors do the same?

⁴⁷ **And if** you only greet your brothers, what are you doing that is out of the ordinary? Do not **even the** Gentiles **do the same?**

³² If **you love those who love you,** what credit is that to you? For **even the** sinners love those who love them.

³³ **And if** you also do good to those who do good to you, what credit is that to you? **Even the** sinners **do the same.**

³⁴ And if you lend to those from whom you expect repayment, what credit is that to you? Even sinners lend to sinners, to receive as much again.

³⁵ Instead, love your enemies, and do good, and lend, expecting nothing back; and your reward will be great, and you will be **children** of the Most High; for he showers kindness **on the** ungrateful **and the evil.**"

⁴⁵ Thus you will become **children** of your Father who is in heaven; **for** he makes his sun rise **on the evil and** on the good, and sends rains on the just and on the unjust."

a Matt 5:43: Matt + "You have heard it said, 'You shall love your countryman and hate your enemy."
b Matt 5:38–39a: Matt + "You have heard that it was said, 'An eye for an eye and a tooth for a tooth.' But I tell you, do not oppose one who is evil. But . . ."
c Matt 5:41: Possibly in Q and omitted by Luke.
d Matt 7:12b: Matt + "for this is the law and the prophets."

On Judging   Q 6:36–37b, 38c

Matt 5:48; 7:1–2	Luke 6:36–38
48 "Be perfect, therefore, as **your** heavenly **Father is** perfect. 1 "**Do not judge,** lest **you be judged.** 2 For with the judgement you pronounce you will be judged, and with	36 "Be merciful, even as **your Father is** merciful. 37 And **judge not,** and **you will not be judged;** condemn not, and you will not be condemned; forgive, and you will be forgiven; 38 give, and it will be given to you; they will put into your lap a full measure, pressed down, shaken together, overflowing. For by
the standard with which you measure, it will be measured to you."	**the standard with which you measure, it will be measured** back **to you."**

Q 6:38c ⇨ Mark 4:24

Blind Guides, Teachers and Pupils   Q 6:39b–40

Matt 15:14	Luke 6:39–40
14 a "Guides of the blind are themselves blind. Now if **a blind man leads a blind man, both will fall into a pit."**	39 b "Surely **a blind man** cannot **lead a blind man? Will they** not **both fall into a pit?**

Matt 10:24–25	
24 "**A disciple is not above the teacher,** nor a servant above his master; 25 it is enough for the disciple to be **like his teacher,** and the servant like his master. c"	40 **A disciple is not above his teacher,** but every one when he is fully trained will be **like his teacher."**

a Matt 15:14a: Matt + "Let them alone;"
b Luke 6:39a: Luke + He also told them a parable:
c Matt 10:25c: Matt + "If they called the master of the house Beelzebul, how much more will they say it of those of his household."

On Hypocrisy   *Q 6:41–42*

Matt 7:3–5   Luke 6:41–42

^{3/41} "Why do you seek the speck that is in your brother's eye, but do not notice the beam that is in your own eye? ^{4/42} ^a How can you say^b to your brother, '^c let me remove the speck that is in^d your eye,' when you yourself do not see^e the beam that is in your own eye? ^{5/} You hypocrite, first remove the beam from your own eye, and then you will see clearly to remove the speck that is in^f your brother's eye."

a Luke; Matt + Or
b Luke; Matt: will you say
c Matt; Luke + Brother
d Luke; Matt: from
e Luke; Matt: and behold, (there is a)
f Luke; Matt: from

Good and Evil Persons   *Q 6:43–45*

Matt 7:16–20	Matt 12:33–35	Luke 6:43–45
¹⁸ "A good **tree** ca**nnot bear** evil **fruit, nor can a rotten tree bear good fruit.** ¹⁶ From their **fruits** you will **know** them. Are **grapes gathered from thorns,** or **figs** from thistles? ^a"	³³ "Either think that the tree is healthy, and its fruit good; or suppose that the tree is rotten and its fruit bad; for by its fruit the tree is known.	⁴³ "For **no** healthy **tree bears** bad **fruit, nor** again **does a rotten tree bear good fruit;** ⁴⁴ for each tree is **known** by its own **fruit.** For **figs** are not **gathered from thorns,** nor are **grapes** picked from a bramble bush. (v. 45c)
	³⁴ ^b For from what over-flows the heart the mouth speaks. ³⁵ From the good storeroom the good person brings out good things, and from an evil storeroom, the evil person brings out evil things;" (v. 34b)	⁴⁵ From the good store-room of the heart the good person produces what is good, from an evil one, the evil pro-duces evil; for from what overflows a heart his mouth speaks."

a Matt + v. 17: So, every healthy tree bears good fruit, but the rotten tree bears bad fruit.
b Matt + v. 34a: You brood of vipers! How can you speak good, if you are evil?

The Parable of the Builders   Q 6:46–49

Matt 7:21–27	Luke 6:46–49

21 "Not every one who says to **me, 'Lord, Lord,'** will enter the kingdom of heaven, but the one who **does** the will of my Father who is in heaven." (vv. 22–23 ⇨ Q 13:26–27)

46 "Why do you call **me 'Lord, Lord'** and not **do** what I tell you?

24 "Therefore **every one** who **hears** these **words of mine and practices them** will be like a wise man who **built** his **house upon the rock;** 25 and the rain fell, and **the torrent**s came, and the winds blew and beat **against that house, and** it did **not** fall, for it had been founded on the rock.

47 **Every one** who comes to me and **hears my words and practices them,** I will show you what he is like: 48 he is like a person **building a house,** who dug down deep, and laid the foundation **upon the rock;** and when a flood came, **the torrent** broke **against that house, and** could **not** shake it, since it was well built.

26 And every **one who hears** these words of mine **and does not practice them** will be like a foolish man who **built** his **house on the** sand; 27 and the rain fell, and **the torrent**s came, and the wind blew and beat against **that house, and it fell; and** its fall **was great."**

49 But **one who hears and does not practice them** is like a person who **built a house on the** ground without a foundation. **The torrent** broke against it, **and** immediately **it collapsed, and the** ruin **of that house was great."**

The Centurion in Capharnaum   Q 7:1–10

Matt 7:28–29	Luke 7:1–10

⟨ 28 And it happened that when Jesus finished these sayings, the crowds were astonished at his teaching,⟩

⟨ 1 After he had completed all his speech in the hearing of the people⟩

Matt 8:5–13

5 When **he entered Capharnaum, a centurion** came forward to him, **appeal**ing **to him** 6 and **saying,** "Lord, my serving boy is lying paralysed at home, suffering dreadfully." 7 And he said to him, "I will **come** and heal him."

he entered Capharnaum. 2 Now **a centurion** had a certain slave who was dear to him, who was sick and at the point of death. 3 When he heard about Jesus, he sent to him elders of the Jews, asking him to **come** and spare his slave. 4 And when they came to Jesus, they **appealed to him** earnestly, **saying,** "He is worthy to have you do this for him, 5 for he loves our nation, and he himself built the synagogue for us." 6 So Jesus went with them. When he was not far from the house, **the centurion** sent friends, saying to him, **"Lord,** do not trouble yourself, for I **am not worthy to have you come under my roof;** 7 that is why I did not consider myself fit to come to you. But **speak a word, and** let **my serving boy be healed.**

8 And **the centurion** answered him, **"Lord, I am not worthy to have you come under my roof;**

but only **speak a word and my serving boy** will **be healed.**

9/8 **For I myself am a man set** a **under authority, with soldiers under me: and I say to one, 'Go,' and he goes; to another, 'Come,' and he comes; and to my slave, 'Do this,' and he does it."**
10/9 **When Jesus heard** this b **he marvelled** at him c, **and** d **to those** e **that followed him, he said "I tell you, I have not found such trust in Israel."**

(vv. 11–12 ⇨ Q 13:28–29)

13 And to the centurion Jesus said, "Depart. As you have trusted, may it be done to you." **And** his serving boy was healed in that hour.

10 **And** when the delegation returned to the house, they found the slave well.

a Luke; Matt: omit
b Luke; Matt: omit
c Luke; Matt: omit
d Matt; Luke + turning
e Matt; Luke: to the crowd

John's Inquiry   Q 7:18–20, 22–23

Matt 11:2–6	Luke 7:18–23

[2] Now when **John** heard in prison about the works of the Christ, he **sent word by his disciples** [3] and said to him, **"Are you the one who is to come, or should we expect** someone else?"

[18] And the disciples of John told him of all these things. [19] And **John**, summoning two of **his disciples, sent** them to the Lord, saying, **"Are you the one who is to come, or should we expect** another?" [20] When the men had come to him, they said, "John the Baptist sent us to you, saying, '**Are you the one who is to come, or should we expect** another?'" [a]

4/22 **And he** [b] **answered them, "Go and tell John what you** have seen and heard [c]: 5/ **the blind recover their sight,** [d] **the lame walk, lepers are cleansed, and the deaf hear,** [d] **the dead are raised up, the poor are given good news.** 6/23 **And whoever is not offended by me is blessed."**

Q 6:22b: Cf. Isa 26:19; 29:18–19; Isa 35:5–6; 42:6–7; 61:1 (LXX).
a   Luke + v. 21: In that hour he cured many of diseases and afflictions and evil spirits, and to many who were blind he granted sight.
b   Luke; Matt: Jesus
c   Luke; Matt: you hear and see
d   Luke; Matt: + and

Jesus' Eulogy of John   Q 7:24–28

Matt 11:7–11	Luke 7:24–28

[7] **Now when** they had gone on their way, Jesus

[24] **Now when** the messengers of John had departed, he

began to speak to the crowds concerning John: "What did you go out into the wilderness to see? A reed shaken by the wind? 8/25 **But what did you go out to see? A man clothed in luxurious clothing? Behold, those** who wear luxurious garments [a] **are in** the royal palaces [b]. 9/26 **But what did you go out to see? A prophet? Yes, I tell you, and more than a prophet.** 10/27 **This is the one about whom it is written,**
'Behold, I send my messenger before your face, who will prepare your way before you.'

11/28 c **I tell you, among those born of women** none
is d **greater than John; yet the least in the kingdom of
God** f **is greater than he."**

Q 7:27b: Mal 3:1; Exod 23:20; cf. Mark 1:2
a   Matt; Luke: who are gorgeously apparelled and live in
    luxury
b   Luke; Matt: houses of kings
c   Luke; Matt: + Amen
d   Luke; Matt: there has not arisen (one)
e   Luke; Matt: the heavens

The Kingdom Suffers Violence   Q 16:16

Matt 11:12–13	Luke 16:16
12 **"From** the days of John the Baptist until now **the reign of** heaven is **seized at, and** the violent grabbed **it.** 13 For all **the prophets and the law** prophesied until **John."**	16 **"The law and the prophets were** until **John. From** then **the reign of** God is proclaimed, **and** everybody **seizes at it."**

The Children in the Agora   Q 7:31–35

Matt 11:16–19	Luke 7:31–35
16 "Now **to what shall I compare this generation?**	31 **"To what** then **shall I compare** the people of **this generation**, and what are they like?
It is **like children seated in the agoras** who **address** their playmates,	32 They are **like children seated in the agora** and **address**ing one another,

17/**"We piped to you, and you did not dance; we sang
a dirge, and you did not** mourn a .' 18/33 **For John** b
came c **neither eating** bread d **nor drinking** wine d;
and they e **say, 'He has a demon.'** 19/34 **The Son of
man** came c **eating and drinking; and they** e **say,
'Behold, a glutton and a drunk, a friend of tax
collectors and sinners!'** /35 **Yet Wisdom is vindicated
by** f **her** children g ."

a   Matt; Luke: weep
b   Matt; Luke: + the Baptist
c   Matt; Luke: has come
d   Luke; Matt: omit bread, wine
e   Matt; Luke: you (pl.)
f   Matt; Luke: + all
g   Luke; Matt: works

Three Followers of Jesus   Q 9:57–60 (61–62)

Matt 8:19–22	Luke 9:57–62
[19] **And** a scribe came up and **said to him,**	[57] **And** as they were going along the road, someone **said to him,**

"I will follow you wherever you go." [20/58] **And Jesus** said[a] **to him, "Foxes have holes, and birds of the sky have nests; but the Son of man has nowhere to lay his head."**

| [21] **And another** of his disciples **said** to him, | [59] **And** to **another** he said, "Follow me." But **he said,** |

"Lord, let me first go and bury my father." [22/60] **But** he[b] **said**[a] **to him,** [c] **"Leave the dead to bury their own dead.** [d]**"**

> ([61] Yet another said, "I will follow you, Lord; but first let me say farewell to those at my home." [62] Jesus said to him, "No one who puts his hand to the plough and looks back is fit for the reign of God.")[e]

a Luke; Matt: says
b Luke; Matt: Jesus
c Luke; Matt: + Follow me and (⇨ Luke 9:59a)
d Matt; Luke: + but as for you, go and proclaim the reign of God.
e Possibly in Q but omitted by Matthew

The Mission Speech   Q 10:2–12

Matt 9:37–38; 10:7–15	Luke 10:2–12
[37] Then **he said** to his disciples,	[2] And **he said** to them,

[38/] **"The harvest is large, but the workers are few; therefore beg the master of the harvest to send out workers into his harvest.**
[16/3] [a] **Behold, I am sending you as sheep among wolves.** [b]

[7] Preach as you go, saying, **'The reign of** heaven **has come near.'** [8] **Heal the sick,** raise the dead, cleanse lepers, exorcise demons. You received without payment, give without charge.

[9] Take **no** gold or silver, nor copper in your belts, [10] **no knapsack** for your journey, nor two tunics, **nor sandals,** nor a staff **for the worker deserves his** food. [11] **Into whatever city** or village **you enter,** determine who in it is worthy, and **stay** with that person until you depart.

[12] As **you enter** the **house,** greet it. [13] **And if** the house **is** worthy, let **your peace** come **upon** it; **but** if it is **not** worthy, let you peace return to **you.**

⇨ v. 4

⇨ Carry **no** purse, **no knapsack, no sandals;** and greet no one on the road.

⇨ v. 7b
⇨ v. 8a

⇨ v. 7a

⇨ v. 9b
⇨ v. 9a

⇨ v. 11b

⇨ v. 10b
⇨ v. 11b
⇨ v. 11a

⇨ v. 8a
⇨ v. 7

[5] Into whatever **house you enter,** first say, 'Peace be to this house!' [6] **And if** a child of peace **is** there, **your peace** shall rest **upon** him; **but if not,** it shall return to **you.**

[7] And **stay** in the same house, eating and drinking whatever they have, **for the worker deserves his** wages. Do not go from house to house.

[8] **And if you enter a city** and they welcome you, eat what is set before you;

[9] and **heal the sick** in it and say to them, **'The reign of** God **has come near** to you.'

[10] But **whatever** city you enter that **does not welcome you, go out** into its streets and say, [11] 'Even **the dust of** your **city** that clings to our **feet,** we wipe off against you; but know this, that the reign of God has come near.'

[14] And **whoever does not welcome you** or listen to your words, as you **go out** of that house or **city** shake off **the dust** from your **feet.**

⇨ v. 7

[15] Amen, **I tell you, it shall be more tolerable on** the **day** of judgment **for** the land of **Sodom** and Gomorrah **than for that city."**

[12] **I tell you** that **it shall be more tolerable on** that **day for Sodom than for that city."**

Q 10:4–11 ⇨ Mark 6:8–13
a Matt; Luke: + Go!
b Luke; Matt add: therefore be as clever as snakes and as innocent as doves.

Woes on the Galilean Towns   *Q 10:13–15*

Matt 11:20–24   Luke 10:13–15

21/13 **"Woe to you, Chorazin! woe to you, Bethsaida!**
for if the miracles done in you had been done in
Tyre and Sidon, they would have repented long ago
a in sackcloth and ashes. 22/14 But b it shall be more
tolerable on the c judgement for Tyre and Sidon
than for you. 23/15 And you, Capharnaum, will you
be exalted to heaven? *You shall descend to Hades!"*
("For if the miracles done in you had
been done in Sodom, it would be
standing today. 24 But I tell you that it
shall be more tolerable on the day of
judgement for the land of Sodom than
for you.")d

Q 10:15b: Isa 14:15
a Matt; Luke: + sitting
b Luke; Matt: + I tell you,
c Luke; Matt: + day of
d Possibly in Q and omitted by Luke

The Authority of the Q Envoys   *Q 10:16*

Matt 10:40	Luke 10:16
40 **"Whoever** welcomes **you** welcomes **me, and whoever** welcomes **me** welcomes **him who sent me."**	16 **"Whoever** hears **you** hears **me, and whoever** rejects you rejects me; but whoever rejects **me** rejects **him who sent me."**

Thanksgiving for Revelation   *Q 10:21–22*

Matt 11:25–27	Luke 10:21–22
25 **At** that time Jesus **said,**	21 **At** that very hour he rejoiced in the Holy Spirit and **said,**

"I praise you Father, Lord of heaven and earth, that
you have hidden these things from sages and the
learned and revealed them to babes. 26/Yes, Father,
for such was your gracious will. 27/22 All things
have been handed over to me by my Father; and no
one knows the son a **except the Father,** or the Fatherb

except the Son and any one to whom the Son wishes to reveal him."

a   Matt; Luke: who the Son is
b   Matt; Luke: and who the Father is

Blessing on the Eye-witnesses   Q 10:23–24

Matt 13:16–17	Luke 10:23–24

16 "But your **eyes are blessed,** because they **see**, and your ears, because they hear.

23 a **"Blessed are the eyes** which **see** what you see!

17/24 **For** b **I tell you that many prophets and** kings c wanted d **to see what you are seeing, and did not see it, and to hear what you are hearing, and did not hear it."**

a   Luke add v. 23a: And turning to the disciples he said
    privately,
b   Luke; Matt: Amen, for
c   Luke; Matt: righteous persons
d   Luke; Matt: desired

The Lord's Prayer   Q 11:2–4

Matt 6:9–13	Luke 11:2–4

9 **Pray** then like this:

a 2 He said to them, "When you **pray,** say:

" b **Father** c**, may your name be holy.**
10/ **May your reign come** d**.**
11/3 **Give us** today e **our daily bread;**
12/4 **and forgive us our** debts f**, even as we** ourselves have **forgiven our** debtors g**;**
13/ **and do not lead us to the test** h**."**

a   Luke + v. 1–2a: And it happened that he was in a certain
    place praying, and when he finished, one of his disciples
    said to him, "Lord, teach us to pray, as John also taught his
    disciples."
b   Luke; Matt: + Our
c   Luke; Matt: + in the heavens
d   Luke; Matt: + Your will be done, on earth as it is in heaven.
e   Matt; Luke: each day
f   Matt; Luke: sins
g   Matt; Luke: for **we** ourselves **also forgive** every one who
    is indebted to **us**
h   Luke; Matt: + but deliver us from the evil one.

Confidence in Prayer   Q 11:9–13

Matt 7:7–11   Luke 11:9–13

7/9 a **"Ask, and it will be given you; seek, and you
will find; knock, and it will be opened to you.**
8/10 **For every one who asks receives, and whoever
seeks finds, and whoever knocks is admitted.**

9 Or who **among you, if his son asks** him for bread, **will give him** a stone? 10 **Or if he asks for a fish, will give him a snake?**	11 What father **among you, if his son asks for a fish, will** instead of a fish **give him** a snake; 12 Or **if he asks for** an egg, **will give him** a scorpion?

11/13 **If you, then, being selfish, know how to give
good gifts to your children, how much more will
the** b **Father** from heaven c **give** good things d **to those
who ask him!"**

a Matt; Luke: + And I tell you,
b Luke; Matt: your
c Luke; Matt: who is in the heavens
d Matt; Luke: the Holy Spirit

The Beelzebul Accusation   Q 11:14–23

Matt 12:22–30	Matt 9:32–34	Luke 11:14–23
22 Then a blind and **mute** man who was demon-possessed was brought to him, and he healed him, so that **the mute spoke** and saw again. 23 **And** all **the crowds** were amazed, and were saying, "Can this be the Son of David?" 24 **But** when the Pharisees heard it **they said,** "This man does not **exorcise the demons, except by Beelzebul, the prince of demons."** ⇨ Matt 12:38 (Q 11:29–32)	32 As they were going away, behold they brought to him a <u>mute</u> who was demon-possessed. 33 And <u>when the demon</u> had been exorcised, <u>the mute</u> spoke, and the crowds marvelled, saying, "Never has anything like this been seen in Israel." 34 But the Pharisees were saying, <u>"It is by the prince of demons that he exor-cises the demons."</u>	14 And he was exorcising a demon that was **mute;** when the demon had gone out, **the mute spoke and the crowds** marvelled. 15 **But** some of them **said,** "It is **by Beelzebul, the prince of demons that he exorcises the demons.**" 16 Now others, to test him, sought from him a sign from heaven.

25/17 **But knowing their** designs a, **he said to them,
"Every kingdom divided against itself is laid waste,
and** a city or household divided against itself will not
survive. b

26/18 **And if Satan** exorcises Satan, he[c] **is divided against himself; how** [d] **will his kingdom endure?** [e] 27/19 And[f] **if I exorcise demons by Beelzebul, by whom do your sons exorcise? Therefore they shall be your judges.** 28/20 **But if it is by the finger**[g] **of God that I exorcise demons, then the reign of God has come upon you.**

29 Or how can one enter a **strong man**'s house and plunder his property, unless he first binds the strong man?
And then he may plunder **his** house.

21 When a **strong man**, fully armed, guards his own courtyard, his goods are safe; 22 but when one stronger than he overpowers him and conquers him, he takes away his armour in which he trusted, **and** divides **his** spoil.

30/23 **Whoever is not with me is against me, and whoever does not gather with me scatters."**

Q 11:14–15, 17–18 ⇨ Mark 3:22–26
Q 11:21–22 ⇨ Mark 3:27
a   Matt; Luke: thoughts
b   Matt; Luke: a house that is against itself collapses.
c   Matt; Luke omit exorcises Satan, he.
d   Luke; Matt + then
e   Matt; Luke + For you say that I exorcise demons by Beelzebul.
f   Matt; Luke: But
g   Luke; Matt: Spirit

The Return of the Evil Spirit   Q 11:24–26

Matt 12:43–45   Luke 11:24–26

43/24 [a] **"When the unclean spirit has gone out of a person, he goes through arid places seeking a resting place** and he finds none.[b]
44/ **Then he says, 'I will return to my house from whence I came.'**
/25 **And when he comes he finds it swept and put in order.**
45/26 **Then he goes and brings** [c] **seven other spirits more evil than himself, and they enter and dwell there; and the last state of that person becomes worse than the first.** [d]"

a   Luke; Matt + Now
b   Matt; Luke: and having found none,
c   Luke; Matt + with himself
d   Luke; Matt + So shall it be also with this evil generation.

True Blessedness   (Q 11:27–28)

(²⁷ As he was saying these things, a
woman from the crowd raised her
voice and said to him, "Blessed is the
womb that bore you, and the breasts
that you sucked!" ²⁸ But he said,
"Blessed rather are those who listen to
the word of God and keep it!")

Vv. 27–28: Possibly in Q and omitted by Matthew.

The Sign of Jonah   Q 11:16, 29–32

Matt 12:38–42	Matt 16:1–2a, 4	Luke 11:16, 29–32
³⁸ Then some of the scribes and Pharisees said to him, "Teacher, we wish to see **a sign** from you." ³⁹ **But** he answered them, "**An evil** and adulterous **generation seeks a sign; and no sign shall be given to it except the sign of Jonah** the prophet.	¹ And the Pharisees and Sadducees came, and to test him they asked him to show them a sign from heaven. ² But he answered them . . . ⁴ "An evil and adulterous generation seeks a sign, and no sign shall be given to it except the sign of Jonah."	¹⁶ Now others, to test him, were seeking from him **a sign** from heaven. ²⁹ **But** as the crowds were increasing, he began to say, "This generation is **an evil generation;** (it) **seeks a sign, and no sign shall be given to it except the sign of Jonah**.
⁴⁰ **For** as **Jonah** was three days and three nights in the belly of the sea monster, **so will the Son of man be** three days and three nights in the heart of the earth.		³⁰ **For** as **Jonah** became a sign to the Ninevites, **so will the Son of man be** to this generation.

⁴²/³¹ **The queen of the South will arise at the
judgment with ᵃ this generation and condemn
them; for she came from the ends of the earth to
hear the wisdom of Solomon, and behold,
something greater than Solomon is here.**
⁴¹/³² **The Ninevite men will arise at the judgment
with this generation and condemn it; for they
repented at the preaching of Jonah, and behold,
something greater than Jonah is here."**

Q 11:16, 29 ⇨ Mark 8:11–12
a Matt; Luke: + the men of

The Lamp and the Eye   Q 11:33–36

Matt 5:14-15	Luke 11:33
[a] [15] "Nor do they light **a lamp** and **put it under a grain basket, but on a lampstand,** and it gives light to all in the house."	[33] "No one having lit **a lamp puts** it in a cellar or **under a grain basket, but on a lampstand,** that those who enter may see the light."

Matt 6:22-23	Luke 11:34-36
[22] **"The eye is the lamp of the body.** So, if **your eye is generous, your whole body** will be **full of light;** [23] but if your eye **is evil, your** whole body will be **full of darkness. If then the light in you is darkness,** how great is the darkness!"	[34] "Your **eye is the lamp of the body;** when **your eye is generous, your whole body** is also **full of light; but** when it **is evil, your body** is also **full of darkness.** [35] Therefore watch lest **the light in you be darkness.** [36] **If then** your whole body is full of light, having no part dark, it will be completely full of light, as when a lamp with its rays illuminates you."

Q 11:33 ⇨ Mark 4:21
a   Matt + v. 14: You are the light of the world. A city set on a hill cannot be hid.

The Woes Against the Pharisees   Q 11:39b–44, 46–52

a. On Tithing

Matt 23:23   Luke 11:42

[23/42] **"Woe to you,** [a] **Pharisees** [b]**, for you tithe mint and dill** [c] **and** cummin [d] **and** neglect [e] [f] **justice and the** love of God [g]. **But these you ought to have done without** neglecting [h] **the others."**

Q 11:42 cf. Mic 6:8
a   Luke; Matt + scribes and
b   Luke; Matt + hypocrites
c   Matt; Luke: rue
d   Matt; Luke: every herb
e   Luke; Matt: leave aside
f   Luke; Matt + the weightier matters of the law,
g   Luke; Matt: mercy and faithfulness.
h   Luke; Matt: leaving aside

b. On Washing Vessels

Matt 23:25–26   Luke 11:39b–41

a 25/39 "Now b **you** c **Pharisees** d,e **cleanse the outside
of the cup and of the** plate f, **but inside** you are g **full
of extortion and** evil h.

26 You blind Pharisee! first cleanse the
inside of the cup, that its outside may
also be **clean.**"

40 You fools! Did not he who made the
outside make the inside also? 41 But
give as alms what is inside; and
behold, everything is **clean** for you."

a Luke + vv. 37–39a: While he was speaking a Pharisee
asked him to dine with him; so he went in and sat at table.
Seeing this, the Pharisee was surprised that he did not first
wash before dinner. 39 But the Lord said to him,
b Luke; Matt: Woe to
c Luke; Matt + scribes and
d Luke; Matt + hypocrites!
e Luke; Matt + for you
f Luke; Matt: dish
g Luke; Matt: they are
h Luke; Matt: rapacity

c. On Seeking Honors

Matt 23:6–7   Luke 11:43

43/6 "Woe to you Pharisees a! for you love b **the front
seat in the assemblies** 7/ **and salutations in the
market places** c."

Q 11:43 ⇨ Mark 12:38–39a
a Luke; Matt: omit
b Luke; Matt: They love the place of honor at feasts and
c Luke; Matt + and being called rabbi by people

d. Unmarked Graves

Matt 23:27–28   Luke 11:44

27 **"Woe to you**, scribes and Pharisees,
hypocrites, **for you are** like white-
washed tombs, which outside seem to
be beautiful, but inside are full of dead
bones and all kinds of uncleanness. 28
Thus you also on the outside seem to
be righteous to people but inside you
are full of hypocrisy and lawlessness."

44 **"Woe to you,**
for you are like unmarked graves, and
the people who walk on them do not
know it."

e. Heavy Burdens

Matt 23:4	Luke 11:46
[4] "They bind heavy **burdens, hard to bear,** and lay them on **people**'s shoulders; but **they themselves** will **not** move them **with (their) finger.**"	[46] He said, "Woe to you lawyers also! for you load **people** with **burdens hard to bear,** and **you yourselves** do **not** touch burdens **with** one of (your) **fingers.**"

f. You Build the Prophets' Tombs

Matt 23:29–32　　Luke 11:47–48

[29/47] **"Woe to you,** [a] **for you build the graves** [b] [c] **of the prophets,**

[30] and you say: If we had lived in the days of our **fathers**, we would not have collaborated with them in shedding the blood of the prophets. [31] Thus you witness against yourselves, that **you are** sons of those who murdered the prophets. [32] Fill up, then, the measure **of your fathers.**" [d]	but your **fathers** killed them. [48] Therefore **you are** witnesses and you consent to the deeds **of your fathers,** for they killed them, but you build (their tombs)."

a Luke: Matt + scribes and Pharisees, hypocrites,
b Luke; Matt: the tombs **of the prophets,**
c Luke; Matt + and beautify **the graves** of the just.
d Matt + v. 33: "You serpents, brood of vipers, how will you flee from the judgment of Gehenna?"

g. Sophia's Oracle

Matt 23:34–36   Luke 11:49–51

34/49 **Therefore,** the Wisdom of God said[a]: **I will**[b] **send them**[c] **prophets and** apostles[d], **some of whom** they[e] **will kill** [f] **and persecute,** [g]

35 so that upon you may come all **the** righteous **blood shed** on earth	50 so that **the blood** of all the prophets that has been **shed** from the foundation of the cosmos will be required of this generation,
from the blood of innocent **Abel to the blood of Zechariah** the son of Barachiah, whom you murdered **between** the sanctuary **and the altar.** 36 Amen, **I tell you,** all this will come upon **this generation."**	51 **from the blood of Abel to the blood of Zechariah** who was killed **between the altar and** the inner temple; Yes **I tell you**, it will be required of **this generation."**

a Luke; Matt: behold
b Luke; Matt: omit (i.e., Matthew's verb is a present tense).
c Luke; Matt: you (pl.)
d Luke; Matt: sages and scribes
e Luke; Matt: you (pl.)
f Luke; Matt + and crucify and some of them you will scourge in your assemblies,
g Luke; Matt + from town to town;

h. You Lock the Kingdom

Matt 23:13	Luke 11:52
13 "But **woe to you,** scribes and Pharisees, hypocrites! **for** you lock the kingdom of heaven away from people; for you **neither enter** yourselves, nor allow **those who are trying to enter** to go in."	52 "**Woe to you** lawyers! **for you have** taken away the key of knowledge; you yourselves **did not enter**, and you prevented **those who were trying to enter**."

Hidden and Revealed   Q 12:2–3

Matt 10:26–27

26 Therefore do not fear them:

Luke 12:2–3

2 a **Nothing has been covered up that will not be revealed or hidden that will not be known.**

27 What I tell you **in the dark, speak in the light and what** you **hear whispered proclaim upon the housetops.**

3 Therefore, whatever **you speak in the dark** will be **heard in the light and what** you have **whispered** in secret rooms shall be **proclaimed upon the housetops.**

Q 12:2 ⇨ Mark 4:22
a Luke; Matt: + For

Appropriate Fear   Q 12:4–7

Matt 10:28–31

28 And **do not fear those who kill the body** but are **not** powerful enough to kill the soul;

fear instead **him who** can destroy both soul and body in **Gehenna.**

29 **Are not** two **sparrows sold for** an *assarion?* **And not one of them** will fall to the ground without your Father's consent.
30 But **even the hairs of your head are all numbered.** 31 **Fear not,** therefore, **you are worth more than many sparrows.**

Luke 12:4–7

4 I tell you my friends, **do not fear those who kill the body** and afterwards are **not** able to do more. 5 But I will warn you whom to fear: **fear him who,** after he has killed, has the power to cast into **Gehenna;** yes, I tell you, fear him!
6 **Are not** five **sparrows sold for** two *assaria?* **And not one of them** is forgotten before God.

7 But **even the hairs of your head are all numbered. Fear not; you are worth more than many sparrows.**

On Confessing Jesus   Q 12:8–9

Matt 10:32–33	Luke 12:8–9

³² So **everyone** who **acknowledges me in public, I also will acknowledge before** my Father who is in the heavens;
³³ **but** whoever **denies me in public, I** also **will den**y before my Father who is in the heavens.

⁸ I tell you, **everyone** who **acknowledges me in public,** the Son of Man **will also acknowledge before** the angels of God;
⁹ **but** whoever **denies me in public will** be **den**ied before the angels of God.

Q 12:8–9 ⇨ Mark 8:38

Blasphemy of the Spirit   Q 12:10

Matt 12:32	Luke 12:10

³² **And whoever says a word** opposing **the Son of man will be forgiven, but** whoever speaks opposing **the Holy Spirit will not be forgiven,** either in this age or in the coming age.

¹⁰ **And** everyone **who says a word** against **the Son of man will be forgiven; but** the one who blasphemes against **the Holy Spirit will not be forgiven.**

Q 12:10 ⇨ Mark 3:28–29

The Spirit's Assistance   Q 12:11–12

Matt 10:19	Luke 12:11–12

¹⁹ **But when they** deliver **you** up, **do not be anxious how or what** you will say;

for what you are to say will be given you in that hour.

¹¹ **But when they** bring **you** before the assemblies and rulers and authorities, **do not be anxious how or what** you are to answer or what you should say;
¹² **for** the Holy Spirit will teach **you** what you ought to say **in that hour.**

Q 12:11–12 ⇨ Mark 13:9–11

Foolish Possessions   *(Q 12:13–14, 16–21)*

Luke 12:13–14, 16–21 [a]

([13] Someone from the crowd said to him, "Teacher, tell my brother to divide the inheritance with me." [14] But he said to him, "Friend, who set me up as a judge or divider over you?")

[b]

([16] He told them a parable, saying, "The land of a rich man produced abundantly, [17] and he thought to himself, saying, "What shall I do, for I have nowhere to store my crops?" [18] And he said, "I will do this: I will tear down my granaries and build bigger ones and I will store all my grain and goods there. [19] And I will say to myself, "Soul, you have many good things laid up for many years; rest, eat, drink, be merry."

[20] But God said to him, "Fool! This night your soul is required of you; the things you have prepared, whose will they be?"

[21] Thus the one who lays up treasure from himself is not rich in the sight of God.)

a   13–14, 16–21: Perhaps from Q; v. 15: Probably Lukan.
b   Luke + v. 15: Then he said, "Take heed, and guard against all greed; for one's life does not consist in the abundance of one's possessions."

Earthly Cares   Q 12:22–31

Matt 6:25–33   Luke 12:22–31

22 He said to his disciples:

25/ **Therefore I tell you, do not be anxious about
your**[a] **soul, what you will eat** [b] **or about your**[a] **body,
what you will wear.** /23 Is not[c] **the soul more than
food and the body more than clothing?** 26/24 Consider the ravens:[d] **for they neither plant seeds nor
harvest nor** do they gather into[e] **granaries, and** God [f]
feeds them. Are you not much[g] **more valuable than
birds**[h]. 27/25 **Who among you is able to add a** [i] **cubit to
his span of life by being anxious?**

28 And **concerning** clothing, **why are you anxious?**	26 If then you are not able to do such a small thing, **why are you anxious concerning** other things?
Learn from **the lilies** of the field, **how they grow: they do not toil or spin.**	27 Consider **the lilies, how they grow: they do not toil or spin.**

29/ **Now I tell you,** [j] **not even Solomon in all his
glory was arrayed like one of these.** 30/28 **But if God
so clothed the grass in**[k] **the field, which is here today
and tomorrow is thrown into the furnace,** how[l]
much more (will he clothe) you, O weak in faith!

31 Therefore **do not** be anxious, saying, "**What will we eat?**" or "**What will** we **drink?**" or "What will we wear?"	29 And you, **do not** seek **what** you **will eat** and **what** you **will drink** and do not be worried.
32 **For all the nations are seeking (these). For your** heavenly **Father knows that you need** all these.	30 **For all the nations** of the world **are seeking (these). But your Father knows that you need** them.
33 But **seek** first God's **reign** and his righteousness **and** all **these things will be added to you.**	31 But **seek** his **reign and these things will be added to you.**

---

a Matt; Luke: the
b Luke; Matt: + or what you will drink
c Matt; Luke: For (i.e., an assertion instead of Matthew's
   question).
d Luke; Matt: Look to the birds of the sky:
e Matt; Luke: do they have storehouses or
f Luke; Matt: your heavenly Father
g Luke; Matt: omit
h Luke; Matt: them.
i Matt; Luke: + single
j Matt; Luke: + that
k Luke; Matt: of
l Luke; Matt: will (he) not

Heavenly Treasures   Q 12:33–34

Matt 6:19–21	Luke 12:33–34
[19] Do not lay up for yourselves treasures on earth, where moth and rust corrode and where thieves dig through and steal, [20] but lay up for yourselves **treasures in heaven where** neither **moth** nor rust corrodes and where **thie**ves do not dig through and steal.	[33] Sell your possessions and give alms; provide yourselves with purses that do not wear out, with an unfailing **treasure in** the **heavens, where** no **thief** approaches and no **moth** destroys.

[21/34] **For where** your[a] **treasure is, there will** your[a] **heart be also.**

a   Matt: your (sing.); Luke: your (pl.)

Watchful Servants   [Q 12:35–38]

Luke 12:35–38

[[35] Let your belts be fastened and your lamps burning, [36] and be like people who are expecting their master to come home from the marriage feast, so that when he comes and knocks they may open the door immediately to him. [37] Blessed are those servants whom the master finds awake when he comes; Amen, I tell you, he will put on an apron and have them recline, and he will come and serve them. [38] Even if he comes in the second watch, or in the third, and finds them so, blessed are those servants!]

vv. 35–38: cf. Matt 25:1–13; Doubtful attribution to Q.

The Householder and the Thief   Q 12:39–40

Matt 24:43–44   Luke 12:39–40

43/39 **But know this**[a], **that if the householder had known in which** part of the night[b] **the thief was coming** he would have watched and[c] **he would not have let**[d] **his house be dug into.** 44/40 [e] **You also must be prepared, for the Son of man is coming at an hour you do not expect.**

Q 12:39–40 ⇨ Mark 13:35
a Luke; Matt: it
b Matt; Luke: hour
c Matt; Luke: omit
d Matt; Luke: left **his house (to) be dug into.**
e Luke; Matt: + Therefore

Faithful and Unfaithful Servants   Q 12:42b-46

Matt 24:45–51   Luke 12:42b-46

45/ [a] **Who then is the faithful and wise** servant[b] **whom his master puts**[c] **in charge of his** household[d] **to give them their food**[e] **on time?** 46/43 **Blessed is that servant whom his master, when he comes, finds doing this.** 47/44 Truly[f] **I tell you, he will put him in charge of all his possessions.** 48/45 **But if that** [g] **servant should say to himself, "My master is delayed** [h]**,"** 49/ **and he should begin to beat** his fellow servants[i] **and to eat and drink** and to get drunk[j] 50/46 **The master of that servant will come on a day when he does not expect it, and at an hour he does not know,** 51/ **and will punish him severely and assign him a place with the** untrustworthy[k] [l].

a Matt; Luke + vv 41–42a: Peter said, "Lord, are you telling this parable for us or for everyone?" And the Lord said,
b Matt: Luke: steward
c Luke; Matt: put
d Matt; Luke: household staff
e Matt; Luke: rations
f Luke; Matt: Amen
g Matt; Luke: + evil
h Matt; Luke: + in coming
i Matt; Luke: the housemen and the maids
j Luke; Matt: with the drunks
k Luke; Matt: hypocrites
l Luke; Matt: + and there will be weeping and gnashing of teeth.

Fire and Division on Earth   Q 12: (49) 51–53

Matt 10:34–36	Luke 12:49–53
	[49] I have come to bring fire upon the earth; and how I wish that it were already kindled! a
[34] Do not think **that** I am come to bring **peace** upon **the earth.** I am not come to bring peace, **but** a sword. [35] **For** I am come to set a man against his **father, and daughter** against her **mother and a daughter-in-law** against **her mother-in-law.**	[51] Do you suppose **that** I have come to give **peace** to **the earth?** No, I tell you, **but** rather division. [52] **For** from now on in one house there will be five divided, three against two and two against three; [53] there will be divided father against son and son against **father,** mother against daughter **and daughter** against **mother,** mother-in-law against **her** daughter-in-law **and daughter-in-law** against **mother-in-law.**
[36] And a man's enemies will be his own kin.	

a   Luke + v. 50: I have a baptism to be baptized with; and how I am in anguish until it is over!

Signs of the Times   Q 12:54–56

Matt 16:2–3	Luke 12:54–56
[2] **But** he answered and said to them, "When it is evening, **you say,** 'Good weather, for the sky is red,' [3] **and** in the morning, 'Today will be stormy, for the sky is red and dark.' You know how to judge **the appearance of the sky, but** cannot judge the signs of the **times.**	[54] **But** he said to the crowds, "When you see a cloud rising in the west, **you say** immediately, 'Rain is coming'; and so it happens. [55] **And** when there is a south wind blowing you say, 'It will be hot'; and it happens. [56] Hypocrites! You know how to interpret **the appearance of the** earth and **sky, but** why do you not know how to interpret this **time?**

Agreeing with One's Accuser   Q 12:57–59

Matt 5:25–26	Luke 12:57–59
	[57] And why do you not judge for yourselves what is right?
[25] Come to terms quickly **with a plaintiff against you** while you are going with **him on the way,** lest the plaintiff **hand you over to the judge, and the judge to the** guard, **and** you be **thrown into prison.**	[58] As you go **with a plaintiff against you** before the magistrate, make an effort to settle with **him on the way,** lest he drag you **to the judge, and the judge hand** you **over to the** bailiff, **and** the bailiff **throw** you **into prison.**
[26] Amen, **I tell you, you will not leave there until you have paid the last** *quadran.*	[59] **I tell you, you will not leave there until you have paid the** very **last** copper.

The Mustard and the Leaven   Q 13:18–21

Matt 13:31–33	Luke 13:18–21
[31] He proposed to them another parable, **saying, "The reign of the** heavens—	[18] He was **saying** therefore, "What is **the reign of** God like and to what shall I liken it?

/[19] It **is like a grain of mustard which someone took and** cast it in his own garden [a], [32]/ [b] and [c] **it grew** [d] **and became a tree** and [e] *the birds of the sky made their nests in its branches.*

[33] He told them another parable:	[20] And he said again:

[f] **The reign** of God [g] **is like leaven which a woman took and hid in three measures of flour, till it leavened the whole mass.**

Q 13:31–32 ⇨ Mark 4:30–32
Q 13:32b: cf. Ezek 31:6; Dan 4:10, 20 (LXX and Theod); Ps 103:10–12 (LXX)
a Luke; Matt: sowed it into his field,
b Luke; Matt + (from Mark): it is the smallest of all the seeds but when
c Luke; Matt: when
d Luke; Matt: + (from Mark): it is the largest of the shrubs,
e Luke; Matt: so that
f Matt; Luke: + To what shall I liken . . . it **is like** . . .
g Luke; Matt: of the heavens

The Narrow Gate and the Closed Door   Q 13:24–27

Matt 7:13–14, 22–23	Luke 13:24–27

[13] **Enter through the narrow** gate; **for** the gate is wide and the way is easy that leads to destruction, and those who **enter** through it are **many.** [14] But how narrow is the gate and how hard the way that leads to life, and those who find it are few.

[24] Strive to **enter through the narrow** door; **for many**, I tell you, will seek to **enter** and will not be able.

[25] When once the house owner has stood up and locked the door, you will begin to stand outside and knock at the door, saying, 'Lord, open for us.' He will answer you, 'I do not know where you come from.'

[22] On that day many will say to me, "Lord Lord, did we not prophesy in your name, **and** exorcise demons in your name **and** perform many miracles in your name?"

[26] Then you will start saying, "We ate **and** drank with you, **and** you taught in our streets."

[23] **And** then I will declare to them, "I never knew **you**; *depart from me, you who act against the Law.*"

[27] **And** he will say to you, "I do not know where you come from; *away from me, all you workers of iniquity.*"

Luke 13:25: Cf. Matt 25:10–12; perhaps in Q.
Q 13:27b: cf. Ps 6:9a

Gentiles in the Kingdom   Q 13:28–30

Matt 8:11–12; 20:16	Luke 13:28–30

[11] I tell you that many **will come from east and west and will sit at table** with **Abraham and Isaac and Jacob in the kingdom** of the heavens,
[12] but the children of **the kingdom will be thrust out** into the outer darkness. **Out there will be weeping and gnashing of teeth.**
⇨ v. 11

⇨ v. 12a
[20:16] Thus the **last will be first and the first last.**

[29] and people **will come from east and west** and from north and south **and will sit at table in the kingdom** of God.

[28] **Out there will be weeping and gnashing of teeth** when you see **Abraham and Isaac and Jacob** and all of the prophets in **the kingdom** of God, but you **thrust out**side.
[30] And behold, those who are **first will be last and** those who are **last** will be **first.**

Q 13:30 ⇨ Mark 10:31

Lament over Jerusalem   Q 13:34–35

Matt 23:37–39   Luke 13:34–35

37/34 **Jerusalem, Jerusalem, you kill the prophets and
stone those who are sent to you! How often would I
have gathered your children together, as a hen**
gathers[a] her[b] **brood under her wings, and you
refused!** 38/35 **Behold, your temple is forsaken** [c].
39/ But[d] **I tell you, you will not see me** [e] **until** [f] **you
say, "Blessed is the one who comes in the name of
the Lord!"**

a Matt; Luke: omit
b Matt; Luke: her own
c Matt; Luke: + and desolate
d Luke; Matt: For
e Luke; Matt: + from now on
f Matt; Luke: + the time comes when

Exalting the Humble   Q 14:11/18:14b

Matt 23:12	Luke 14:11; 18:14b
12 Now whoever **exalts himself will be humbled, and** whoever **humbles himself will be exalted.**	11 For everyone who **exalts himself will be humbled, and** the one who **humbles himself will be exalted.** 14 [a] For everyone who **exalts himself will be humbled,** but the one who **humbles himself will be exalted.**

a Luke + v. 14a: I tell you, this one [i.e., the tax collector]
  went down [from the temple] to his house justified rather
  than the other;

The Great Supper   Q 14:16–24

Matt 22:1–10	Luke 14:16–24
1 And Jesus again answered and **spoke** in parables to them saying, 2 "The reign of the heavens is like **a man**, a king, who **gave** a wedding feast for his son. 3 **And he sent out his servant**s to **summon** those who had been invited to the wedding feast, but they did not want to come.	16 Now he **spoke** to him, a certain **man gave** a large banquet, and he **summon**ed many 17 **and he sent out his servant** at the hour of the banquet to **tell those who have been invited:** 'Come, for it is **ready.'**

⁴ Again he sent out other servants saying, '**Tell those who have been invited**: Behold, I have prepared my dinner; my oxen and by fat calves are killed and everything is **ready**. Come to the wedding.'
⁵ But they made light of it and departed, one to his own **farm**, another to his business,
⁶ and the rest seized his servants, abused them and killed them.
⁷ **The** king **was angry** and dispatching his troops his destroyed those murderers and razed their city.
⁸ Then he says **to his servant**s, 'The wedding feast is ready, but those who had been invited were not worthy;
⁹ go therefore into the byways **and** invite as many as you find to the feast.
¹⁰ And those servants **went out onto the roads** and gathered everyone they found, both evil and good. And the when they all sat down, the wedding hall was full.

¹⁸ And they began one by one to make excuses: The first said to him, 'I have bought **a farm** and I must go to inspect it. I ask, have me excused.'
¹⁹ And another said, 'I have bought give yokes of oxen, and I am going to examine them. I ask, have me excused.'
²⁰ And another said, 'I have married as wife and therefore I am unable to come.'
²¹ And the servant came and told this to his master. Then **the** householder **was angry** and said **to his servant,** 'Go out quickly into the plazas and alleys of this city **and** bring the poor and maimed and blind and lame here.'
²² And the servant said, 'Sir, what you commanded has been done, and still there is room.' ²³ And the master said to the servant, '**Go out onto the roads** and hedges and compel them to enter, so that my house will be full.
²⁴ For I tell you that none of those men who had been invited will taste of my banquet.

Being My Disciple   Q 14:26–27; 17:33

Matt 10:37–39	Luke 14:26–27; 17:33
³⁷ Whoever loves **father** or **mother** more than me **is not** worthy **of me,** and whoever loves son or daughter more than me is not worthy of me.	²⁶ If someone comes to me and does not hate his own **father** and **mother** and wife and children and brothers and sisters, and indeed even his own life, he ca**nnot be my** disciple.
³⁸ And whoever **does not** take his **cross and** follow **after me is not** worthy **of me.**	²⁷ Whoever **does not** bear his own **cross and** come **after me is not** able **to be my** disciple.
³⁹ Whoever finds **his life will lose it,** and whoever **loses** his life for my sake will find **it.**	17:33 Whoever seeks to gain **his life will lose it,** but whoever **loses** (it) will keep **it.**

Q 14:27 ⇨ Mark 8:34
Q 17:33 ⇨ Mark 8:35

Savorless Salt   Q 14:34–35

Matt 5:13	Luke 14:34–35

¹³ You are **the salt** of the earth; **but if salt becomes insipid, with what** could it be salted?
It is no longer good **for** anything except to be **thrown out** and trodden under foot by people.

³⁴ **Salt** is good; **but if salt becomes insipid, with what** could it be seasoned?
³⁵ It is fit neither **for** soil nor for the dunghill. They **throw it out.** Let whoever has ears listen.

Q 14:34–35 ⇨ Mark 9:49–50

The Lost Sheep and Lost Coin   Q 15:4–7 (8–10)

Matt 18:12–13	Luke 15:4–7 (8–10)

¹² **What** do you think? If a certain **man** had **a hundred sheep and one of them** went astray, will he not leave **the ninety-nine** on the hills **and go** in search of the one that was lost?
¹³ **And** if he should **find it,**

⁴ **What man** among you having **a hundred sheep and** if he lost **one of them**, will not leave **the ninety-nine** in the wilderness **and go** after the lost one until he finds **it.**
⁵ **And find**ing (it) he puts it on his shoulders, **rejoic**ing
⁶ and coming home he invites his friends and neighbours, saying to them, 'Rejoice with me, for I have found my sheep which was lost.'
⁷ Likewise, **I tell you that** there will be more joy in heaven **over** one sinner who repents **than over ninety-nine** righteous persons who do not need repentance.

amen, **I tell you that** he will **rejoice over** it more **than over** the **ninety-nine** that did not go astray.

(⁸ What woman having ten drachmae, if she should lose one drachma, will not light a lamp and sweep the house and seek diligently until she finds it?
⁹ And finding (it) she invites her friends and neighbours, saying, 'Rejoice with me, for I have found the drachma which was lost.' ¹⁰ Likewise, I tell you that there will be joy among the angels of God over one sinner who repents.)

Luke 15:8–10: Possibly in Q and omitted by Matthew.

God and Mammon   Q 16:13

Matt 6:24   Luke 16:13

24/13 **No one**[a] **can serve two masters; for either he will hate the one and love the other, or he will be loyal to the one and despise the other. You cannot serve God and mammon.**

a   Matt; Luke: **no** servant

The Kingdom, the Law and Divorce   Q 16:16–18

Matt 11:12–13	Luke 16:16–18

13 For all **the prophets and the law** prophesied until **John.**
12 **From** the days of John the Baptist until now **the reign of** heaven is **seized at, and** the violent grabbed **it.**

16 **The law and the prophets** were until **John. From** then **the reign of** God is proclaimed, **and** everybody **seizes at it.**

Matt 5:18

18 Amen I tell you, till **heaven and earth pass away,** not one iota **or one serif** will pass from **the Law** until all is accomplished.

17 But it is easier for **heaven and earth to pass away than** for **one serif of the Law** to be dropped.

Matt 5:32

32 But I tell you that **everyone who divorces his wife** except on the ground of unchastity, forces her **to commit adultery, and** whoever **marries a divorcee** commits adultery.

18 **Everyone who divorces his wife** and marries another **commits adultery and** he who **marries a divorcee** is an adulterer.

Q 16:18 ⇨ Mark 10:11–12

On Scandals   Q 17:1-2

Matt 18:7, 6	Luke 17:1-2
[7] [a] "For it is necessary for **scandals to come, but woe** to the person **through whom** scandal **comes;** [6] Whoever **leads astray one of the least of these** who believe in me, it would be better **for him** to have a millstone fastened **around his neck and** to be drowned in the depth of **the sea."**	[1] [b] **"Scandals** are sure **to come, but woe** (to the one) **through whom** they **come.** [2] It would be better **for him** if a millstone were hung **around his neck and** he were cast into **the sea** than that he **lead astray one of the least of these."**

Q 17:2 ⇨ Mark 9:42
a   Matt + v. 7a: Woe to the world because of scandals;
b   Luke + v. 1a: He said to his disciples,

Forgiveness   Q 17:3b-4

Matt 18:15, 21-22	Luke 17:3-4
[15] "Now **if your brother should sin** against you, go and correct **him** between you and him alone. If he should listen to you, you have gained a brother." [21] [b] "Lord, how often shall my brother **sin against** me and I **forgive him? Seven times?"** [22] Jesus said to him, "I tell you not **seven times** but seventy-seven times."	[3] [a] **"If your brother should sin,** rebuke **him** and **if** he should repent, forgive him. [4] And if he should **sin against** you **seven times** a day and turns to you **seven times** saying, 'I repent,' **forgive him."**

a   Luke + v. 3a: Take heed to to yourselves;
b   Matt + v. 21a: Then Peter came up and said to him,

On Having Faith   Q 17:6b

Matt 17:20b	Luke 17:6
[20] [a] "For amen I tell you, if **you have faith as a grain of mustard,** you will say **to this** mountain, 'Move from here to there,' **and** it will move; and nothing will be impossible **for you."**	[6] [b] "If **you have faith as a grain of mustard,** you could say **to this** syca-mine tree, 'Be uprooted and be planted in the sea,' **and** it would be obedient **to you."**

Q 17:6b ⇨ Mark 11:22-23
a   Matt + v. 19-20a (from Mark): Then the disciples came to
    Jesus privately and said, "Why could we not exorcise it?"
    He said to them, "Because of your weak faith."
b   Luke + v. 6a: The Lord said,

Coming of the Son of Man   Q 17:23–24, 26–30, 34–35, 37

Matt 24:26–28, 38–41	Luke 17:23–24, 26–30, 34–35, 37

26 "Therefore, if **they say to you, 'Lo,** he is in the desert,' **do not go out; 'Lo,** in the secret chambers,' **do not** believe. 27 **For as the lightning** goes out from the east and flashes to the west, **so will be** the Parousia of **the Son of man.**

23 "And **they will say to you, 'Lo** here,' or 'Lo, there.' **Do not go out, do not** follow. 24 **For as the lightning** flashes and lights up the sky from one side to the other, **so will the Son of man be** in his day.

28/37 a **Where the** corpse b **is, there the eagles** c **gather.**

37 For as were **the days of Noah, so will be** the Parousia of **the Son of man;** 38 for just as in those days before the flood they were eating and **drinking, marrying** and **being married, up to the day when Noah entered the ark,** 39 **and** they did not know until **the flood came and** took them all,

26 And as it happened in **the days of Noah, so will it be** also in the days of the **Son of man.**

27 they were dining, **drinking, marrying, being married, up to the day when Noah entered the ark, and the flood came and** destroyed everybody. (28 Similarly, as it was in the days of Lot: they were dining, drinking, buying, selling, planting, building, 29 but on the day that Lot went out from Sodom fire and sulphur rained down from heaven and destroyed everybody—)d

so also **will be** the Parousia of **the Son of man.**

so **will it be** on the day when **the Son of Man** is revealed.

40/34 I tell you, on that night e **there will be two in the** field f, **one will be swept away and one** g **left behind;** 41/35 **two women** (will be) **grinding** at the millstone h, **one will be swept away** and one g **left behind."**

Q 17:23 ⇨ Mark 13:21–23
a Luke: repositions Q 17:37b after Q 17:34–35; + v. 37a: And answering they said to him, "Where, Lord?" And he said,
b Matt; Luke: body
c Matt; Luke + also
d Luke 17:28–29: Possibly in Q and deleted by Matthew.
e Luke; Matt: Then
f Matt; Luke: on one couch
g Matt; Luke: the other
h Matt; Luke: together

The Parable of the Entrusted Money   Q 19:12–26

Matt 25:14–30	Luke 19:12–27

[14] "For it is like **man** going on a long journey (who) **summon**ed his own **servants** and entrusted to them his possessions. [15] To one **he gave** five talents, to another, two, to another, one, to each according to his own ability. Then he departed. Immediately [16] the one who had received five talents went and traded with them and gained another five.

[12] Therefore he said, "A certain noble **man** went into a far country to receive a kingdom for himself, and (then) to return.
[13] **Summon**ing ten of his **servants, he gave** them ten minas and said to them, 'Do business with these until I return.'
[a]

[17] In the same way the one with two gained another two.
[18] But the one who had received one departed and dug in the ground and hid his master's money.
[19] After a considerable time the master of those **servants** came and had a reckoning of accounts with them.

[15] And it happened that when he returned, having received his kingdom, and he gave orders to call these **servants** to whom he had given the money, so that he know what they had made in business.
[16] **The** first **one** came **saying, 'Lord,** your mina has made ten minas.'

[20] And approaching, **the one** who had received the five talents presented the other five talents **saying, 'Lord,** you entrusted me with five talents; see, I have gained another five talents.'
[21] His master said **to him, 'Well done, good** and reliable **servant**; you have been **reliable** in small matters; I will set you over many things. Enter into the joy of your master.'
[22] **Also approach**ing, **the one** who had two talents said, 'Lord, you entrusted me with two talents; see, I have gained another two talents.'
[23] His master said to him, 'Well done, good and reliable servant; you have been reliable in small matters; I will set you over many thing. Enter into the joy of your master.'

[17] And he said **to him, 'Well done, good servant**; because you were **reliable** in a little thing, you will have authority over ten cities.

[18] **And the** second **one approach**ed, saying, 'Your mina, **Lord,** made five minas.'

[19] He also said to this one, 'And you will be over five cities.'

24 Now the one who had received one talent also approached and said, 'Lord, I know about you, that you are a hard man, reaping where you did not sow and gathering where you did not scatter.
25 And being fearful, I went and hid your talent in the ground. See, take what belongs to you.

26 But his master answered and said to him, 'Evil and slothful servant! You knew that I reap where I did not sow and gather where I did not scatter?

27 Then you should have put my money with the money lenders, and when I came I would have received what belonged to me with interest.
28 Therefore take from him the talent and give it to him who has the ten talents.

29 For to everyone who has it will be given and he will have in abundance, and from the one who has not, even what he has will be taken from him.
b"

20 And the other one approached, saying, 'Lord, see your mina which I have kept stored in a napkin.

21 For I was fearful of you, for you are a severe man, drawing what you did not deposit, and reaping what you did not sow.
22 He said to him, 'From your own mouth I judge you, evil servant! You knew that I am a severe man, withdrawing what I did not deposit, and reaping what I did not sow.
23 Why did you not give my money to the bank, and when I came, I might have collected it with interest?'
24 And he said to the bystanders, 'Take from him the mina and give it to him who has the ten minas'.
25 And they said to him, "Lord, he (already) has ten minas."
26 "I tell you, to everyone who has it will be given, and from the one who has not, even what he has will be taken."
c

a Luke + v 14 (from another parable, or from a historical ancedotes): 14 But his citizens hated him and sent elders after him saying, 'We do not wish him to reign over us.'
b Matt + v. 30: "And cast the worthless servant into outer darkness; out there will be weeping and gnashing of teeth."
c Luke + v. 27 (cf. v. 14): "But as for these enemies of mine who did not want to reign over them, bring them here and slay them before me."

Judging Israel   *Q 22:28–30*

Matt 19:28b	Luke 22:28–30
[28] a **"You who** followed **me**—in the regeneration, when the Son of man shall sit upon a throne of his glory— **you** yourselves also **will sit upon** twelve **thrones, judging the twelve tribes of Israel."**	[28] "Now **you** are those **who** have persevered with **me** in my trials; [29] And I assign to you the kingdom, just as my father assigned (it) to me, [30] so that you may eat and drink at my table in my kingdom, and **you will sit upon thrones, judging the twelve tribes of Israel."**

Matt + v. 28a (see Mark 10:29a): Jesus said to them, "Amen, I
tell you that

The Gospel
of Thomas

The Gospel of Thomas

INTRODUCTION

Introduction

The early Christians were a very diverse group of persons, with a wide variety of opinions about who Jesus might have been, and what significance was to be attached to his life and death. This realization, more than any other, could be said to characterize the consensus of modern critical scholarship on the problem of how the Christian church began. This diversity, of course, can be seen even within that relatively unified corpus of books and letters later Christian generations came to recognize as the New Testament canon. But the full extent of this diversity is realized first when one includes in the data base for studying early Christianity the many writings which derive from that earliest formative period of the infant church, before any particular set of ideas had gained such prominence as to command the designation "orthodoxy," tractates and documents of every stripe which gradually fell into disuse as early Christians battled slowly to a consensus about what would be considered normative in its thought and practice. Many of these early Christian writings, so valuable for reconstructing the history of the earliest Christian communities, faded from the scene and were eventually lost, their only footprints to be found in the occasional reference, or perhaps even a brief quote, in the writings of the church leaders who emerged in later years. Such writings as the Gospel of the Hebrews, or the Gospel of the Ebionites, are known to us only through the various references and brief quotations to be found in Cyril of Jerusalem, Jerome, Origen, Clement, Epiphanius, and other early Fathers of the church.

Such was also the fate of the ancient Gospel of Thomas. Scholars have known of the existence of a Gospel of Thomas for many years. Origen mentions it, as does Jerome.[1] Hippolytus even quotes a saying from Thomas, which has now come to be recognized as at least a version of Saying 4:

> They (the Naassenes) say that not only the mysteries of the Assyrians and Phrygians, but also those of the Egyptians support their account of the blessed nature of the things which were, are, and are yet to be, a nature which is both hidden and revealed at the same time, and which he calls the sought-for kingdom of heaven which is within man. They transmit a tradition concerning this in the Gospel entitled *According to Thomas*, which states expressly, "The one who seeks me will find me in the children from seven years of age and onwards. For there, hiding in the fourteenth aeon, I am revealed."[2]

But none of these early church leaders had much regard for the book. As one can see from Hippolytus' treatment above, by the third century it was already being associated with heretical and unacceptable teaching. Cyril of Jerusalem even went so far as to forbid its reading, under the erroneous assumption that it had been written by Thomas, the disciple of the arch-heretic Mani.[3] Of course, the fact that Cyril would take such a strong position means that the Gospel of Thomas must have still enjoyed a significant following even in the fourth century, when Cyril wrote. Still, with such powerful leaders turned so vehemently against it, it is small wonder that the Gospel of Thomas eventually disappeared from the scene, a victory perhaps for the orthodox church, but a loss for the historian of earliest Christianity.

Were it not for a quirk of fate and the extraordinary good luck of an Egyptian farmer, that would have been the the final chapter in the history of the Gospel of Thomas. This unusual book would have remained a relatively obscure footnote in the annals of primitive Christian history and theology. But one need only glance at the plethora of recent discussions of the problem of Christian origins to realize that this was not the case. The Gospel of Thomas is back, and it is at the heart of the current debate about the diversity of early Christian theology. Its obscure demise at the end of the early Christian period turned out to be but an extended episode in its history. That episode was brought to an end by a spectacular discovery, an event of momentous consequences for the history of New Testament scholarship and our understanding of Christian origins. That is where the new episode in the discussion of this gospel begins.

Nag Hammadi Discovery

Made in 1945 by a local peasant beneath a boulder near the base of the Jabal al-Tarif cliff about 6.2 miles northeast of the city of Nag Hammadi, near the village of Hamra Dom. References on the papyrus cartonnage of the covers indicate that the codices come from the region around Chenoboskion, a center of monastic life, and date to the fourth century.

Description
Twelve codices and part of a thirteenth. The codices consist of folded papyrus leaves assembled into one or more quires and sewn into a leather cover. To date at least 1,139 complete or partial pages have been identified.

Language
The Nag Hammadi Library represents a large collection of original Gnostic writings. All are in Coptic, the late form of Egyptian written mostly in Greek uncial letters and used in Christian times, but the dialects are neither uniform nor pure. The working hypothesis of almost all scholars is that one is dealing with Coptic translations of works originally written in Greek.

Catalogue of the Nag Hammadi Library

Codex I
The Prayer of the Apostle Paul
The Apocryphon of James
The Gospel of Truth
The Treatise on Resurrection
The Tripartite Tractate
Colophon

Codex II
The Apocryphon of John
The Gospel of Thomas
The Gospel of Philip
The Hypostasis of the Archons
On the Origin of the World
The Exegesis on the Soul
The Book of Thomas the Contender
Colophon

Codex III
The Apocryphon of John
The Gospel of the Egyptians
Eugnostos the Blessed
The Sophia of Jesus Christ
The Dialogue of the Saviour

Codex IV
The Apocryphon of John
The Gospel of the Egyptians

Codex V
Eugnostos the Blessed
The Apocalypse of Paul
The (First) Apocalypse of James
The (Second) Apocalypse of James
The Apocalypse of Adam

Codex VI
The Acts of Peter and the Twelve
    Apostles
The Thunder: Perfect Mind
Authoritative Teaching
The Concept of our Great Power
Plato, Republic 588B–589B
The Discourse on the Eighth and Ninth
The Prayer of Thanksgiving
Scribal Note
Asclepius 21–29

Codex VII
The Paraphrase of Shem
The Second Treatise of the Great Seth
The Apocalypse of Peter
The Teachings of Silvanus
The Three Steles of Seth
Colophon

Codex VIII
Zostrianos
The Letter of Peter to Philip

Codex IX
Melchizedek
The Thought of Norea
The Testimony of Truth

Codex X
Marsanes

Codex XI
The Interpretation of Knowledge
A Valentinian Exposition
On the Anointing
On Baptism A
On Baptism B
On the Eucharist A
On the Eucharist B
Allogenes
Hypsiphrone

Codex XII
The Sentences of Sextus
The Gospel of Truth
Fragments

Codex XIII
Trimorphic Protennoia
On the Origin of the World

The Discovery of the Gospel of Thomas

The Nag Hammadi Library

In December of 1945 an Egyptian farmer named Muhammed 'Ali went out to the cliffs that skirt the Nile as it winds its way through Upper Egypt near the town of Nag Hammadi. The farmers of Nag Hammadi mine the nitrogen-rich deposits of soil which collect at their base. As he and his brother searched for the naturally occurring form of fertilizer to be spread on their fields, they came across an earthenware jar of obviously ancient origin. When they broke open the jar, they discovered inside a cache of thirteen leather-bound codices—papyrus books—containing more than 50 individual tractates of various origin. It was not the treasure they had hoped for, but even in 1945 the antiquities trade in Upper Egypt was brisk enough that Muhammed 'Ali could guess that such a collection of crusty ancient books would have some value in the marketplace. What he did not know, and what no one would know for some time to come, was that he had just uncovered one of the most important archaeological finds in the history of New Testament scholarship and the study of early Christianity. Though perhaps less widely known, the Nag Hammadi library has been called a discovery every bit as revolutionary for the study of the New Testament as the Dead Sea Scrolls were for the study of the Hebrew Bible.[4]

The significance of the find first became evident some three years later, when the French scholar and dealer in antiquities, Jean Doresse, working for a Cairo antiquities dealer, first made an inventory of the tractates contained in these papyrus codices. Among them he found a variety of treatises, some of them previously known, others known only through references to them in various ancient authors, many with an obviously gnostic orientation, some ascetic, some Jewish, and, though unrecognized by Doresse at the time, even one classical text, a short excerpt from Plato's *Republic*. At the end of the second tractate in the codex now designated Codex II, Doresse found the subscript title of a text which had been lost for at least a thousand years: *Peuaggelion Pkata Thomas*. A new episode in the history of the "Gospel According to Thomas" had begun.

The Coptic Gospel of Thomas: A Collection of Sayings

Like all the tractates from the Nag Hammadi library, the copy of the Gospel of Thomas found there is a Coptic translation of a Greek original. Coptic was the latest form of the native ancient Egyptian language. Prior to the period of Christian evangelization in Egypt, the Egyptian language was written in hieroglyphic form, or in hieratic or demotic, the cursive forms of this ancient script. But in the second century C.E., when Christian missionaries set out from Alexandria to proselytize the countryside, they chose to translate their sacred texts into Egyptian using Greek characters instead of the older, native, demotic forms. The transliterated form of the language, known as Coptic, may have been easier for the Greek-educated missionaries to pronounce; or perhaps the older demotic script simply had too many indigenous religious associations. At any rate, the Nag Hammadi library, and the Coptic Gospel of Thomas within it, are part of the legacy of Coptic literature produced by this early Christian missionary effort in Upper Egypt.

Work on the publication of the Nag Hammadi texts proceeded slowly. The ensuing years in Egypt, which saw the assassination of a president and the Suez crisis, did not provide a hospitable climate for the tedious scholarly work necessary to bring these fragile manuscripts to publication. These major political problems were compounded by smaller political struggles for scholarly turf, and attempts to monopolize access and publication rights to the exciting new texts. It was not until 1957 that the director of the Coptic Museum in Cairo, Pahor Labib, decided to place a small portion of these texts in the public domain by publishing a number of pages in photographic form; among them were the pages from Codex II containing the Coptic Gospel of Thomas.[5] Soon thereafter the East German scholar, Johannes Leipoldt, published a German translation of the Gospel of Thomas.[6] Leipoldt's translation made this important text available for the first time to a large number of specialists in the field of New Testament and early Christianity. A critical edition of the Coptic text of Thomas would appear within a year.[7]

The new gospel created quite a sensation. One reason for the excitement was the type of book Thomas turned out to be. Since the nineteenth century scholars have operated under the assumption that Matthew and Luke used a source of Jesus' sayings in the writing of their respective gospels. Today, as then, this source is commonly known as "Q." Though widely accepted, one of the major difficulties with this hypothesis was the fact that it could not be shown that such a book would even be plausible as a form of early Christian literature. There were simply no extant examples of the genre. The discovery of the Gospel of Thomas altered this state of affairs, for the new gospel turned

Final Page of
Coptic Thomas

The final page of the Coptic Gospel of Thomas
with the subscript title "The Gospel according to
Thomas." Below the title is the beginning of the
Gospel of Philip.

out to be just that. It is a collection of 114 sayings of Jesus, listed serially, each introduced by the simple formula "Jesus said," or alternatively "he said." Only occasionally are sayings introduced together with a brief, orienting setting. For all practical purposes, the Gospel of Thomas is a gospel without narrative—a "sayings gospel." Though careful study was to reveal immediately that the new gospel was not the long lost document known as Q, the discovery of the Coptic Gospel of Thomas did provide us at long last with an example of what many had argued was one of the oldest known forms of Christian literature: the sayings collection.

The Oxyrhynchus Fragments of the Gospel of Thomas

Ironically enough, the first chapter in the tale of this fascinating discovery was not written at Nag Hammadi, but approximately 150 miles downstream, near El Bahnasa, at an archaeological site known as Oxyrhynchus. There, at the end of the last century, a team of British archaeologists sponsored by the Egypt Exploration Fund uncovered a great mass of papyrus fragments from an ancient trash heap. Over the course of eight centuries this dump had served as the inauspicious repository for documents and books of the richest assortment, whose accidental survival has today provided us with one of the most important sources for understanding everyday life in the Greco-Roman world. Among the first papyrus fragments published in 1897 by the excavators, Bernard Grenfell and Arthur S. Hunt, was a small leaf measuring 14.5 × 9.5 cm. Numbered POxy 1, the fragment is a single leaf from a papyrus codex. Its Greek text, dated orthographically to around 200 C.E., is part of a series of sayings of Jesus. Grenfell and Hunt later published two other similar fragments from this find, POxy 654 and POxy 655. The former is a single fragment from a papyrus roll. The latter is actually several fragments from another roll, only six of which survive today at Harvard University's Houghton Library. Both, like POxy 1, were recognized as the fragmentary remains of a collection of Jesus' sayings written in Greek. Grenfell and Hunt referred to them simply as Λόγια ’Ιησοῦ ("Sayings of Jesus").[8]

Though discussed from time to time by interested scholars, the full significance of these fragments for the history of early Christianity was not realized until the 1950's, after the publication of the Coptic version of the Gospel of Thomas. It was the French scholar, Henri-Ch. Puech, who made the connection that would pull these ancient fragments back into the limelight. Puech noticed that the sayings of POxy 654 actually corresponded to the Prologue and first seven sayings of the newly discovered Coptic Gospel of Thomas, the six sayings of POxy 1 to Sayings 28–33, and the fragmentary sayings of POxy 655 to Sayings 37–40.[9] It had been suspected that perhaps POxy 654 and POxy 1 represented two fragments of the same text, but this was not suggested for POxy 655. After studying the Coptic version of Thomas in Nag Hammadi Codex II, Puech could argue that all three fragments were witnesses to the original Greek text of the Gospel of Thomas. The newly discovered text was not really so new after all; at least parts of it, in its original language, had been available since the turn of the century. Today, the Coptic version of Thomas, together with the Greek fragments, provide us with the only surviving exemplars of this important early Christian document.

Placing the Gospel of Thomas

The Literary Place of Thomas

Perhaps the most vigorous part of the Thomas discussion over the years has been the debate over its relationship to other early Christian writings, in particular to the synoptic gospels, Matthew, Mark, and Luke. At issue has been the question of whether the Gospel of Thomas represents an independent codification of the Jesus' sayings tradition, or whether it is dependent on written versions of the canonical gospels. On the latter view, it would be easy to regard Thomas as a relatively late collection of materials excerpted from the canonical sources, and then modified to reflect the particular theological views of the later collector. It would also be rather easy to dismiss Thomas as largely irrelevant for the discussion of Christian origins. It would belong, on this view, to the rise of second or third century Christian heresies opposed by the emerging orthodox church. However, on the view that Thomas represents an independent stream of the Jesus tradition, it would have to be taken seriously as another important witness to the origin and development of the early Christian sayings tradition, and perhaps relevant to the problem of Christian origins after all. It is this view that has come to prevail particularly among American New Testament scholars. But it is a view which cannot be taken for granted. Many European scholars, for example, continue to oppose this thesis even today. It is necessary, therefore, to review this discussion before proceeding with such matters as Thomas' date and authorship.

Opponents of the thesis that the Gospel of Thomas represents an early collection of the sayings of Jesus have generally argued that its author knew the synoptic gospels, and drew from them material which was then twisted and contorted to reflect the theological position of the author of Thomas. The German New Testament scholar Wolfgang Schrage has even gone so far as to argue that the Coptic Gospel of Thomas is directly dependent upon the Coptic translation of the synoptic gospels, a thesis which, given the dating of the materials involved, is all but impossible.[10] The more firmly grounded arguments for this thesis have proceeded on the following premise: if the text of Thomas can be found to reproduce elements from the synoptic gospels which can be identified as redactional changes unique to one or another of the individual synoptic evangelists, then one must conclude that the author of Thomas has taken the text directly from these canonical sources.

This, of course, makes sense, *provided* that the pattern of dependence is shown to be both consistent and extensive. This, however, is not the case. There are perhaps five instances in the entire text of Thomas in which one must conclude that the canonical texts have indeed influenced Thomas to some degree.[11] To these may be added another three cases in which the canonical order of particular sayings may have influenced the order in which the same sayings are ordered in Thomas.[12]

How does one interpret this data? Several factors must be considered. First, in the case of Thomas we are dealing for the most part with a single manuscript witness; *as with all ancient manuscripts*, one must reckon with a goodly number of scribal errors and emendations. Secondly, the phenomenon of harmonization, whereby a scribe transcribes a text incorrectly in order to bring it into closer conformity with a parallel text known to the scribe from another gospel, is well known among text critics. Practically every New Testament gospel manuscript has problems of this nature, and those in the Coptic translational tradition are particularly noted for it.[13] Given these conditions of ancient scribal practice, and in view of the fact that there are more than 70 parallels between Thomas and the synoptic texts, the handful of cases in which some degree of dependence may be demonstrated does not seem to build a very strong case for an over-all compositional theory involving direct dependence upon the synoptic texts. Rather, the very small number of places in which one must reckon with some degree of dependence is accounted for more easily by positing a reasonable amount of scribal harmonization. There is no reason to assume that our copies of Thomas, in distinction from most other manuscripts of like age, would be immune to this phenomenon.

Moreover, several factors mitigate strongly against such a compositional theory. First, scholars of the history of the gospel tradition have worked for many years to sort out the way in which the sayings tradition developed. Characteristics such as the allegorical interpretation of parables, the pairing of sayings of like form or content, or the use of language reminiscent of the Greek version of the Hebrew Bible, the Septuagint, have long been recognized as secondary accretions to the more primitive gospel tradition. By noting such secondary characteristics it is usually relatively easy to tell which of two versions of a given saying is the more primitive. If Thomas had taken its sayings directly from the synoptic gospels one would expect to find that in most cases the synoptic version of the saying, whether from Matthew, Mark, or Luke, is more primitive than its Thomas counterpart. But this is not the case. In fact precisely the opposite is true. Most of the sayings in Thomas which have synoptic parallels occur in forms which are more primitive than their synoptic parallels. To be sure, Thomas' sayings often exhibit characteristics of a secondary nature, but with few exceptions (see preceding paragraph) these secondary features are unique to the Thomas version, and have affixed themselves to a form of the saying which is itself more primitive than the synoptic version.[14] This means that although Thomas' sayings generally show the same sorts of secondary developments one finds in the synoptic tradition, it is clear that they have undergone this process of development independently from the parallel synoptic tradition.

Secondly, those sayings with parallels in the synoptic gospels comprise roughly only half of the total number of sayings in Thomas. These other sayings, of course, are not accounted for under the theory that the author of Thomas was merely a pirater of synoptic texts. Rather, they prove beyond doubt that Thomas' author had access to non-canonical sources. This, of course, should not be surprising. If one dates this gospel in the last three decades of the first century (see below), one can only assume that there were available to its author any number of collections of Jesus' sayings, not to mention the oral tradition, which was a living phenomenon well into the second century.

Thirdly, as a sayings collection, the Gospel of Thomas represents a genre of early Christian literature that does not really presuppose the narrative gospel as precursor. Rather, in a series of articles in the 1960s James M. Robinson and Helmut Koester were able to show that the opposite is true: it was the narrative gospel form that tended to absorb and replace the sayings tradition, not the other way around. This was the case with Q, which survived only because Matthew and Luke took it up and used it. It was also the case with the collection of parables in Mark 4. Thus, as a sayings collection, Thomas is one of a very few extant examples of a primitive Christian literary genre, whose members were, for the most part, side-tracked and swallowed up by the narrative gospel form.[15]

Narrative overtook sayings.

All of this does not add up to a very strong case for Thomas' dependence upon the canonical gospels. To the contrary, so long as the number of instances in which some 'cross-fertilization' from the canonical tradition has taken place is limited to but a few examples, and so long as the mitigating factors weigh so heavily against the thesis of Thomas' dependence upon the canonical gospels, one may only conclude that Thomas represents essentially an autonomous tradition, relying for its material upon roots imbedded deeply into the same early Christian traditions also tapped by the canonical gospels and their sources.

Dating the Gospel of Thomas

Though one may rule out dependence upon the canonical gospels, this does not automatically suggest a date for the Gospel of Thomas. To be sure, the fact that Thomas represents an autonomous tradition means that it need not necessarily be dated later than the canonical gospels. But this only widens the range of possible dates for Thomas. One could conceivably date it anytime between the birth of the Jesus movement at the earliest, and the end of the second century at the latest (the date for POxy 1, the oldest manuscript evidence for the Gospel of Thomas.) But assigning a more precise date within this range still poses a number of difficulties.

At the root of the problem is the general instability of the gospel tradition in its early years. We know that even the canonical gospels, Matthew, Mark, Luke, and John, were not entirely stable until relatively late in the history of their transmission, so that one must frequently distinguish between earlier and later materials contained within them.

The best illustration of this phenomenon of relative instability is the Gospel of Mark. Scholars generally hold that both Matthew and Luke made use of Mark in the composition of their respective gospels. But Luke strangely omits an entire section of Mark (6:45–8:26), which Matthew for his part includes. This has prompted many to suggest that Matthew and Luke had different versions of Mark, one with this section, one without it. Presumably Matthew's copy would have been an expanded version of the Mark used by Luke. Furthermore, a recently discovered letter fragment of Clement of Alexandria (ca. 150–215) quotes Markan verses known to Clement which no longer appear in the Markan manuscripts that survived antiquity. This means that not only was Mark expanded, it may have also been abbreviated, even as late as the second or third century.[16]

[handwritten margin note: Exc luded Mark in Luke.]

As a sayings collection, the Gospel of Thomas presents one with difficulties of this nature, but of a far greater magnitude. Without the necessity of having to look after the narrative quality of the overall work, each new curator of the collection could have added new sayings, or sloughed away outmoded sayings, with little difficulty. Thus, such a collection would quite naturally have been a cumulative product, whose content might have easily changed from generation to generation. Which form of the text then does one date? Many of these sayings undoubtedly derive from the very earliest period of the Jesus movement, perhaps some even from Jesus himself. But these cannot be used to date the formation of the collection as a whole. On the other extreme, a few of these sayings will no doubt have been added to the collection in a much later period, conceivably as late as the third or fourth century. But these, too, are not necessarily relevant for dating the collection as a whole. Bracketing out the extremes, however, there are at least a few facts which make it possible to suggest an approximate period within which at least the torso of this collection was most likely assembled.

First, as Koester has pointed out, the collection must come from a period in which the church was still appealing to the authoritative position of particular apostles within particular communities as a way of guaranteeing the reliability of its traditions.[17] The *incipit* and the title certainly function in this way (see below). But one might also point to Saying 12, which appeals to James, and to Saying 13, which appeals to the authority of Thomas, to illustrate the trend. In this sense the Gospel of Thomas is comparable to the canonical gospels, all of which appeal to the authority of apostolic figures, or to the deutero-Pauline epistles, which appeal to the figure of Paul in like manner. All of these texts derive from the last three decades of the first century C.E.

Secondly, it should also be noted that Thomas does not treat the "the twelve" as a unified, sanctified group of quasi-saints. The authority of each is not taken for granted by virtue of the status earned simply through being part of "the twelve." In Saying 13, for example, Thomas' answer is held up as exemplary, but those of Peter and Matthew are deprecated as inadequate. The text thus dates to a time before that in which the disciples as a group were idolized to the degree that would have made this impossible. Mark, written around 70 C.E., is comparable; Acts, written around 100 C.E., marks the emergence of the later phenomenon. This, again, suggests a date for Thomas in the last three decades of the first century.

Didymos Judas Thomas

The title of this book, *Peuaggelion Pkata Thomas* ("The Gospel According to Thomas"), occurs at the end of the book, written by a scribe in subscript fashion (typical of ancient scribal practice). As such, it was probably added secondarily. Originally the text would have been referred to by its opening lines, or *incipit*, which reads: "These are the secret sayings that the living Jesus spoke and Didymos Judas Thomas recorded." Thus, the name of the person to whom the tradition has assigned this collection of sayings is actually Didymos Judas Thomas. Of the three names strung together here only one is a bona fide given name. Thomas is simply the Semitic word for "twin." Didymos, on the other hand, is its Greek translation. Only Judas here is a real name. The others are variants of a nick-name, "the twin." Apparently in the bilingual world of the eastern reaches of the Roman Empire, this redundancy was not noticed, and the name of this author was taken to be Judas Thomas the Twin. Thus it is Judas the Twin to whom this text appeals as the guarantor of its traditions.

Who was this Judas? Of course the most famous Judas in the gospels is Judas Iscariot, who, according to tradition, betrayed Jesus to the authorities just before his execution. But it is not likely that this infamous Judas is the one to whom the sayings tradition would appeal as the guarantor of its reliability. There is, however, another Judas mentioned in the gospels, a certain Judas, "not the Iscariot" (John 14:22). Curiously, in the later Syriac translation of John 14:22 this Judas is identified as Judas Thomas, or Judas the Twin. Yet whose twin? Turning again to the New Testament for clues, there is still another Judas mentioned in the gospels, who likewise is not to be identified with Judas Iscariot, namely Judas, the brother of Jesus mentioned in Mark 6:3 and Matt 13:55. And yet a fourth Judas, "Judas, a servant of Jesus Christ and brother of James," is said to have written the Epistle of Jude. James, of course, is also named as a brother of Jesus in Mark 6:3 and Matt 13:55, so that we may have here a kind of family portrait, even though the author piously demures from claiming the status of "brother" with respect to Jesus, replacing it with the deprecating term "servant."

This odd series of connections has led Koester to suggest that the *incipit* to the Gospel of Thomas intends to claim as its author Judas, the twin brother of Jesus.[18] This suggestion is not as far-fetched as it may initially seem. After all, throughout the Gospel of John the apostle Thomas, to whom the subscript title assigns the Gospel of Thomas, is consistently referred to as "Thomas the Twin" (11:16; 14:5; 20:24-28; 21:2). And in later Syrian tradition, the Acts of Thomas, whose author likely knew the Gospel of Thomas, preserves a tradition that precisely this apostle Thomas was in fact the twin of Jesus (cf. Acts of Thomas 11).

Of course, however intriguing, all of these claims probably do not tell us much about the actual authorship of the Gospel of Thomas. They belong, rather, to the common early Christian phenomenon of assigning important accounts of the tradition to prominent apostolic figures as a means of asserting their reliability. That is the intent of both the *incipit* of the Gospel of Thomas and its subscript title. The fact that they do not exactly agree is not particularly significant. It is likely that over time, and especially in Syria, the figure of Judas, the brother of Jesus, came to be identified with the apostle Thomas, perhaps since both were known in some circles as "the Twin." Such identification is not uncommon among the great legends and heroes of the past. For all practical purposes, we simply do not know who really wrote this gospel.

Provenance

In the period of Christian beginnings it may frequently be observed that the names of certain apostles came to have special significance within a particular geographical area. This phenomenon may have its roots in the actual history of the evangelization of these areas, or the associations may be purely legendary. Whatever may be the case, this phenomenon provides a useful method for locating various texts geographically within the general area of early Christian influence.

Of course, the most important clue of this nature in the Gospel of Thomas is the figure Judas Thomas, or Didymos Judas Thomas. As noted above, in the Syriac version of the Gospel of John, "Judas who was not Iscariot" is referred to as Judas Thomas in John 14:22. Judas Thomas is also named in the Prologue of The Book of Thomas the Contender (NHC II 138.2), the Abgar legend (Euseb., *Ecclesiastical History*. I. xiii.11), and in the *Sermons* of Ephraem (VII. xi. 3), all of eastern Syrian origin. Perhaps more important, however, is the fact that the main character of the Acts of Thomas (also of eastern Syrian origin) is named "Judas Thomas, who is also called Didymos." Apart from the Gospel of Thomas, this is the only other place where one finds this curious combination of names. The association of the apostle Thomas with eastern Syria is also made by Origen (in Eusebius, *Ecclesiastical History*. III.i.1) and in the pseudo-Clementines (*Recognitions* IX.29). All of this offers a relatively strong case for locating the Gospel of Thomas, with its appeal to Didymos Judas Thomas, in eastern Syria as well.

Yet all of these witnesses for the Thomas tradition in the east are relatively late, post-dating the Gospel of Thomas by a century and more. This raises a question of origins: was the apostolic authority of Thomas claimed for the Gospel of Thomas because it was assembled originally in eastern Syria, or could the Gospel of Thomas itself be partially responsible for bringing the Thomas tradition to eastern Syria in the first place, it having been composed earlier in another place. The latter option may be suggested by two factors. First, as a collection of Jesus' sayings, a large part of its material, if not the collection as a whole, would have come originally out of Palestine, the center of activity for the earliest Jesus movement. Secondly, if one returns once again to the issue of names and the phenomenon of geographical specificity to claims of apostolic authority, it is noteworthy that aside from Didymos Judas Thomas, the other authority figure to which the Gospel of Thomas appeals is "James the Just" (Saying 12), that is, James the brother of Jesus. He, in contrast to Thomas, was not associated with the east, but with Jerusalem, where, according to Josephus, he was martyred under the High Priest Ananus the Younger in 62 C.E. (*Antiquities* XX. 197–203). If one may assume that the sayings tradition, generally speaking, has its origins in Palestine with the emergence of the Jesus movement, then it seems that the best way to account for both the James and Thomas traditions in the Gospel of Thomas would be to postulate that at least part of the collection was assembled originally in Palestine. Later a group of early Christians would have taken the collection with it as it migrated east, to eastern Syria, where the Judas Thomas tradition was indigenized and gradually attained a level of prominence there that would account for its appearance in the Acts of Thomas, Thomas the Contender, Ephraem, and the like.

The Theology of the Gospel of Thomas

Sayings Collections and Wisdom

The Gospel of Thomas is a sayings collection. As such it stands as one among several early Christian sayings collections, such as Q and the parables collection in Mark 4 already mentioned above, but also the core of the Epistle of James and the first six chapters of the early Christian manual known as the Didache. But the larger literary context of this type of literature is the Wisdom literature of late Judaism, which produced such sayings collections as Ecclesiastes and those imbedded in Proverbs (e.g., chs. 1–9; 22:17–24:22; 24:23–34) in the Hebrew Bible, and the Wisdom of Solomon and Sirach in the so-called Apocrypha. Thus, Thomas, as a wisdom collection, would have been right at home within the larger Jewish literary culture within which the first Christian writings began to appear.

As such Thomas naturally contains a number of proverbs, whose common, everyday wisdom is consistent with the general orientation of such collections: its sayings speak of what is true about people, about life and the world, and about how one may cultivate a proper attitude about the world and thereby survive its often jolting vicissitudes. They speak about human destiny and what is worthwhile in the world and beyond. It is in this spirit that the Gospel of Thomas, like other Jewish and Christian sayings collections, contains sayings that reveal something fundamental about people and their behavior, sayings such as Thom 45:2–4:

> [2]"A good person brings forth good from the storehouse; [3]a bad person brings forth evil things from the corrupt storehouse in the heart, and says evil things. [4]For from the the abundance of the heart this person brings forth evil things."

Others offer wisdom's critique of foolish human behavior:

[1]Jesus said, "Why do you wash the outside of the cup? [2]Do you not understand that the one who made the inside is also the one who made the outside?"
—Thom 89

Still others are suggestive of the comportment proper to one who correctly understands the tenuous nature of a person's sojourn in the world:

[1]Jesus said, "There was a rich person who had a great deal of money. [2]He said, 'I shall invest my money so that I may sow, reap, plant, and fill my store-houses with produce, that I may lack nothing.' [3]These were the things he was thinking in his heart, but that very night he died. Whoever has ears should hear."   —Thom 63

Thomas and Counter-Cultural Wisdom

This parable in Thom 63 introduces a theme that is extremely important in the Gospel of Thomas, a theme that finds its most succinct expression in Saying 110:

Jesus said, "Let one who has found the world, and has become wealthy, renounce the world."

Or again in Saying 111:3:

[3]Does not Jesus say, "Whoever has found oneself, of that person the world is not worthy?"

For Thomas Christianity the world is not a hospitable place. Its standards, its values are to be rejected and despised. Thus, the wisdom of the Gospel of Thomas is not unlike the wisdom of which Paul speaks in 1 Cor 2:6:

[6]Yet among the mature we do impart wisdom, *although it is not a wisdom of this age or of the rulers of this age,* who are doomed to pass away.

Thomas' wisdom, like that of which Paul speaks, is not exactly standard wisdom fare. It has a kind of anti-cosmic bent, it rejects the world and the dominant interpretation of reality in the world.

This antithetical or counter-cultural way in which wisdom is interpreted in the Gospel of Thomas is communicated also in the way the parables tradition is mediated here. The parables in Thomas function to underscore the way in which the Thomas Christian chooses to relativize human values and achievement in the face of a surprising discovery. Each of the following parables from Thomas focuses on a character who abandons all common sense, ignores the dictates of prudence, and lunges after a single object discovered at an unexpected moment in the work-a-day world.

> [1]And he said, "The human one is like a wise fisherman who cast his net into the sea and drew it up from the sea full of little fish. [2]Among them the wise fisherman discovered a fine large fish. [3]He threw all the little fish back into the sea, and without any effort chose the large fish. [4]Whoever has ears to hear should hear."   —Thom 8

> [1]Jesus said, "The kingdom of the Father is like a merchant who had a supply of merchandise, and then found a pearl. [2]That merchant was prudent; he sold the merchandise and bought the single pearl for himself. [3]So also with you, seek his treasure that is unfailing, that is abiding, where no moth comes to consume and no worm destroys."   —Thom 76

> [1]Jesus said, "The kingdom is like a shepherd who had a hundred sheep. [2]One of them, the largest, went astray. He left the ninety-nine and sought the one until he found it. [3]After he had toiled, he said to the sheep, 'I love you more than the ninety-nine.'"   —Thom 107

No fisher throws *all* of the fish back into the sea simply because he has discovered one particularly large fish! What merchant sells all the stock to buy a single fascinating bauble? And would a shepherd leave ninety-nine sheep unattended and at the mercy of predators in order to search for a single stray, no matter how large?! Yet, from the Thomas point of view, to discover one's true identity results in just such enthusiasm, such a fixation on that newly discovered, highly prized thing, that the world and the world's 'sense' is suddenly and dramatically relativized. When one discovers the truth about the human self, then the world and its demands no longer matter. One is freed from the sense of the work-a-day world to pursue life in a different mode.

the nearness of Jesus.

All except a few of the above quoted sayings from Thomas should sound at least somewhat familiar; Sayings 45, 89, 63, 8, 76, and 107 all have very close parallels in the synoptic gospels. In the case of the parables, at least two of their synoptic counterparts have been transformed by the early church into allegories for salvation conceived within a more apocalyptic framework. But this is a later development. Originally these, and many of the other sayings Thomas and the synoptics share in common, would have formed the common stock of early Christian counter-cultural wisdom to which all branches of the tradition were heir.

Beyond Wisdom

But what is the truth about the human self that the words of Jesus in the Gospel of Thomas reveal? What is the insight that causes one to reject the world and its values in the way the Thomas folk have done? To be sure, there are sayings in Thomas which answer this question in ways that will seem quite conventional with respect to wisdom literature, generally speaking: People tend to be selfish (Thom 41), vain (Thom 36), judgmental (Thom 26), foolish and easily led astray (Thom 34), etc. But Thomas has much more to say about the secrets of human nature than this. It is at this point that the Gospel of Thomas begins to extend beyond what may sound familiar as wisdom. Thomas includes sayings which speak about what is not obvious, about that which is hidden and must be revealed (Thom 5), secrets which reveal themselves only after much searching (Thom 2). This is wisdom of a hidden, more speculative sort, which speaks of human origins and the destiny to which a fully cognizant person may aspire. Typical of this train of thought in Thomas are Sayings 49–50:

> 49 ¹Jesus said, "Blessed are those who are alone and chosen, for you will find the kingdom. ²For you have come from it, and you will return there again."
> 50 ¹Jesus said, "If they say to you, 'Where have you come from?', say to them, 'We have come from the light, from the place where the light came into being by itself, established [itself], and appeared in their image.' ²If they say to you, 'Is it you?', say, 'We are its children, and we are the chosen of the living Father.' ³If they ask you, 'What is the evidence of your Father in you?', say to them, 'It is motion and rest.'"

In this sequence of sayings the Gospel of Thomas has moved beyond the realm of conventional wisdom and into a perspective more akin to Gnosticism. Gnostics believed that they were ultimately not of the present, evil world at all, but rather were descended from the one high God who lives aloft in heavenly remove from the cosmos. Their presence in the world is due to a great tragic mistake whereby the demiurge, a rebellious angel, had sought to create something of its own volition apart from God. The result was the creation of the earth, and at the same time a rupture in the primeval perfection of the divine realm. In this rupture, parts of the divine realm became trapped in the evil creation of the demiurge, spirits (πνεύματα) embodied in persons, who someday must win their release from the evil world, and return to the divine realm from whence they have come. This, or a similar mythological framework, is presupposed in Sayings 49–50. The Thomas Christian is told of his/her origin and ultimate destiny, and finally, is given the secret passwords to be used in the re-ascent past the many heavenly guardians who would block their path.

However, this moment of return to which the Thomas Christian aspires requires preparation beyond the simple memorization of passwords. One must also cultivate the proper understanding of the world that will enable one to leave its confines when the time comes. Thom 56 speaks of such an understanding:

> [1]Jesus said, "Whoever has come to know the world has discovered a carcass, [2]and whoever has discovered a carcass, of that person the world is not worthy."

This saying identifies the world with death and lifelessness, a thing above which one must ultimately rise. Its doublet in Thom 80 provides a clue to how one accomplishes this feat:

> [1]Jesus said: "Whoever has come to know the world has discovered the body, [2]and whoever has discovered the body, of that person the world is not worthy."

Here proper understanding of the world (as ultimately dead) leads inevitably to a proper understanding of the body and corporeal existence. In Thomas, becoming superior to the world involves deprecation of the flesh in favor of the spirit. Saying 29 marvels in bewilderment over how it is that something so glorious as the spirit has become mired in flesh:

> [1]Jesus said, "If the flesh came into being because of spirit, it is a marvel, [2]but if spirit came into being because of the body, it is a marvel of marvels. [3]Yet I marvel at how this great wealth has come to dwell in this poverty."
>
> —Thom 29

In the Gospel of Thomas, flesh and spirit, body and soul are separate components in human being, joined in an unholy mix which spells doom for both:

> [1]Jesus said, "Woe to the flesh that depends on the soul. [2]Woe to the soul that depends on the flesh."   —Thom 112

Like many gnostic groups, Thomas Christians were not interested simply in freeing the soul from the body, as if one could exist as a disembodied spirit, wandering abstractly through the cosmos without form and identity. Separating the soul from the corporeal existence of this world frees it to enter into a new identity, a new kind of corporeal

The Gospel of Thomas

existence which awaits it in the heavenly realm. In gnostic circles this new "body" is often spoken of as one's heavenly twin, or "image," which awaits the soul of the gnostic, guarded and enclosed in the safety of the god-head until it can properly be claimed. Thus, Thomas speaks of the "images," for the present concealed in the Father, but waiting for that moment when their splendor will be revealed to their rightful claimants:

> 83 ¹Jesus said: "Images are visible to people, but the light within them is hidden in the image of the Father's light. ²He will be disclosed, but his image is hidden by his light." 84 ¹Jesus said: "When you see your likeness, you are happy. ²But when you see your images that came into being before you and that neither die nor become visible, how much you will bear!"
>
> —Thom 83–84

Behind this notion of rediscovering one's heavenly image is a particular understanding of human being common in late Jewish wisdom speculation, as well as in Gnosticism, which takes as its point of departure Adam's primordial fall from perfection. Such groups held that prior to the fall, Adam was not male, nor female, but rather both—a perfect and complete androgynous being. This androgynous state was lost in the fall, a fall from perfection. The result was that human existence is condemned to the imperfection of sexual differentiation until such time as the primordial state of androgyny could be restored (cf. Thom 11:4). But according to Thomas, with the proper self-awareness it is possible now to reverse this piece of cosmic history, and to begin the process of returning to that primordial state of perfection. Thom 22:4–7 speaks of this moment of salvation when one recovers one's pre-Adamic androgynous state:

> ⁴Jesus said to them, "When you make the two into one, and when you make the inner like the outer and the outer like the inner, and the upper like the lower, ⁵and when you make male and female into a single one, so that the male will not be male nor the female be female, ⁶when you make eyes in place of an eye, a hand in place of a hand, a foot in place of a foot, an image in place of an image, ⁷then you will enter [the kingdom]."

The sense in Thomas of the fallenness of the world extends to human being itself, and in fact seems even to focus on one's corporeal existence as that reality in which one experiences imperfection most acutely. This saying suggests that the old body of imperfection may gradually be replaced with a new, more perfect body (perhaps through asceticism) until one gradually recovers the primordial state of non-differentiation (cf. Thom 106).

Is then the Gospel of Thomas gnostic? Even though it does not presuppose all of the complex mythological framework to be found in the writings of some of the later second and third century gnostic schools, such as that of Valentinus or the Sethians, in view of the kinds of sayings cited above, one must say that in the most general sense, it is indeed gnostic. But it is also undeniably a work of late Jewish wisdom. In fact, perhaps one of the most important things Thomas tells us about the theological trends of the first century is how easily the sort of counter-cultural wisdom promulgated in Thomas, and elsewhere in early Christianity, could modulate into a purely gnostic way of thinking.[19] The counter-cultural bent of Thomas' wisdom sayings is not far from the anti-cosmic stance taken by Gnosticism; it is but a small step from wisdom's quest for meaning and insight into the human condition to the gnostic notion of self-recognition as the key to salvation. In the Gospel of Thomas, proper understanding of the world and true self-recognition is made possible through the hearing of Jesus' words of wisdom.

The Reign of God in the Gospel of Thomas

As a sayings collection, that Thomas should place so much weight on insight gained through hearing the words of Jesus is understandable. Hearing the words and understanding their implications is, from a soteriological standpoint, of paramount importance in Thomas. Saying 1 could not express this perspective more strongly: "Whoever discovers the interpretation of these sayings will not taste death." With so much resting on the understanding the "word," one might well ask whether there is any room left in the Thomas schema for something like the early Christian notion of the Reign of God. On the one hand, in the Gospel of Thomas there is no future or apocalyptic notion of the Reign of God, such as one finds, for example, in the synoptic gospels or Paul. Rather, what one finds is a concept of the Reign of God, whose chief characteristic is its present-ness for those who are able correctly to perceive it:

> [1]His disciples said to him, "When will the kingdom come?" [2]"It will not come by waiting for it. [3]It will not be said 'Behold, here,' or 'Behold, there.' [4]Rather, the kingdom of the Father is spread out upon the earth, and people do not see it."
> —Thom 113

This present-ness, as one may readily see, is conceived not only in temporal terms, but in spatial terms as well. It is a reality both *now* and *here.* This point is driven home with a sense of humor in Saying 3:1:

¹Jesus said, "If your leaders say to you, 'Behold, the kingdom is in heaven,' then the birds of heaven will precede you. ²If they say to you 'It is in the sea,' then the fish will precede you. ³Rather, the kingdom is within you, and it is outside you."   —Thom 3:1–3

As elsewhere in Thomas, in this saying the element of recognition is crucial. For what is offered here as the Reign of God spread out among persons is not present reality simply as it is, as interpreted through a conventional lens. Rather, the Reign of God is fully present only when one's interpretation of the present moment is focused through a proper understanding of oneself as a child of God. The continuation of Saying 3 illustrates this most clearly:

⁴"When you know yourselves, then you will be known, and you will understand that you are children of the living Father. ⁵But if you do not know yourselves, then you dwell in poverty, and you are the poverty."
—Thom 3:4–5

For the Thomas Christian, to know the Reign of God is to know one's true identity as "children of the Living Father." This reign cannot be associated with a future event, as though one's true identity as a child of God is something that will be revealed only at some future time. Nor can it be associated solely with a transcendent realm, as though this identity cannot be realized even in the midst of life's concrete situations. In the Gospel of Thomas, the presence of the Reign of God here and now represents a radical insistence upon the true identity and grounding of human being in God, a fact which the presence of the world or the nature of the present age cannot be allowed to obstruct.

Social Radicalism and the Gospel of Thomas

But though the Thomas tradition places much weight upon "knowing," and attaining the proper frame of mind for understanding the world, one must not assume that the religious life in Thomas Christianity was simply an intellectual exercise. Thomas Christianity was not a conclave of meditating elites cloistered off from the masses, spiritualizing the gospel away from its concrete relationship to the world. There are many sayings in Thomas (a number of which Thomas shares with the canonical gospels), gathered together for the purpose of specifying the kind of behavior and mode of living in the world that duly reflects the identity of its adherents with the heavenly god-head, the "Father." At the heart of this life-style is a kind of social radicalism that rejects the commonly-held values of the world. The sayings speak of rejecting the ideal of house and home, of settled living in the world:

> Jesus said, "Be passersby." —Thom 42

of rejecting family:

> [1]Jesus said, "Whoever does not hate father and mother cannot be a disciple of me, [2]and whoever does not hate brothers and sisters, and bear the cross as I do, will not be worthy of me." —Thom 55

of rejecting popular piety:

> [1]Jesus said to them, "If you fast, you will bring sin upon yourselves, [2]and if you pray, you will be condemned, [3]and if you give alms, you will harm your spirits." —Thom 14:1–3

and of rejecting shrewd business sense:

> [1][Jesus said], "If you have money, do not lend it at interest. [2]Rather, give [it] to someone from whom you will not get it back." —Thom 95

Instead, Thomas offers up a new set of values that are fundamentally opposed to those of the world. The poor are blessed (Thom 54), as are the suffering (Thom 58), the persecuted (Thom 68), and those who hunger (Thom 69).

Thus, to be a "child of the living father" is to see oneself as free, as one not inextricably bound to the world and its values, as one whose worth, whose "blessedness" does not depend upon the marks of success in the world. For the Thomas Christian, laying claim to one's identity as a child of God means the rejection of every other identity that the world might offer up as valuable: householder, family member, religious leader, successful business person. "Jesus said: 'Let one who has found the world, and has become wealthy, renounce the world.'" (Thom 110).

But how far were the Thomas Christians willing to take this kind of social radicalism? Thomas' Parable of the Tenants provokes the imagination to consider just to what extent they were ready consciously to overturn the rules that governed their times:

> [1]He said, "A [. . .] person owned a vineyard and rented it to some farmers, that they might work it and he might collect its produce from them. [2]He sent his servant that the farmers might give the servant the produce of the vineyard. [3]They seized, beat, and almost killed his servant, and the servant returned and told his master. [4]His master said, 'Perhaps the servant did not know them.' [5]He sent another servant, and the farmers beat that one as well. [6]Then the master sent his son and said, 'Perhaps they will show my son some respect.'

7Because the farmers knew that he was the heir to the vineyard, they seized him and killed him. 8Whoever has ears should hear."   —Thom 65

When one compares this version of the Parable of the Tenants to those which occur in Mark, Matthew, and Luke, one notices immediately its distinguishing characteristic: this version is a true parabolic story, not an allegory. Form critics have long held that allegorization of the parables was a relatively late development in the history of their early interpretation. In fact, even without access to the Coptic Gospel of Thomas, the great parables scholar C. H. Dodd had offered a conjectural reconstruction of the Parable of the Tenants as it would have read before the synoptic tradition had allegorized it. His reconstruction matched Saying 65 almost to the word.[20]

But what does this ancient Christian parable mean? Its interpretation is complicated by a troublesome lacuna, or hole in the papyrus, in its very first line. The missing word is an adjective which would have modified the word "person" in some way. The extant letters around the edges of the hole permit a reconstruction of the word "good," so that one could speak here of a "good person" who rented the farm to "evil" tenants, just as one finds in the synoptic versions of the story. But the extant letters also permit the reconstruction of the word for "creditor" or "usurer," which would make this person one of the absentee landlords so much hated among the land-poor peasants of Galilee. One wonders, in the rural areas of Palestine and Syria among the dispossessed and poor—the tenant class—how this parable would have been heard. Were these evil tenants, or were they brave tenants?

For the modern who has come to think of Christian faith in terms of non-violence or pacifism, such a suggestion may seem shocking. But Palestine in the first century was a very brutal place to live. To persons not accustomed to witnessing willful brutality as part of one's daily existence, Thomas' radical images of the Reign of God can be shocking indeed. Perhaps none is more foreign to us in this respect than Thomas' Parable of the Assassin:

1Jesus said, "The kingdom of the Father is like a person who wanted to put someone powerful to death. 2He drew his sword at home and thrust it into the wall to find out whether his hand would go in. 3Then he killed the powerful one."   —Thom 98

Thomas Christianity saw itself as engaged in a struggle with the world in which it sought to live out its understanding of Jesus' words. Whether this parable in fact advocates armed struggle against the powerful is questionable. Nevertheless, it demonstrates the extent to which a violent context may have come to shape the way early Christians imagined their task as disciples faithful to Jesus' words.

The Gospel of Thomas and Early Christianity

The Gospel of Thomas and Synoptic Christianity

The Gospel of Thomas, as noted above, shares a great deal of the material it draws from the early Christian Jesus tradition with the synoptic gospels, Matthew, Mark, and Luke. Consequently, much of the critical discussion of the Gospel of Thomas over the years has been devoted to its relationship to the synoptic gospels. One of the most important issues in this discussion has already been mentioned: whether or not Thomas is directly dependent upon the synoptic gospels for this traditional material. But if one sides with the majority of scholars on this issue, and supposes that Thomas did not use these canonical gospels, but indeed represents a new and independent witness to the Jesus tradition, the Gospel of Thomas presents us with a unique and very important opportunity to gain new insight into ways in which this tradition was originally formulated and subsequently developed by the early church. One might describe the situation thusly: since Thomas and the synoptic gospels both witness to a common tradition that precedes them, a comparison of these two independent witnesses could tell us much about this earlier common tradition and its theological potential. Those elements shared by both witnesses would have to be considered as belonging to the *earlier* character of the tradition; those elements occurring in only one of the surviving versions should likely be assessed in terms of the *later* development of the tradition.

An example of how this works has already been given above, with the Parable of the Tenants. It was noted, for example, that both the synoptic gospels and the Gospel of Thomas presented the rudiments of a parabolic story; only the synoptic version was also presented as an allegory. Thus, the allegorization of the original parabolic story could rightly be identified as a relatively late development. Form critics had already surmised that this was the case with parables; the Gospel of Thomas verified the theory. In fact, very few of Thomas' parables show much effect of the later tendency in the early church toward allegorization. Thus Thomas has become a rich field for studying the parables tradition in its more original state.

The discovery of the Gospel of Thomas has aided in this sort of tradition-historical study of Jesus' sayings generally speaking. Thomas does not by any means always present one with a more original form of any given saying it shares with the canonical gospels. But by comparing two independently attested versions of a saying, it is often possible to get a better idea of how the earlier version of a Jesus saying might have sounded. At the same time, of course, one becomes much more aware of the way each branch of the tradition has chosen to alter and interpret the saying. Such research stands to help fill in our still sketchy knowledge of the theology of the respective gospel writers. Once one realizes how an author has edited the tradition, one may then ask why, a question, the answer to which is often a theological motivation of one sort or another.

For example, we have seen how easily wisdom speculation of the sort found in Thomas could modulate into a more gnostic understanding of the sayings tradition. This may in fact have been the reason, according to James M. Robinson, that no sayings collections seem to have survived in orthodox Christian circles, and that Q only survived as it was imbedded in the narratives of Matthew and Luke. This gnosticizing tendency, built into the wisdom sayings tradition, may well have cast a pall of suspicion over all sayings collections within orthodox circles. Embedding the sayings of Jesus into a narrative context would have "protected" them from this sort of free-wheeling gnostic interpretation.[21]

One important theological difference between Thomas and the synoptic gospels is the fact that all three of the latter framed the gospel within the overall context of apocalypticism. For all three, Jesus is the Son of Man, who in Jewish mythology was thought of as God's wrathful agent, who would come at the end of time to judge the good and the evil. Thus one finds in Mark 13, and its parallels in Matthew and Luke, Jesus depicted as the Son of Man coming on clouds of glory to judge the wicked and unfaithful. Even Q seems to have understood Jesus in such terms. But as we have seen, this was not the case with Thomas. The words "son of man" occur only once in Thomas, and then only in the non-technical sense of this term, "human being" (Thom 86).[22] Moreover, it has no apocalyptic sections, and in fact speaks out directly against this interpretation of who Jesus was (Thom 3 and 113).

In this instance one might well suppose that Thomas' anti-apocalyptic stance is late, the result of the failure of early Christianity's apocalyptic expectations to materialize. But this may not necessarily be the case.

John Kloppenborg's recent study of Q has argued that this synoptic sayings collection may have undergone considerable editing at some point in its history. The first draft of Q would not have contained the apocalyptic and angry tones of judgment to be found in the final copy used by Matthew and Luke. This first edition, rather, was a collection of wisdom speeches, a "wisdom gospel" not unlike the Gospel of Thomas. The addition of apocalyptic material to Q would have occurred only after the initial Q community had begun to realize how small it really was, and how few had taken their proclamation of Jesus' words seriously.[23]

The confluence of Thomas and the first edition of Q on this issue represents an extremely important discovery. For it has long been assumed by New Testament scholars that the beginnings of early Christian theology are to be found in Jewish apocalyptic thought. In fact, it is usually assumed that Jesus himself was an apocalyptic preacher. But if both branches of the sayings tradition, at least in their beginning stages, agree in presenting Jesus' teaching in non-apocalyptic terms, these assumptions will have to be scrutinized very carefully. It appears more and more likely that Jesus' teaching, and the beginnings of early Christian theology, may not be rooted in Jewish apocalyptic thought after all, but rather in Jewish Wisdom.

The Gospel of Thomas and the first edition of Q are in agreement on one other matter, which may seem equally striking. As opposed to the synoptic gospels and John, each of which ends with a passion narrative culminating with the death of Jesus, Thomas and Q have no passion narrative at all. In fact, neither seems very interested in the death of Jesus; they are certainly not interested in it as a saving event. Thomas never even mentions the crucifixion. This is not to suggest that Jesus was not crucified, or some such thing. But the silence of these two early Christian documents on this crucial matter does raise acutely the question of how it was that the death of Jesus eventually came to be the fulcrum of early Christian theological reflection. One can no longer take it for granted that Jesus' death was the main point of departure for all the groups claiming allegiance to Jesus.

But the editorial or redactional activity of an author is not always determined by strictly theological considerations. Sometimes theological considerations may combine with factors of a more sociological or social-historical nature to affect the way the tradition is formulated. Thus, a comparison of Thomas and the synoptic gospels may also improve our understanding of the over-all social-historical development of the various early Christian groups which transmitted the sayings of Jesus.

For example, much of the socially radical sayings material cited above finds close parallel in the synoptic tradition as well. Its presence there led Gerd Theissen to the conclusion that those who transmitted these early sayings of Jesus were engaged in a socially radical style of living, a life-style he called "itinerant radicalism." But alongside this material one also finds in the synoptic tradition much that seems to relativize this radical tradition, and promote a more conventional, more settled life-style. Thus Theissen also posited, in addition to these radical wandering folk, groups of settled Christians which could give shelter and lend support to the itinerants when they wandered through.[24] By contrast, when one examines the Thomas side of the tradition, one finds plenty to support the radical existence of the itinerants, but nothing to justify the more conventionally situated support groups. Thus, one might hypothesize that the radical behavior of the itinerants, attested in both halves of the tradition, derives from an early stage in the Jesus movement, while the settlement of support groups was a phenomenon which developed somewhat later, and primarily in the synoptic half of the tradition. Among Thomas Christians the radical lifestyle of the wandering itinerant remained the dominant ethos.

The Gospel of Thomas and Johannine Christianity

Since its discovery the Gospel of Thomas has invited comparison with the Gospel of John, not so much for any close verbal correspondence between specific traditions they hold in common, as is the case with the synoptic gospels, but more for the similarities in their respective theological points of view. Of all the gospels, John, with its dualities of darkness and light, spirit and flesh, its often paradoxical language, and its own affinities with gnostic thought seems to speak from a theological perspective most akin to that of Thomas. Two aspects of Johannine and Thomas thought in particular are worth comparing.

First, there is in both John and Thomas a focus on Jesus' words. As noted above, in Thomas it is Jesus' words which bring eternal life (Thom 1). That seems in fact to be the very *raison d'être* of this collection of sayings. Likewise in John 6:63 Jesus reveals: "the words I have spoken to you are spirit and life." And again in John 8:51: "Truly I say to you, whoever keeps my word will never taste death." In 6:68 it is Peter who proclaims: "You [Lord] have the words of eternal life." For both Thomas and John, hearing and understanding ("keeping") the words of Jesus is the key to salvation.

John and Thomas also share a basic christological assumption, though in each it is developed to different degrees. In both gospels Jesus is thought of essentially as the redeemer who descends to earth to sojourn for a time among people, but then re-ascends to heaven from whence he has come. In John, of course, the notion of the descending/ascending redeemer is applied to Jesus most clearly in the Prologue to the gospel:

> 9The true light that enlightens every person was coming into the world. 10He was in the world, and the world was made through him, yet the world knew him not.   —John 1:9–10

The rest of this gospel could be described as the account of this sojourn, and throughout John, Jesus speaks as the redeemer. In John 7:28b-29, for example, Jesus says to the crowds in Jerusalem: "But I have not come of my own accord; the one who sent me is true, and that one you do not know. I know that one, for I come from that one, and that one sent me." Then further in vv. 33–34: "I shall be with you a little longer, and then I go to the one who sent me; you will seek me and you will not find me; where I am you cannot come." Thomas' Jesus speaks of his "mission" in similar terms, as a divine messenger who has descended to earth to enlighten lost souls:

> 1Jesus said, "I took my stand in the midst of the world, and in flesh I appeared to them. 2I found them all drunk, and I did not find any of them thirsty. 3My soul ached for the children of humanity, because they are blind in their hearts and do not see, for they came into the world empty, and they also seek to depart from the world empty. 4But now they are drunk. When they shake off their wine, then they will repent."   —Thom 28

In Saying 38 Jesus speaks of his future re-ascent:

> 1Jesus said, "Often you have desired to hear these sayings that I am speaking to you, and you have no one else from whom to hear them. 2There will be days when you will seek me and you will not find me."

And in both John and Thomas, throughout his sojourn, Jesus, as the redeemer, has a special relationship with God; it is Jesus the redeemer to whom God has given "all things." In John 3:35 Jesus says of this relationship: "The Father loves the Son and has given all things into his hand." Saying 61:3 in the Gospel of Thomas expresses the same enigmatic idea, though in terms slightly less imposing: "I am the one who derives from what is whole. I was granted from the things of my Father."

Yet when one compares these gospels more carefully on this point, it is clear that the redeemer mythology is much less developed in Thomas than in John. In the latter, almost the entire gospel seems devoted to making this point: Jesus is the redeemer sent from God. In Thomas, apart from these few sayings, there is little that one could link specifically to this Christology. It is as though we are encountering it in Thomas in a fledgling form, long before Johannine Christianity had worked out all of the details. The kernel of the idea must be very old indeed. One even finds its rudiments in Q:

> [22]"All things have been handed over to me by my Father; and no one knows who the Son is except the Father, or who the Father is except the Son and any one to whom the Son wishes to reveal him." —Luke 10:22 (par. Matt 11:27)

If Thomas can be said to offer an early form of the redeemer Christology one finds in John's gospel, further comparisons of the Thomas and Johannine traditions may help to explain other aspects of the earlier stages in the development of Johannine thought. For example, it has long been conjectured that the lengthy and complex discourses one finds on the lips of Jesus in John's gospel are the end product of a good deal of theological reflection. The point of departure for such reflection would have been individual sayings or small clusters of sayings, elements of which may still be seen in the end product. However, until now the thorough-going way in which the Johannine community recast its sayings into its characteristically complex discourses has made it all but impossible to recover anything from this early Johannine sayings tradition. But Thomas may be able to help remedy this situation. Helmut Koester has made a start in this direction by identifying several sayings in Thomas, whose Johannine parallels suggest that they were known and used also in the Johannine community.[25] It remains to be seen how far such analysis will take us in understanding the complex background of Johannine thought, but the Gospel of Thomas has opened up significant new possibilities for research along these lines.

The Gospel of Thomas and Paul

One of the perennial difficulties with understanding Paul within the development of earliest Christianity has been explaining his relationship to the early sayings tradition. The dilemma is this: on the one hand

Parallels with the Gospel of John

Thom 13:5

[5]Jesus said, "I am not your teacher. Because you have drunk, you have become intoxicated from the bubbling spring that I have tended."

John 4:14; 7:37–38

[14] "but whoever drinks of the water that I shall give him will never thirst; the water that I shall give him will become in him a spring of water welling up to eternal life."

[37] On the last day of the feast, the great day, Jesus stood up and proclaimed, "If any one thirst, let him come to me and drink. [38] He who believes in me, as the scripture has said, 'Out of his heart shall flow rivers of living water.'"

Thom 24:1–3

[1]His disciples said, "Show us the place where you are, for we must seek it."
[2]He said to them, "Whoever has ears should hear. [3]There is light within a person of light, and it shines on the whole world. If it does not shine, it is dark."

John 11:9–12

[9]Jesus answered, "Are there not twelve hours in the day? If any one walks in the day, he does not stumble, because he sees the light of this world. [10]But if any one walks in the night, he stumbles, because the light is not in him." [11]Thus he spoke, and then he said to them, "Our friend Lazarus has fallen asleep, but I go to awake him out of sleep." [12]The disciples said to him, "Lord, if he has fallen asleep, he will recover."

Thom 92:1–2

[1]Jesus said, "Seek and you will find. [2]In the past, however, I did not tell you the things about which you asked me then. Now I am willing to tell them, but you are not seeking them."

John 16:23–24, 30

[23] "In that day you will ask nothing of me. Truly, truly, I say to you, if you ask anything of the Father, he will give it to you in my name. [24]Hitherto you have asked nothing in my name; ask, and you will receive, that your joy may be full."

[30] "Now we know that you know all things, and need none to question you; by this we believe that you came from God."

Thom 38:1–2

[1]Jesus said, "Often you have desired to hear these sayings that I am speaking to you, and you have no one else from whom to hear them. [2]There will be days when you will seek me and you will not find me."

John 7:33–34; 8:21; 13:33

[33]Jesus then said, "I shall be with you a little longer, and then I go to him who sent me; [34]you will seek me and you will not find me; where I am you cannot come."

[21]Again he said to them, "I go away, and you will seek me and die in your sin; where I am going, you cannot come."

[33] "Little children, yet a little while I am with you. You will seek me; and as I said to the Jews so now I say to you, 'Where I am going you cannot come.'"

Paul quotes so few sayings of Jesus in his letters one has been forced to conclude either that Paul did not know about the sayings tradition, or that he knew of the sayings tradition, but was uninterested in it. On the other hand, by all accounts Paul became a Christian in the region of Syria, and spent the first fifteen or so years of his ministry in and around those environs, precisely the area in which the sayings tradition appears to have been strongest in the first century. How can we imagine Paul becoming deeply involved in the Syrian Christian movement and not coming under the profound influence of the sayings tradition?

The dilemma, as I have summarized it, assumes more or less that the root of the problem is Paul's virtual silence on the sayings tradition; this is in fact the way the problem is usually formulated. But the discovery of the Gospel of Thomas has reminded us that the sayings tradition that survived antiquity does not necessarily represent the full range of theological possibilities and potentialities within that tradition. In other words, the problem was not just Paul's silence on the sayings tradition. Important also was the silence of the sayings tradition *as we knew it* on positions traditionally associated with Paul. Happily, the Gospel of Thomas offers new information that alters this state of affairs. There is a handful of sayings in Thomas which show, on the one hand, how Pauline theology might well have developed out of elements already present within the sayings tradition, and on the other hand, why Paul may have come eventually to avoid using the sayings tradition in his letters.

Thomas shows, for example, that Paul was neither the only, nor perhaps even the first person within the early Christian movement to oppose the circumcision of Gentiles before their inclusion in Christian communities. Saying 53 reads:

> [1]His disciples said to him, "Is circumcision useful or not?" [2]He said to them, "If it were useful, their father would produce children already circumcised from their mother. [3]Rather, the true circumcision in spirit has become profitable in every respect."

Jesus' piquant reply to the question here may seem trite when compared to the sophisticated theological arguments against the circumcision of Gentiles Paul offers in Galatians or Romans. Nonetheless it illustrates the fact that Paul may not have been as "out on a limb" on this matter within early Christianity as is often assumed. Rather, it appears that elements of the sayings tradition had already begun the process of including Gentiles apart from Paul's own efforts. This is indicated also by Saying 14:4–5 in Thomas, which reads as follows:

> ⁴"When you go into any country and walk from place to place, when the people receive you, eat what they serve you and heal the sick among them. ⁵For what goes into your mouth will not defile you; rather, it is what comes out of your mouth that will defile you."

The first part of the saying is simply good advice for homeless beggars such as those who promulgated the Thomas tradition. But the second part makes it clear that the saying's intent is not simply to address the question of how to obtain food. The real question is whether one must seek to obtain only *kosher* food, a question which arises only when Jews have crossed over the social boundaries that separate Jews from Gentiles. The Thomas Christians, like Paul, had clearly crossed those boundaries, and made a practice of visiting both Jewish and Gentile homes.

Another social boundary which scholars are coming more and more to recognize as abrogated in the Pauline communities is that between men and women. While the sayings tradition, as preserved for example in Q, does not explicitly exclude women from participation or leadership in the Jesus movement, one does not find much positive evidence there for their participation either. Could Paul then have been the initiator of this practice? Thomas gives us new information on this front as well. Saying 114 reads:

> ¹Simon Peter said to them, "Let Mary leave us, for females are not worthy of life." ²Jesus said, "Behold, I shall guide her to make her male, so that she too may become a living spirit resembling you males. ³For every female who makes herself male will enter the kingdom of heaven."

Now, as is obvious, this saying does not really free itself from the mistaken notions of its day about the relative worth of men and women. Nonetheless, what it says, in its own "back-handed" way, is very important for the history of early Christianity. First, it probably indicates that not all were in agreement on whether women should be allowed to participate fully in the Jesus movement. The opposition to women voiced by Peter in this saying is not isolated, but reminds one of later evidence of a similar dispute in the Gospel of Mary (BG 8502 17,7–18,15) and Pistis Sophia (I, 36; II, 72). This dispute was likely one which would be carried on within early Christianity for many years to come. The Gospel of Thomas, of course, comes down here in favor of women's participation, provided they engage in the same sort of regimen required of the men in the group. What is more, Mary (it is not clear which Mary is intended here) is taken as the predecessor of all women who would become disciples. This stands in contrast to the more traditional feminine roles assigned to Mary in the synoptic and Johannine traditions (whether one speaks of Mary the mother of Jesus or of Mary Magdelene). In Thomas, Mary is presented as the first female disciple of Jesus. Thus, Paul may well have had good precedent, even from out of the sayings tradition, for including both women and men in the organization of the Christian communities he founded.

While the Gospel of Thomas provides these ways of imagining how Paul may have arrived at his interpretation of the gospel even through the sayings tradition, it also may help explain how it was that Paul eventually broke from the sayings tradition, or at least became reluctant to make use of it in his correspondence. In 1 Corinthians Paul is adamant in his opposition to a group which has arisen among the Christians at Corinth, whose orientation seems to have been rooted in a kind of Hellenistic Jewish wisdom speculation, such as one finds, for example, in Philo of Alexandria. Their claim is to special knowledge, an elitist wisdom, through which they also seek to claim a special status within the community (1:10–4:21). Moreover, their knowledge has already projected them on into the new age that is to come. They have already begun "to rule" (4:8); they have already become immortal (ch. 15); they have begun already to practice the freedom that will accompany the new age (6:12; 10:23). Paul for his part responds by stressing that the wisdom of God cannot be the basis of special claims to status within the community, that the consummation of the Reign of God is yet to come, and that as Christ was raised from death, new life only comes through the future resurrection from death (ch. 15). Furthermore, he argues that freedom cannot be made an absolute principle governing all behavior. Rather freedom may be exercised only in deference to concern for the entire community's well-being (chs. 5–14).

Now, it is noteworthy that in the context of dealing with these problems Paul quotes a saying from the Gospel of Thomas. The quotation comes in the little wisdom speech Paul himself composes in 2:6–16, in which Paul borrows the wisdom style of his opponents, only to correct their views with a few well-designed alterations:

> [9]But as it is written, "What no eye has seen, nor ear heard, nor the human heart conceived, what God has prepared for those who love him," [10]God has revealed to us through the Spirit.   —1 Cor 2:9–10a

Thomas' version is not an exact replica, but reflects the sort of differences one would expect to have resulted from oral transmission:

> Jesus said, "I shall give you what no eye has seen, what no ear has heard, what no hand has touched, what has not arisen in the human heart."   —Thom 17

In view of the fact that Paul in this letter is struggling *against* the kind of esotericism promoted by this saying, it is not likely that he has quoted it here simply because he liked it. Rather, he must have drawn it from the repertoire of his opponents, only to fill it with new content more amenable to his version of the gospel. According to Paul, that which has been revealed is not the knowledge (γνῶσις) that has "puffed up" the "wise" in Corinth, but the crucifixion, the "word of the cross" as Paul himself puts it (1:18). Paul in a sense co-opts the methods of his opponents in order to correct their message.

May one therefore say that the opponents of Paul in Corinth are Thomas Christians? If one locates the Gospel of Thomas in eastern Syria, the geography alone would make this difficult. Nonetheless, the views one finds Paul opposing in 1 Corinthians cannot be far from those of Thomas Christianity. They, like Thomas Christians, were clearly interested in the saving power of secret words of wisdom. Furthermore, because of the immediacy of insight as a vehicle of salvation, they have jumped ahead of Paul's time table: "already you have become kings!" Paul rebukes, "And would that you did reign, so that we might share the rule with you!" (4:8b) This last charge is particularly interesting in view of Thom 2, in which the successful outcome of one's quest for saving knowledge and insight is described precisely with the metaphor of "reigning":

> [1]Jesus said, "Let one who seeks not stop seeking until one finds. [2]When one finds, one will be disturbed. [3]When one is disturbed, one will marvel, and one will reign over all."   —Thom 2

Throughout 1 Corinthians Paul argues against those in Corinth whose enthusiasm has carried them into the Reign of God ahead of Paul's schedule. The Thomas tradition clearly stands with these enthusiasts against Paul. They might well have taken great stock in sayings such as Thomas 3, 113, and especially 51:

> [1]His disciples said to him, "When will the rest for the dead take place, and when will the new world come?" [2]He said to them, "What you look for has come, but you do not know it."

One thinks here of 1 Corinthians 15, where Paul argues against the view that the resurrection is not a future event, and that the wise have been assured of their immortality already in the present.

But perhaps most important, throughout 1 Corinthians Paul seems so intent upon reminding the church over and over again of the particular significance of Jesus' death, one might well guess that Paul's opponents here would have assigned little importance to any of the content of the early Christian creedal formula Paul cites in 15:3: "... that Christ died for our sins in accordance with the scriptures, that he was buried, that he was raised on the third day according to the scriptures. . . ." They were not interested in Jesus' death as a saving event. One is reminded that within the earliest sayings tradition, not only in Thomas, but also in the earliest version of the synoptic sayings source, Q, there is virtually nothing to indicate that its tradents—those responsible for handing the tradition on—would have had any use for such a formula. But this is natural enough: in the Gospel of Thomas it is insight gained through Jesus' words which can bring about the presence of the Reign of God here and now (Thom 3).

Even though one should not press the point as far as saying Paul's opponents in 1 Corinthians were Thomas Christians, the Gospel of Thomas does give us some basic insights into the potential of the sayings tradition to produce precisely the sort of views Paul was in fact combatting in Corinth. Thus, it may not have been the case that Paul was simply uninterested in the sayings tradition, or even that because of his experience of the Risen Lord Paul was unconcerned with the Jesus of history. Paul may have come to reject the tradition of Jesus' sayings (despite the fact that he himself would have originally come into the Christian movement via the the sayings tradition) because in the form in which he later encountered it among other missionaries to the West, its theological tendencies turned out to be unacceptable to him.

The Gospel of Thomas and Jesus

The Gospel of Thomas and the Quest of the Historical Jesus

One of the reasons the discovery and publication of the Gospel of Thomas created so much excitement in both the academic community and the public at large was, of course, the fact that it is not just a random collection of wisdom sayings, but a collection of *Jesus'* sayings. Thus the new gospel generated a host of great expectations for new and exciting information about Jesus. Though in some circles the excitement far exceeded what could reasonably be expected from any ancient document, there was indeed some grounds for the enthusiasm. The early 1950's saw the beginning of the "new quest of the historical Jesus." The "old quest," largely the product of nineteenth century liberal theology, had dribbled to a close in the previous generation, when it was realized that the gospels as we have them are not history books, but products of the early Christian preaching about Jesus. It was therefore no longer possible to write a biography of Jesus; nor was it possible to examine Jesus' psychological development or the unfolding of his own self understanding. Perhaps Rudolf Bultmann, more than anyone else, coined its epitaph in a now famous quote from his book *Jesus and the Word:*

> I do indeed think that we can know almost nothing concerning the life and personality of Jesus, since the early Christian sources show no interest in either, are moreover fragmentary and often legendary; and other sources about Jesus do not exist. Except for the purely critical research, what has been written in the last hundred and fifty years on the life of Jesus, his personality and the development of his inner life, is fantastic and romantic.[26]

But Bultmann did not with these remarks intend to close the door completely on historical research on Jesus; they were, after all, made in the introduction to his own book on this very subject! Rather, what Bultmann signaled was a shift in effort, away from interest in the person of Jesus, that is, his biography and psychology, and toward that in which Jesus himself would have been interested: his teaching. This shift required a new focus in research efforts, away from using the gospels to attempt to reconstruct a biography of Jesus, and onto Jesus' sayings as that part of the tradition within which Jesus' teaching may have survived. This was the point of departure for that entire generation of Bultmann's pupils who initiated the new quest of the historical Jesus in the 1950's: the analysis of Jesus' sayings. And in the midst of this new wave of interest precisely in Jesus' sayings, Pahor Labib published his photographs of the Gospel of Thomas, a collection of Jesus' sayings.

Yet the wheels of scholarship grind slowly, and they grind exceedingly small. There would be years filled with much critical analysis before the new collection could be made useful for the new questers. Thomas' date, authorship, and provenance, and most importantly, the nature of Thomas' relationship to the synoptic gospels, all had to be worked out before any sayings from Thomas could be used in the new

Jesus discussion. For neither Bultmann nor the new questers were willing to accept any single saying prima facia as an authentic saying of Jesus. They realized that the sayings tradition, too, had to a large extent been formed by the preaching activities of the early church. Sayings had been adapted to later situations, others had been added to the corpus. Methods and criteria had to be applied to each saying to determine its origin, and ultimately to adjudicate whether any part or version of it might have in fact come from Jesus himself. Bultmann had already started this work years before with those sayings imbedded in the synoptic tradition with his landmark book, *The History of the Synoptic Tradition*.[27] With the Gospel of Thomas, the process had to begin again from scratch.

Now more than thirty years after its publication, the Gospel of Thomas has begun to find its place in the discussion of the historical Jesus. The contribution it has made, and continues to make as research proceeds, is three-fold.

Thomas and the Analysis of the Sayings Tradition

First, before any saying can be attributed to the historical Jesus it must first be examined for signs of later alteration in the hands of the early church. When a saying survives only in one source, let us say for example, in Luke, it is often difficult to determine what if anything about the saying is ancient, and what represents later reworking. Scholars generally know enough about Luke's own theology that sometimes they are able to tell whether Luke has created the saying of his own accord, or reworked an earlier saying to better complement his own interpretation of the gospel. But even when Luke's work can be identified, this is only the first step in critical analysis. If Luke has taken the saying from tradition, one may still have to identify various ways in which the preaching of the early church may have affected the saying over a long process of oral transmission. It may be, and often is the case that the early church itself was responsible for creating the saying or assigning it to Jesus.

When the tradition-history of a saying is not entirely clear, a parallel version of the saying can often help to clarify this history. For, as an independent attestation to the saying, it can function as a kind of "control" over against which another version of the saying may be compared. The advantages may be illustrated using as an example the saying preserved in Luke 17:20–21 and Saying 113 of the Gospel of Thomas. The two versions are laid out in parallel columns below.

Luke 17:20–21	Thom 113:1–4
[20] When he was asked by the Pharisees when the reign of God would come, he answered them, "You cannot tell with careful observation when the reign of God is coming; [21] nor can people say, 'Look, here it is!' or 'There!' For behold, the reign of God is among you."	[1] His disciples said to him, "When will the kingdom come?" [2] "It will not come by watching for it. [3] It will not be said, 'Behold, here' or 'Behold, there.' [4] Rather, the kingdom of the Father is spread out upon the earth, and people do not see it."

A comparison of the two versions of this saying tells one a number of things about it. First, an independent attestation of the saying in the Gospel of Thomas indicates immediately that Luke's author is not responsible for creating the saying, even though it complements well one of the themes running throughout his gospel, the delay of the parousia. He, like the author of Thomas, has rather chosen it from the tradition because it meets his needs. Secondly, one notices that each introduces the saying using a different setting: in Luke Jesus responds to the query of the Pharisees, in Thomas he responds to the disciples. Such settings were often judged by Bultmann to be entirely artificial and secondary; the discrepancy noticed here would seem to confirm that judgment in this case. Thirdly, Luke's version of the saying mentions the observation of "signs to be observed," a feature not found in Thomas. When one notices that Luke has used the saying to introduce a traditional apocalyptic passage adapted from his source, Q (17:22–37; cf. Matt 24:23, 26–27, 37–39, 17–18; 10:39; 24:40–41, 28), which speaks of such signs, it seems evident that Luke would have added this part of the saying to tailor it to his own purposes. Finally, Luke's version of the saying has always posed difficulties of understanding because of the ambiguities of the Greek in its final phrase: "for behold, the reign of God is $\grave{\epsilon}\nu\tau\grave{o}s$ $\grave{v}\mu\hat{\omega}\nu$." This phrase, $\epsilon\nu\tau\grave{o}s$ $\grave{v}\mu\hat{\omega}\nu$, may mean either "inside of you (pl.)" (for example as a spiritual reality within the person), or "in the midst you" (for example as a corporate reality experienced in a communal relationship). How did the early Christians understand this saying? It would be helpful if the oral transmission of this saying had left us with a little different wording that would not be quite so ambiguous. Thomas, in this case, provides just that: "the kingdom of the Father is spread out upon the earth, and people do not see it." Thus, early Christians apparently did not read this saying as a spiritualizing of the reign of God, but an expression of its corporate potential in the present.

Such analysis has helped to identify an earlier version of this saying, and even clarified its meaning to early Christians, but it has not yet revealed whether or not the saying should be attributed to Jesus. Thomas gives us no new criteria that could make this part of the task any easier. This saying, as all other sayings in the corpus of material the early church attributed to Jesus, must now be subjected to the historical criteria used by various new questers in the evaluation of individual sayings. What Thomas can do, however, is add much clarity to what exactly it is that should be evaluated. Scholars are currently engaged in duplicating this procedure for all the sayings in the tradition for which there are Thomas parallels.

New Sayings in Thomas

Of course, not all of Thomas' sayings have parallels in other, previously known gospels. Thus Thomas has been significant in the quest of the historical Jesus in another respect as well: it has significantly expanded the corpus of sayings known to have been attributed to Jesus. These new sayings, of course, must now be evaluated like any other saying traditionally ascribed to Jesus, using critically developed and consistently applied criteria. A few attempts at this systematic task were made early on in the Thomas discussion. For example, the well-known parables scholar, Joachim Jeremias, made use of several of Thomas' sayings to help reconstruct the original preaching of Jesus in the last edition of his book on parables, among them Saying 82:[28]

> [1]Jesus said, "Whoever is near me is near the fire, [2]and whoever is far from me is far from the kingdom."

Johannes Bauer argued for regarding Saying 82 as authentic, as well as Sayings 81, 58, 51, and 52.[29] R. McL. Wilson thought that Sayings 39, 102, and 47, among others should be given consideration, but he was seldom willing to commit firmly to an opinion favoring their authenticity.[30] But none of these early attempts to evaluate Thomas' sayings was marked by a carefully defined method and consistently applied criteria. Thus, most of this evaluative work remains yet to be done.

Thomas' Interpretation of Jesus

While the critical analysis and evaluation of individual sayings will go on, and perhaps eventually make a significant contribution to our knowledge of Jesus' teaching, there is yet another way in which the Gospel of Thomas may help us to understand what Jesus said. Most of what we know about Jesus must be deduced indirectly from the way various early Christian communities remembered him and interpreted his teaching. Without a reliable account of Jesus' life, scholars are left to study the "Jesus event" largely through the interpretations of that event which gradually emerged in the early Christian communities, which began to gather for meals and common life after Jesus' death. Thus, apart from the new sayings Thomas may provide the scholar as primary data, another and equally important contribution Thomas makes to the Jesus discussion is simply its presentation of yet another way in which Jesus was understood and interpreted as a significant event.

For the Gospel of Thomas, the significance of Jesus was that when he spoke, the Reign of God became a present reality for those who heard and understood what he was saying. What he said, according to the Gospel of Thomas, was that a person's worth as a human being does not depend upon how one fares in the world. The concerns of the world: home, family, business, synagogue, temple—all of these are relatively unimportant. One's worth as a human being is inherent, and fully realized simply and only when one truly knows oneself to be a child of God. Thus, the presence of the Reign of God is not something for which one must wait, a future event. The Reign of God becomes possible, a real potentially present thing whenever this word is preached and accepted as true. The Gospel of Thomas criticized other early Christian interpretations of Jesus which understood him within the context of apocalyptic eschatology, which looked to the future for the Reign of God, placing responsibility for its fulfillment solely in the hands of God, or of Jesus as the Son of Man coming on clouds of glory to initiate a final judgment and the beginning of a new age. Thomas' Jesus preaches a Reign of God that is actualizing itself even as Jesus preaches his word. As persons accept his social critique and his basic human affirmation, the Reign of God becomes a present reality.

Yet, while stressing the presence of the Reign of God, Thomas' Jesus also speaks of salvation in transcendental terms. The one who under-

[margin note: Present reality of God's reign]

stands Jesus' words not only experiences the Reign of God here and now, she also receives the promise that she will "not taste death." The one who hears and understands is given the words to re-ascend to the heavenly heights. For such a one there is the promise of paradise. Thomas' Jesus is not really out to change the world. He aims rather to change people's perception of the world and their role in it. The Thomas kerygma—or preaching—is essentially one of non-participation, not transformation. Though one's view of the world may change, the world, rest assured, remains the same.

The question is: what does this Jesus have to do with the Jesus of history? Perhaps nothing; perhaps everything. These questions are just now being asked.

About the Translation

The text presented here is a new translation of the Gospel of Thomas. There are several things distinguishing it from previous translations, which should be noted.

First, the number of texual emendations has been kept to a minimum. Likewise, lacunae have been filled in only where enough text exists around the holes to provide a relative degree of certainty about how the missing text is to be read. Particularly suggestive emendations or completions have been duly recorded in the footnotes, but the text itself is basically only that which is provided by the manuscript evidence.

Second, it has become customary to divide the Gospel of Thomas into 114 sayings. Once we have reached a better understanding of this gospel and its sayings, it may be that some of the divisions this system has provided will turn out to have been misleading. Nonetheless, the present text, for convenience sake, makes use of this conventional numbering system. In addition, however, each saying has been further divided into identifiable sub-units. Hopefully this will provide a useful way of referencing the Gospel of Thomas with greater precision.

Finally, some effort has been made to render the Coptic (and Greek where applicable) into an English prose that avoids as much as possible language that is gender-biased. This should not mislead the English reader into thinking that the Gospel of Thomas had somehow risen above the gender bias of its day and age. This was certainly not the case. This bias will occasionally appear in the translation in places where an inclusive language translation would have obscured something of importance for understanding the text (for example, in the rendering of possessive pronouns). Such difficult spots have been left unresolved intentionally, under the assumption that to destroy all evidence of gender bias in one's translation may serve to mask a bias problem that runs deeper than language, which itself may be important for understanding aspects of the text. Still, whenever an inclusive way of rendering the text into English readily suggested itself, this option was taken.

Notes

1. Origen mentions it in his homilies on the Gospel of Luke (*In Luc. hom.* 1); Jerome mentions it in his commentary on Matthew (*Comm. in evang. Matth.*, Prologue). For a full account of the Greek and Latin *testamonia* to the Gospel of Thomas, see H. Attridge,"Appendix: The Greek Fragments," in B. Layton, ed., *Nag Hammadi Codex II,2-7, together with XII,2, Brit. Lib. Or. 4926 (1), and POxy 1, 654, 655*; Volume 1: *Gospel According to Thomas, Gospel According to Philip, Hypostasis of the Archons, and Indexes*; Nag Hammadi Studies XX (Leiden: Brill, 1989) 103–9.

2. Hippolytus, *Refutatio* 5.7.20; trans. from Attridge, "Appendix: The Greek Fragments," 103.

3. *Catechesis* 6.31; see Attridge 105–6.

4. The story of the discovery of the Nag Hammadi library is told by James M. Robinson in *The Nag Hammadi Library in English*; Rev. ed. (San Francisco: Harper and Row, 1988) 10–26; see also his articles "The Discovery of the Nag Hammadi Codices," and "Getting the Nag Hammadi Library into English," *Biblical Archaeologist* 42,4 (1979) 206–24 and 239–48 respectively.

5. *Coptic Gnostic Papyri in the Coptic Museum at Old Cairo*, Vol. 1 (Cairo: Government Press [Antiquities Department] 1956).

6. "Ein neues Evangelium: Das Koptisch Thomasevangelium übersetzt und besprochen." *TLZ* 83 (1958) cols. 481–96.

7. A. Guillaumont, H.-Ch. Puech, G. Quispel, W.C. Till, Y. 'Abd al Masih, *The Gospel According to Thomas: Coptic Text Established and Translated* (Leiden: Brill/ London: Collins/New York: Harper, 1959); published simultaneously in Dutch (Leiden: Brill); German (Leiden: Brill); and French (Paris: Presses Universitaires de France/Leiden: Brill).

8. Grenfell and Hunt originally published POxy 1 in a pamphlet by this title: ΛΟΓΙΑ ΙΗΣΟΥ: *Sayings of Our Lord* (Egypt Exploration Fund; London: Henry Frowde, 1897). They published POxy 654 and 655 seven years later as *New Sayings of Jesus and Fragment of a Lost Gospel from Oxyrhynchus* (Egypt Exploration Fund; London: Henry Frowde, 1904).

9. "Une collection des paroles de Jésus récemment retrouvée: L'Evangile selon Thomas," in Académie des inscriptions et de belles lettres, *Comptes rendus des séances de l'année 1957* (1958) 146–66; see also "The Gospel of Thomas," in

Hennecke and Schneemelcher, *New Testament Apocrypha*, Vol I: *Gospels and Related Writings* (Philadelphia: Westminster, 1963) 278–307.

10. *Das Verhältnis des Thomas-Evangeliums zur Synoptischen Tradition und zu den koptischen Evangelienübersetzungen. Zugleich ein Beitrag zur gnostischen Synoptikerdeutung*; BZNW 29 (Berlin: Töpelmann, 1964).

11. Sayings 32 (cf. Matt 5:14b); 39 (cf. 23:13); 45b (cf. Luke 6:45); 104a (cf. Luke 5:33); and 104b (cf. Luke 5:33–35).

12. Sayings 32, 33b (cf. Matt 5:14b-15); 65, 66 (cf. Mark 12:31–35, pars.); and 92a, 93–94 (cf. Matt 7:6–7).

13. J. Horman, "The Parable of the Sower in the Gospel of Thomas," *NovT* 21 (1979) 328–29, 355–57.

14. S. J. Patterson, "The Gospel of Thomas within the Development of Early Christianity," (Diss., Claremont, 1988) 84–118. See also idem., *The Gospel of Thomas in the Jesus tradition* (Sonoma, CA: Polebridge, forthcoming 1990).

15. Robinson and Koester collected these and other essays into a book: *Trajectories Through Early Christianity* (Philadelphia: Fortress, 1971). The pertinent chapters are "LOGOI SOPHON: On the Gattung of Q" (ch. 3 by Robinson), "GNOMAI DIAPHOROI: The Origin and Nature of Diversification in the History of Early Christianity" (ch. 4 by Koester), and "One Jesus and Four Primitive Gospels" (ch. 6 by Koester). A summary of their contribution to this discussion is to be found in Patterson, "The Gospel of Thomas," 39–51. More recently Robinson has defended this approach in an essay entitled "On Bridging the Gulf from Q to the Gospel of Thomas (or vice versa)" in C. W. Hedrick and R. Hodgson, Jr. eds., *Nag Hammadi, Gnosticism, and Early Christianity* (Peabody, MA: Hendrickson Publishers, 1986) 127–55.

16. For a sketch of this problem see H. Koester, "History and Development of Mark's Gospel (From Mark to *Secret Mark* and 'Canonical' Mark)," in Bruce Corley, ed., *Colloquy on New Testament Studies: A Time for Reappraisal and Fresh Approaches* (Macon, Georgia: Mercer University Press, 1983) 35–57.

17. "Introduction (to the Gospel of Thomas)," in B. Layton, ed., *Nag Hammadi Codex II,2–7 together with XII,2, Brit. Lib. Or. 4926 (1), and POxy 1, 654, 655*; Volume 1: *Gospel According to Thomas, Gospel According to Philip, Hypostasis of the Archons, and Indexes*; Nag Hammadi Studies XX (Leiden: Brill, 1989) 40–41.

18. "Introduction," 39.

19. This was the basic insight of James M. Robinson in his landmark article "LOGOI SOPHON" (see above, note 15).

20. *The Parables of the Kingdom* (New York: Charles Scribner's Sons, 1961) 96–102. Dodd's hypothetical non-allegorized version of the parable differed from Thomas' version only insofar as Dodd included as original to the parable the question posed by Jesus in Mark 12:9: "What will the owner of the vineyard do?"

21. "LOGOI SOPHON," 113.

22. Son of man is originally a Semitic idiom meaning simply "person" or "human being."

23. *The Formation of Q: Trajectories in Ancient Wisdom Collections*; Studies in Antiquity and Christianity (Philadelphia: Fortress, 1987).

24. "Itinerant Radicalism: The Tradition of Jesus Sayings from the Perspective

of the Sociology of Literature," *Radical Religion* 2 (1976) 84–93. A more complete sketch of the thesis is to be found in his *Sociology of Palestinian Christianity* (Philadelphia: Fortress, 1978).

25. "Gnostic Sayings and Controversy Traditions in John 8:12–59," in C. W. Hedrick and R. Hodgson, Jr. eds., *Nag Hammadi, Gnosticism, and Early Christianity* (Peabody, MA: Hendrickson Publishers, 1986) 97–110.

26. Trans. by Louise Pettibone Smith and Erminie Huntress Lantero (Rev. ed. 1958; New York: Charles Scribner's Sons, 1934) 8.

27. (New York: Harper and Row, 1963). The German original (*Die Geschichte der synoptischen Tradition*) was first published in 1921 (Göttingen: Vandenhoeck & Ruprecht).

28. Jeremias, *Die Gleichnisse Jesu* (10. Aufl.; Göttingen: Vandenhoeck & Ruprecht, 1984) 195.

29. "Echte Jesusworte," in W.C. van Unnik, *Evangelien aus dem Nilsand* (Frankfurt: Verlag Heinrich Scheffer, 1960) 124–30.

30. *Studies in the Gospel of Thomas* (London: A.R. Mowbray, 1960) 75–78.

The Gospel of Thomas

SUGGESTED READING

J. Dominic Crossan. *In Fragments: The Aphorisms of Jesus*. San Francisco: Harper and Row, 1983.

> Crossan includes sayings from the Gospel of Thomas in his major tradition-historical study of the early Christian sayings tradition. As such it represents one of the few attempts to integrate information derived from Thomas into our overall understanding of the development of the Jesus tradition.

Stevan Davies. *The Gospel of Thomas and Christian Wisdom*. New York: Seabury, 1983.

> A unique, though highly polemical attempt to read Thomas strictly in terms of Jewish Wisdom tradition. His aversion to finding anything Gnostic in Thomas is too extreme, but he provides a counterpoint to those who would impart a Gnostic meaning to every detail in Thomas.

F. T. Fallon and Ron Cameron. "The Gospel of Thomas: A *Forschungsbericht* and Analysis." Pp. 41–95 in W. Haase and H. Temporini, *Aufstieg und Niedergang der Römischen Welt (Rise and Decline of the Roman World)*. Teil II: Principat, Band 25:6. Berlin / New York: Walter De Gruyter, 1988.

> The best and most recent review of scholarship on the Gospel of Thomas in English.

Robert W. Funk. *New Gospel Parallels*. Vol. 2. Philadelphia: Fortress, 1985.

> Volume 2 contains the Gospel of Thomas and presents in parallel columns parallel texts from other ancient sources. Available from Polebridge Press.

Robert M. Grant and David N. Freedman. *The Secret Sayings of Jesus, with an English Translation of the Gospel of Thomas by William R. Schoedel.* Garden City: Doubleday / London: Collins, 1960.

> An early comprehensive study of the Gospel of Thomas by two prominent biblical historians. The thesis that Thomas is a Gnostic attempt to corrupt the canonical gospel tradition is no longer regarded as plausible by most scholars, but Grant and Freedman have tracked down much material from the period of early Christianity that is helpful for understanding the Gospel of Thomas.

Bernard P. Grenfell and Arthur S. Hunt. ΛΟΓΙΑ ΙΗΣΟΥ: *Sayings of Our Lord.* Egypt Exploration Fund. London: Henry Frowde, 1897. And *New Sayings of Jesus and Fragment of a Lost Gospel from Oxyrhynchus.* Egypt Exploration Fund. London: Henry Frowde, 1904.

> Grenfell and Hunt's original publication of the Greek fragments of the Gospel of Thomas found at Oxyrhynchus.

Kendrick Grobel. "How Gnostic Is the Gospel of Thomas?" *New Testament Studies* 8 (1961/1962) 367–73.

> An important early study which cautioned against reading Gnosticism into every saying in the Gospel of Thomas, Grobel's study pointed the way to a more nuanced understanding of Thomas' theology.

A. Guillaumont, H.-Ch. Puech, G. Quispel, W. C. Till, Yassah 'Abd al Masiḥ. *The Gospel According to Thomas: Coptic Text Established and Translated.* Leiden: Brill / London: Collins / New York: Harper, 1959. Published simultaneously in Dutch (Leiden: Brill), German (Leiden: Brill), and French (Paris: Presses Universitaires de France / Leiden: Brill).

> The *editio princeps* (first published edition) of the Gospel of Thomas. These books present the text of Thomas and a translation on facing pages.

Ernst Haenchen. *Die Botschaft des Thomas-Evangeliums.* Theologische Bibliotek Töpelmann 6. Berlin: Töpelmann, 1961.

> In the German language, perhaps the finest attempt to understand the Gospel of Thomas as an early Gnostic gospel. Though scholars today are less inclined to accept such a thoroughly gnostic reading of Thomas, Haenchen presents a plausible reading of how Thomas would have been received by later Gnostic groups.

James M. Robinson and Helmut Koester. *Trajectories Through Early Christianity.* Philadelphia: Fortress, 1971.

This collection of essays contains some of the most important work on the Gospel of Thomas by these two scholars, among them the following studies: "LOGOI SOPHON: On the Gattung of Q," pp. 71–113, by J. M. Robinson; "GNOMAI DIAPHOROI: The origin and Nature of Diversification in the History of Early Christianity," pp. 114–57, by H. Koester; "One Jesus and Four Primitive Gospels," pp. 158–204, by H. Koester.

Bentley Layton, ed., *Nag Hammadi Codex II,2–7 together with XII,2, Brit. Lib. Or. 4926 (1), and POxy 1, 654, 655*. Vol. 1: *Gospel According to Thomas, Gospel According to Philip, Hypostasis of the Archons, and Indexes*. Nag Hammadi Studies XX. Leiden: Brill, 1989.

This volume contains the most up-to-date critical text of the Coptic Gospel of Thomas by Bentley Layton, a new critical edition of the Greek fragments by H. Attridge, an excellent translation of Thomas by Thomas O. Lambdin, an introduction to Thomas by Helmut Koester, and helpful indexes. It should become the standard critical tool for future Thomas scholars.

Harvey K. McArthur. "The Dependence of the Gospel of Thomas on the Synoptics." *Expository Times* 71 (1959/1960) 286–87.

An eloquent attempt to argue for the position that Thomas is dependent upon the canonical gospels.

Marvin W. Meyer. "Making Mary Male: The Categories 'male' and 'female' in the Gospel of Thomas." *New Testament Studies* 31 (1985) 554–70.

A contribution to our understanding of some of the more obscure theological categories of the Gospel of Thomas.

H. W. Montefiore. "A Comparison of the Parables of the Gospel According to Thomas and the Synoptic Gospels." *New Testament Studies* 7 (1960/1961) 220–48.

An important early study of the parables in the Gospel of Thomas, which, using the methods of form criticism and tradition-historical analysis, demonstrates that Thomas could not have borrowed its parables from the canonical tradition. This was a landmark study in establishing Thomas as an independent witness to the Jesus sayings tradition.

Kurt Rudolph. *Gnosis: The Nature and History of Gnosticism*. Trans. by R. Mcl. Wilson. San Francisco: Harper and Row, 1983.

The most recent and thorough introduction to Gnosticism.

Wolfgang Schrage. *Das Verhältnis des Thomas-Evangeliums zur Synoptischen Tradition und zu den koptischen Evangelienübersetzungen. Zugleich ein Beitrag zur gnostischen Synoptikerdeutung.* BZNW 29. Berlin: Töpelmann, 1964.

In the German language, the most thorough-going attempt to prove Thomas' dependence upon the canonical gospels.

R. Mcl. Wilson. *Studies in the Gospel of Thomas.* London: A. R. Mowbray, 1960.

A balanced, though often indecisive, treatment of the tradition-historical problems in the Gospel of Thomas by a prominent scholar of early Christianity and Gnosticism. Wilson's concern is to sift the Thomas tradition for sayings that might plausibly be attributed to Jesus.

Sigla Used for the Text & Translation

[   ]   Square brackets indicate a lacuna or gap in the manuscript. When the text cannot be reconstructed with confidence, three dots are placed within brackets in the translation, and a sufficient number of dots are placed within brackets in the Coptic text to indicate the approximate number of letters missing in the manuscript.

. . .   Three dots used without brackets in the translation indicate a series of Coptic letters that do not constitute a translatable sense unit.

⟨   ⟩   Pointed brackets indicate a correction of a scribal omission or error.

(   )   Parentheses in the translation indicate material, not present in the manuscript but supplied by the translator, that is helpful for a clear understanding of the translation.

*   Asterisks in the translation indicate notes to the translation. The notes are assembled at the end of the translation.

The Gospel of Thomas

TEXT & TRANSLATION

ⲚⲀⲈⲒ ⲚⲈ Ⲛ̄ϢⲀϪⲈ ⲈⲐⲎ⳿ ⲈⲚⲦⲀⲒ̅Ⲥ̅
ⲈⲦⲞⲚⳞ ϪⲞⲞⲨ ⲀⲨⲰ ⲀϤⲤ̇ⳞⲀⲒⲤⲞⲨ
Ⲛ̄ϬⲒ ⲆⲒⲆⲨⲘⲞⲤ Ⲓ̈ⲞⲨⲆⲀⲤ ⲐⲰⲘⲀⲤ

1 ⲀⲨⲰ ⲠⲈϪⲀϤ ϪⲈ ⲠⲈⲦⲀⳞⲈ
ⲈⲐⲈⲢⲘⲎⲚⲈⲒⲀ Ⲛ̄ⲚⲈⲈⲒϢⲀϪⲈ ϤⲚⲀϪⲒ
ϮⲠⲈ ⲀⲚ Ⲙ̄ⲠⲘⲞⲨ

2 ¹ⲠⲈϪⲈ Ⲓ̅Ⲥ̅ ⲘⲚ̄ⲦⲢⲈϤⲖⲞ Ⲛ̄ϬⲒ
ⲠⲈⲦϢⲒⲚⲈ ⲈϤϢⲒⲚⲈ ϢⲀⲚⲦⲈϤϬⲒⲚⲈ
²ⲀⲨⲰ ⳞⲞⲦⲀⲚ ⲈϤϢⲀⲚϬⲒⲚⲈ
ϤⲚⲀϢⲦⲢ̄Ⲧ̄Ⲣ̄ ³ⲀⲨⲰ ⲈϤϢⲀⲚϢⲦⲞⲢⲦⲢ̄
ϤⲚⲀⲢ̄ ϢⲠⲎⲢⲈ ⁴ⲀⲨⲰ ϤⲚⲀⲢ̄ Ⲣ̄ⲢⲞ ⲈⲬⲘ̄
ⲠⲦⲎⲢϤ

3 ¹ⲠⲈϪⲈ Ⲓ̅Ⲥ̅ ϪⲈ ⲈⲨϢⲀϪⲞⲞⲤ
ⲚⲎⲦⲚ̄ Ⲛ̄ϬⲒ ⲚⲈⲦⲤⲰⲔ ⳞⲎⲦ ⲐⲎⲨⲦⲚ̄ ϪⲈ
ⲈⲒⲤⳞⲎⲎⲦⲈ ⲈⲦⲘⲚ̄ⲦⲈⲢⲞ ⳞⲚ̄ ⲦⲠⲈ ⲈⲒⲈ
Ⲛ̄ⳞⲀⲖⲎⲦ ⲚⲀⲢ̄ ϢⲞⲢⲠ ⲈⲢⲰⲦⲚ̄ Ⲛ̄ⲦⲈ
ⲦⲠⲈ ²ⲈⲨϢⲀⲚϪⲞⲞⲤ ⲚⲎⲦⲚ̄ ϪⲈ ⲤⳞⲚ̄
ⲐⲀⲖⲀⲤⲤⲀ ⲈⲒⲈ Ⲛ̄ⲦⲂⲦ ⲚⲀⲢ̄ ϢⲞⲢⲠ
ⲈⲢⲰⲦⲚ̄ ³ⲀⲖⲖⲀ ⲦⲘⲚ̄ⲦⲈⲢⲞ
ⲤⲘ̄ⲠⲈⲦⲚ̄ⳞⲞⲨⲚ ⲀⲨⲰ ⲤⲘ̄ⲠⲈⲦⲚ̄ⲂⲀⲖ
⁴ⳞⲞⲦⲀⲚ ⲈⲦⲈⲦⲚ̄ϢⲀⲚⲤⲞⲨⲰⲚ ⲐⲎⲨⲦⲚ̄

Prologue

These are the secret sayings that the living Jesus spoke and Didymos Judas Thomas recorded.

1 And he said, "Whoever discovers the interpretation of these sayings will not taste death."

2 ¹Jesus said, "Let one who seeks not stop seeking until one finds. ²When one finds, one will be disturbed. ³When one is disturbed, one will marvel, ⁴and will reign over all."

3 ¹Jesus said, "If your leaders say to you, 'Behold, the kingdom is in heaven,' then the birds of heaven will precede you. ²If they say to you, 'It is in the sea,' then the fish will precede you. ³Rather, the kingdom is within you and it is outside you. ⁴When you know yourselves, then you

129

ⲦⲞⲦⲈ ⲤⲈⲚⲀⲤⲞⲨⲰⲚ ⲦⲎⲚⲈ ⲀⲨⲰ
ⲦⲈⲦⲚⲀⲈⲒⲘⲈ ⲬⲈ ⲚⲦⲰⲦⲚ ⲠⲈ ⲚϢⲎⲢⲈ
ⲘⲠⲈⲒⲰⲦ ⲈⲦⲞⲚϨ ⁵ⲈϢⲰⲠⲈ ⲆⲈ
ⲦⲈⲦⲚⲀⲤⲞⲨⲰⲚ ⲦⲎⲨⲦⲚ ⲀⲚ ⲈⲈⲒⲈ
ⲦⲈⲦⲚϢⲞⲞⲠ ϨⲚ ⲞⲨⲘⲚⲦϨⲎⲔⲈ ⲀⲨⲰ
ⲚⲦⲰⲦⲚ ⲠⲈ ⲦⲘⲚⲦϨⲎⲔⲈ

4 ¹ⲠⲈⲬⲈ ⲒⲤ ϤⲚⲀⲬⲚⲀⲨ ⲀⲚ ⲚϬⲒ
ⲠⲢⲰⲘⲈ ⲚϨⲖ̄ⲖⲞ ϨⲚ ⲚⲈϤϨⲞⲞⲨ ⲈⲬⲚⲈ
ⲞⲨⲔⲞⲨⲈⲒ ⲚϢⲎⲢⲈ ϢⲎⲘ ⲈϤϨⲚ ⲤⲀϢϤ̄
ⲚϨⲞⲞⲨ ⲈⲦⲂⲈ ⲠⲦⲞⲠⲞⲤ ⲘⲠⲰⲚϨ
ⲀⲨⲰ ϤⲚⲀⲰⲚϨ ²ⲬⲈ ⲞⲨⲚ ϨⲀϨ
ⲚϢⲞⲢⲠ ⲚⲀⲢ̄ ϨⲀⲈ ³ⲀⲨⲰ ⲚⲤⲈϢⲰⲠⲈ
ⲞⲨⲀ ⲞⲨⲰⲦ

5 ¹ⲠⲈⲬⲈ ⲒⲤ ⲤⲞⲨⲰⲚ ⲠⲈⲦⲘ̄ⲠⲘ̄ⲦⲞ
ⲘⲠⲈⲔϨⲞ ⲈⲂⲞⲖ ⲀⲨⲰ ⲠⲈⲐⲎⲠ ⲈⲢⲞⲔ
ϤⲚⲀϬⲰⲖⲠ ⲈⲂⲞⲖ ⲚⲀⲔ ²ⲘⲚ ⲖⲀⲀⲨ
ⲄⲀⲢ ⲈϤϨⲎⲠ ⲈϤⲚⲀⲞⲨⲰⲚϨ ⲈⲂⲞⲖ ⲀⲚ

6 ¹ⲀⲨⲬⲚⲞⲨϤ ⲚϬⲒ ⲚⲈϤⲘⲀⲐⲎⲦⲎⲤ
ⲠⲈⲬⲀⲨ ⲚⲀϤ ⲬⲈⲔⲞⲨⲰϢ
ⲈⲦⲢⲚ̄Ⲣ̄ⲚⲎⲤⲦⲈⲨⲈ ⲀⲨⲰ ⲈϢ ⲦⲈ ⲐⲈ
ⲈⲚⲀϢⲖⲎⲖ ⲈⲚⲀϮ ⲈⲖⲈⲎⲘⲞⲤⲨⲚⲎ
ⲀⲨⲰ ⲈⲚⲀⲢ̄ⲠⲀⲢⲀⲦⲎⲢⲈⲒ ⲈⲞⲨ
ⲚϬⲒⲞⲨⲰⲘ

²ⲠⲈⲬⲈ ⲒⲤ ⲬⲈ ⲘⲠⲢ̄ⲬⲈ ϬⲞⲖ ³ⲀⲨⲰ
ⲠⲈⲦⲈⲦⲘ̄ⲘⲞⲤⲦⲈ ⲘⲘⲞϤ ⲘⲠⲢ̄ⲀⲀϤ
⁴ⲬⲈ ⲤⲈϬⲞⲖⲠ ⲦⲎⲢⲞⲨ ⲈⲂⲞⲖ
ⲘⲠⲈⲘⲦⲞ ⲈⲂⲞⲖ ⲚⲦⲠⲈ ⁵ⲘⲚ ⲖⲀⲀⲨ
ⲄⲀⲢ ⲈϤϨⲎⲠ ⲈϤⲚⲀⲞⲨⲰⲚϨ ⲈⲂⲞⲖ ⲀⲚ
⁶ⲀⲨⲰ ⲘⲚ ⲖⲀⲀⲨ ⲈϤϨⲞⲂⲤ̄ ⲈⲨⲚⲀϬⲰ
ⲞⲨⲈϢⲚ ϬⲞⲖⲠϤ

7 ¹ⲠⲈⲬⲈ ⲒⲤ ⲞⲨⲘⲀⲔⲀⲢⲒⲞⲤ ⲠⲈ
ⲠⲘⲞⲨⲈⲒ ⲠⲀⲈⲒ ⲈⲦⲈ ⲠⲢⲰⲘⲈ
ⲚⲀⲞⲨⲞⲘϤ ⲀⲨⲰ ⲚⲦⲈ ⲠⲘⲞⲨⲈⲒ
ϢⲰⲠⲈ Ⲣ̄ⲢⲰⲘⲈ ²ⲀⲨⲰ ϤⲂⲎⲦ ⲚϬⲒ
ⲠⲢⲰⲘⲈ ⲠⲀⲈⲒ ⲈⲦⲈ ⲠⲘⲞⲨⲈⲒ
ⲚⲀⲞⲨⲞⲘϤ ⲀⲨⲰ ⲠⲘⲞⲨⲈⲒ ⲚⲀϢⲰⲠⲈ
Ⲣ̄ⲢⲰⲘⲈ

will be known, and you will
understand that you are children
of the living Father. ⁵But if you
do not know yourselves, then
you dwell in poverty, and you
are the poverty."

4 ¹Jesus said, "The person old
in days will not hesitate to ask a
little child seven days old about
the place of life, and that person
will live. ²For many of the first
will be last, ³and will become a
single one."

5 ¹Jesus said, "Know what is
before your face, and what is
hidden from you will be disclosed to you. ²For there is
nothing hidden that will not be
revealed."

6 ¹His disciples asked him and
said to him, "Do you want us to
fast? How shall we pray? Shall
we give alms? What diet shall we
observe?"

²Jesus said, "Do not lie, ³and do
not do what you hate, ⁴because
all things are disclosed before
heaven. ⁵For there is nothing
hidden that will not be revealed,
⁶and there is nothing covered
that will remain without being
disclosed."

7 ¹Jesus said, "Blessed is the
lion that the human will eat, so
that the lion becomes human.
²And defiled is the human that
the lion will eat, and the lion will
become human."

8 ¹ⲁⲩⲱ ⲡⲉⲭⲁϥ ⲭⲉ ⲉⲡⲣⲱⲙⲉ
ⲧⲛ̄ⲧⲱⲛ ⲁⲩⲟⲩⲱϩ̄ⲉ ⲣ̄ⲣⲙⲛ̄ϩⲏⲧ ⲡⲁⲉⲓ
ⲛ̄ⲧⲁϩⲛⲟⲩⲭⲉ ⲛ̄ⲧⲉϥⲁⲃⲱ
ⲉⲑⲁⲗⲁⲥⲥⲁ ⲁϥⲥⲱⲕ ⲙ̄ⲙⲟⲥ ⲉϩⲣⲁⲓ̈
ϩⲛ̄ ⲑⲁⲗⲁⲥⲥⲁ ⲉⲥⲙⲉϩ ⲛ̄ⲧⲃⲧ
ⲛ̄ⲕⲟⲩⲉⲓ ²ⲛ̄ϩⲣⲁⲓ̈ ⲛ̄ϩⲏⲧⲟⲩ ⲁϥϩⲉ
ⲁⲩⲛⲟϭ ⲛ̄ⲧⲃⲧ̄ ⲉⲛⲁⲛⲟⲩϥ ⲛ̄ϭⲓ
ⲡⲟⲩⲱϩ̄ⲉ ⲣ̄ⲣⲙⲛ̄ϩⲏⲧ ³ⲁϥⲛⲟⲩⲭⲉ
ⲛ̄ⲛ̄ⲕⲟⲩⲉⲓ ⲧⲏⲣⲟⲩ ⲛ̄ⲧⲃⲧ ⲉⲃⲟⲗ
ⲉ[ⲡⲉ]ⲥⲏⲧ ⲉⲑⲁⲗⲁⲥⲥⲁ ⲁϥⲥⲱⲧⲡ
ⲙ̄ⲡⲛⲟϭ ⲛ̄ⲧⲃⲧ̄ ⲭⲱⲣⲓⲥ ϩⲓⲥⲉ ⁴ⲡⲉⲧⲉ
ⲟⲩⲛ̄ ⲙⲁⲁⲭⲉ ⲙ̄ⲙⲟϥ ⲉⲥⲱⲧⲙ̄
ⲙⲁⲣⲉϥⲥⲱⲧⲙ̄

9 ¹ⲡⲉⲭⲉ ⲓ̄ⲥ̄ ⲭⲉ ⲉⲓⲥϩⲏⲏⲧⲉ ⲁϥⲉⲓ
ⲉⲃⲟⲗ ⲛ̄ϭⲓ ⲡⲉⲧⲥⲓⲧⲉ ⲁϥⲙⲉϩ ⲧⲟⲟⲧϥ̄
ⲁϥⲛⲟⲩⲭⲉ ²ⲁϩⲟⲉⲓⲛⲉ ⲙⲉⲛ ϩⲉ ⲉⲭⲛ̄
ⲧⲉϩⲓⲏ ⲁⲩⲉⲓ ⲛ̄ϭⲓ ⲛ̄ϩⲁⲗⲁⲧⲉ
ⲁⲩⲕⲁⲧϥⲟⲩ ³ϩⲛ̄ⲕⲟⲟⲩⲉ ⲁⲩϩⲉ ⲉⲭⲛ̄
ⲧⲡⲉⲧⲣⲁ ⲁⲩⲱ ⲙ̄ⲡⲟⲩⲭⲉ ⲛⲟⲩⲛⲉ
ⲉⲡⲉⲥⲏⲧ ⲉⲡⲕⲁϩ ⲁⲩⲱ ⲙ̄ⲡⲟⲩⲧⲉⲩⲉ
ϩⲙ̄ⲥ̄ ⲉϩⲣⲁⲓ̈ ⲉⲧⲡⲉ ⁴ⲁⲩⲱ ϩⲛ̄ⲕⲟⲟⲩⲉ
ⲁⲩϩⲉ ⲉⲭⲛ̄ ⲛ̄ϣⲟⲛⲧⲉ ⲁⲩⲱϭⲧ
ⲙ̄ⲡⲉⲃⲣⲟϭ ⲁⲩⲱ ⲁⲡϥⲛ̄ⲧ ⲟⲩⲟⲙⲟⲩ
⁵ⲁⲩⲱ ⲁϩⲛ̄ⲕⲟⲟⲩⲉ ϩⲉ ⲉⲭⲛ̄ ⲡⲕⲁϩ
ⲉⲧⲛⲁⲛⲟⲩϥ ⲁⲩⲱ ⲁϥϯ ⲕⲁⲣⲡⲟⲥ
ⲉϩⲣⲁⲓ̈ ⲉⲧⲡⲉ ⲉⲛⲁⲛⲟⲩϥ ⲁϥⲉⲓ ⲛ̄ⲥⲉ
ⲉⲥⲟⲧⲉ ⲁⲩⲱ ϣⲉⲭⲟⲩⲱⲧ ⲉⲥⲟⲧⲉ

10 ⲡⲉⲭⲉ ⲓ̄ⲥ̄ ⲭⲉ ⲁⲉⲓⲛⲟⲩⲭⲉ
ⲛ̄ⲟⲩⲕⲱϩ̄ⲧ ⲉⲭⲛ̄ ⲡⲕⲟⲥⲙⲟⲥ ⲁⲩⲱ
ⲉⲓⲥϩⲏⲏⲧⲉ ϯⲁⲣⲉϩ ⲉⲣⲟϥ
ϣⲁⲛⲧⲉϥⲭⲉⲣⲟ

11 ¹ⲡⲉⲭⲉ ⲓ̄ⲥ̄ ⲭⲉ ⲧⲉⲉⲓⲡⲉ
ⲛⲁⲣ̄ⲡⲁⲣⲁⲅⲉ ⲁⲩⲱ ⲧⲉⲧⲛ̄ⲧⲡⲉ ⲙ̄ⲙⲟⲥ
ⲛⲁⲣ̄ⲡⲁⲣⲁⲅⲉ ²ⲁⲩⲱ ⲛⲉⲧⲙⲟⲟⲩⲧ
ⲥⲉⲟⲛϩ ⲁⲛ ⲁⲩⲱ ⲛⲉⲧⲟⲛϩ
ⲥⲉⲛⲁⲙⲟⲩ ⲁⲛ ³ⲛ̄ϩⲟⲟⲩ
ⲛⲉⲧⲉⲧⲛ̄ⲟⲩⲱⲙ ⲙ̄ⲡⲉⲧⲙⲟⲟⲩⲧ
ⲛⲉⲧⲉⲧⲛ̄ⲉⲓⲣⲉ ⲙ̄ⲙⲟϥ ⲙ̄ⲡⲉⲧⲟⲛϩ

8 ¹And he said, "The human one is like a wise fisherman who cast his net into the sea and drew it up from the sea full of little fish. ²Among them the wise fisherman discovered a fine large fish. ³He threw all the little fish back into the sea, and without any effort* chose the large fish. ⁴Whoever has ears to hear should hear."

Following of new + only new poh.

9 ¹Jesus said, "Behold, the sower went out, took a handful (of seeds), and scattered (them). ²Some fell on the road, and the birds came and gathered them. ³Others fell on rock, and they did not take root in the soil and did not produce heads of grain. ⁴Others fell on thorns, and they choked the seeds and worms consumed them. ⁵And others fell on good soil, and it brought forth a good crop: it yielded sixty per measure and one hundred twenty per measure."

10 Jesus said, "I have cast fire upon the world, and behold, I am guarding it until it blazes."

11 ¹Jesus said, "This heaven will pass away, and the one above it will pass away. ²The dead are not alive, and the living will not die. ³During the days when you ate what is dead, you made it alive. When you are in

ⲐⲞⲦⲀⲚ ⲈⲦⲈⲦⲚϢⲀⲚϢⲰⲠⲈ ⲐⲘ̄
ⲠⲞⲨⲞⲈⲒⲚ ⲞⲨ ⲠⲈⲦⲈⲦⲚⲀⲀϤ ⁴ⲐⲘ̄
ⲫⲞⲞⲨ ⲈⲦⲈⲦⲚⲞ Ⲛ̄ⲞⲨⲀ ⲀⲦⲈⲦⲚ̄ⲈⲒⲢⲈ
Ⲙ̄ⲠⲤⲚⲀⲨ ⲐⲞⲦⲀⲚ ⲆⲈ
ⲈⲦⲈⲦⲚ̄ϢⲀϢⲰⲠⲈ Ⲛ̄ⲤⲚⲀⲨ ⲞⲨ ⲠⲈ
ⲈⲦⲈⲦⲚ̄ⲚⲀⲀϤ

12 ¹ⲠⲈⲬⲈ Ⲙ̄ⲘⲀⲐⲎⲦⲎⲤ Ⲛ̄Ⲓ̄Ⲥ̄ ⲬⲈ
ⲦⲚ̄ⲤⲞⲞⲨⲚ ⲬⲈ ⲔⲚⲀⲂⲰⲔ Ⲛ̄ⲦⲞⲞⲦⲚ̄
ⲚⲒⲘ ⲠⲈ ⲈⲦⲚⲀⲢ̄ ⲚⲞϬ Ⲉ2ⲢⲀⲒ̈ ⲈⲬⲰⲚ

²ⲠⲈⲬⲈ Ⲓ̄Ⲥ̄ ⲚⲀⲨ ⲬⲈ ⲠⲘⲀ
Ⲛ̄ⲦⲀⲦⲈⲦⲚ̄ⲈⲒ Ⲙ̄ⲘⲀⲨ ⲈⲦⲈⲦⲚⲀⲂⲰⲔ
ϢⲀ Ⲓ̈ⲀⲔⲰⲂⲞⲤ ⲠⲆⲒⲔⲀⲒⲞⲤ ⲠⲀⲈⲒ Ⲛ̄ⲦⲀ
ⲦⲠⲈ ⲘⲚ̄ ⲠⲔⲀ2 ϢⲰⲠⲈ ⲈⲦⲂⲎⲦϤ̄

13 ¹ⲠⲈⲬⲈ Ⲓ̄Ⲥ̄ Ⲛ̄ⲚⲈϤⲘⲀⲐⲎⲦⲎⲤ ⲬⲈ
ⲦⲚ̄ⲦⲰⲚⲦ Ⲛ̄ⲦⲈⲦⲚ̄ⲬⲞⲞⲤ ⲚⲀⲈⲒ ⲬⲈ
ⲈⲈⲒⲚⲈ Ⲛ̄ⲚⲒⲘ

²ⲠⲈⲬⲀϤ ⲚⲀϤ Ⲛ̄ϬⲒ ⲤⲒⲘⲰⲚ ⲠⲈⲦⲢⲞⲤ
ⲬⲈ ⲈⲔⲈⲒⲚⲈ Ⲛ̄ⲞⲨⲀⲄⲄⲈⲖⲞⲤ
Ⲛ̄ⲆⲒⲔⲀⲒⲞⲤ

³ⲠⲈⲬⲀϤ ⲚⲀϤ Ⲛ̄ϬⲒ ⲘⲀⲐⲐⲀⲒⲞⲤ ⲬⲈ
ⲈⲔⲈⲒⲚⲈ Ⲛ̄ⲞⲨⲢⲰⲘⲈ Ⲙ̄ⲫⲒⲖⲞⲤⲞⲫⲞⲤ
Ⲛ̄ⲢⲘ̄Ⲛ̄2ⲎⲦ

⁴ⲠⲈⲬⲀϤ ⲚⲀϤ Ⲛ̄ϬⲒ ⲐⲰⲘⲀⲤ ⲬⲈ
ⲠⲤⲀ2 2ⲞⲖⲰⲤ ⲦⲀⲦⲀⲠⲢⲞ
ⲚⲀϢ(ϣ)ⲀⲠϤ ⲀⲚ ⲈⲦⲢⲀⲬⲞⲞⲤ ⲬⲈ
ⲈⲔⲈⲒⲚⲈ Ⲛ̄ⲚⲒⲘ

⁵ⲠⲈⲬⲈ Ⲓ̄Ⲏ̄Ⲥ̄ ⲬⲈ ⲀⲚⲞⲔ ⲠⲈⲔⲤⲀ2
ⲀⲚ ⲈⲠⲈⲒ ⲀⲔⲤⲰ ⲀⲔ†2Ⲉ ⲈⲂⲞⲖ 2Ⲛ̄
ⲦⲠⲎⲄⲎ ⲈⲦⲂ̄Ⲣ̄ⲂⲢⲈ ⲦⲀⲈⲒ ⲀⲚⲞⲔ
Ⲛ̄ⲦⲀⲈⲒϢⲒⲦⲤ̄

⁶Ⲁ ⲨⲰ ⲀϤⲬⲒⲦϤ̄ ⲀϤⲀⲚⲀⲬⲰⲢⲈⲒ
ⲀϤⲬⲰ ⲚⲀϤ Ⲛ̄ϢⲞⲘⲦ Ⲛ̄ϢⲀⲬⲈ

⁷Ⲛ̄ⲦⲀⲢⲈ ⲐⲰⲘⲀⲤ ⲆⲈ ⲈⲒ ϢⲀ
ⲚⲈϤϢⲂⲈⲈⲢ ⲀⲨⲬⲚⲞⲨϤ ⲬⲈ Ⲛ̄ⲦⲀ Ⲓ̄Ⲥ̄
ⲬⲞⲞⲤ ⲬⲈ ⲞⲨ ⲚⲀⲔ

⁸ⲠⲈⲬⲀϤ ⲚⲀⲨ Ⲛ̄ϬⲒ ⲐⲰⲘⲀⲤ ⲬⲈ
ⲈⲒϢⲀⲚⲬⲰ ⲚⲎⲦⲚ̄ ⲞⲨⲀ 2Ⲛ̄ Ⲛ̄ϢⲀⲬⲈ
Ⲛ̄ⲦⲀϤⲬⲞⲞⲨ ⲚⲀⲈⲒ ⲦⲈⲦⲚⲀϤⲒ ⲰⲚⲈ

---

the light, what will you do? ⁴On the day when you were one, you became two. But when you become two, what will you do?"

12 ¹The disciples said to Jesus, "We know that you will leave us. Who is going to be our leader?"

²Jesus said to them, "No matter where you are, you are to go to James the Just, for whose sake heaven and earth came into being."

13 ¹Jesus said to his disciples, "Compare me to something and tell me what I am like."

²Simon Peter said to him, "You are like a just angel."

³Matthew said to him, "You are like a wise philosopher."

⁴Thomas said to him, "Teacher, my mouth is utterly unable to say what you are like."

⁵Jesus said, "I am not your teacher. Because you have drunk, you have become intoxicated* from the bubbling spring that I have tended."

⁶And he took him, and withdrew, and spoke three sayings to him.

⁷When Thomas came back to his friends, they asked him, "What did Jesus say to you?"

⁸Thomas said to them, "If I tell you one of the sayings he spoke to me, you will pick up rocks and stone me, and fire will come from

ⲛ̄ⲧⲉⲧⲛ̄ⲛⲟⲩϫⲉ ⲉⲣⲟⲉⲓ ⲁⲩⲱ ⲛ̄ⲧⲉ
ⲟⲩⲕⲱϩⲧ ⲉⲓ ⲉⲃⲟⲗ ϩⲛ̄ ⲛ̄ⲱⲛⲉ
ⲛ̄ⲥⲣⲱϩⲕ ⲙ̄ⲙⲱⲧⲛ̄

14 ¹ⲡⲉϫⲉ ⲓ̅ⲥ̅ ⲛⲁⲩ ϫⲉ
ⲉⲧⲉⲧⲛ̄ϣⲁⲛⲣ̄ⲛⲏⲥⲧⲉⲩⲉ ⲧⲉⲧⲛⲁϫⲡⲟ
ⲛ̄ⲏⲧⲛ̄ ⲛ̄ⲛⲟⲩⲛⲟⲃⲉ ²ⲁⲩⲱ
ⲉⲧⲉⲧⲛ̄ϣⲁⲛϣⲗⲏⲗ
ⲥⲉⲛⲁⲣ̄ⲕⲁⲧⲁⲕⲣⲓⲛⲉ ⲙ̄ⲙⲱⲧⲛ̄ ³ⲁⲩⲱ
ⲉⲧⲉⲧⲛ̄ϣⲁⲛϯ ⲉⲗⲉⲏⲙⲟⲥⲩⲛⲏ
ⲉⲧⲉⲧⲛⲁⲉⲓⲣⲉ ⲛ̄ⲟⲩⲕⲁⲕⲟⲛ
ⲛ̄ⲛⲉⲧⲙ̄ⲡⲛ̄ⲁ̄ ⁴ⲁⲩⲱ ⲉⲧⲉⲧⲛ̄ϣⲁⲛⲃⲱⲕ
ⲉϩⲟⲩⲛ ⲉⲕⲁϩ ⲛⲓⲙ ⲁⲩⲱ
ⲛ̄ⲧⲉⲧⲛ̄ⲙⲟⲟϣⲉ ϩⲛ̄ ⲛ̄ⲭⲱⲣⲁ
ⲉⲩϣⲁⲣ̄ⲡⲁⲣⲁⲇⲉⲭⲉ ⲙ̄ⲙⲱⲧⲛ̄
ⲡⲉⲧⲟⲩⲛⲁⲕⲁⲁϥ ϩⲁⲣⲱⲧⲛ̄ ⲟⲩⲟⲙϥ̄
ⲛⲉⲧϣⲱⲛⲉ ⲛ̄ϩⲏⲧⲟⲩ ⲉⲣⲓⲑⲉⲣⲁⲡⲉⲩⲉ
ⲙ̄ⲙⲟⲟⲩ ⁵ⲡⲉⲧⲛⲁⲃⲱⲕ ⲅⲁⲣ ⲉϩⲟⲩⲛ
ϩⲛ̄ ⲧⲉⲧⲛ̄ⲧⲁⲡⲣⲟ ϥⲛⲁϫⲱϩⲙ̄ ⲑⲩⲧⲛ̄
ⲁⲛ ⲁⲗⲗⲁ ⲡⲉⲧⲛ̄ⲛⲏⲩ ⲉⲃⲟⲗ ϩⲛ̄
ⲧⲉⲧⲛ̄ⲧⲁⲡⲣⲟ ⲛ̄ⲧⲟϥ ⲡⲉⲧⲛⲁϫⲁϩⲙ̄
ⲑⲩⲧⲛ̄

15 ⲡⲉϫⲉ ⲓ̅ⲥ̅ ϫⲉ ϩⲟⲧⲁⲛ
ⲉⲧⲉⲧⲛ̄ϣⲁⲛⲛⲁⲩ ⲉⲡⲉⲧⲉ
ⲙ̄ⲡⲟⲩϫⲡⲟϥ ⲉⲃⲟⲗ ϩⲛ̄ ⲧⲥϩⲓⲙⲉ
ⲡⲉϩⲧ ⲑⲩⲧⲛ̄ ⲉϫⲙ̄ ⲡⲉⲧⲛ̄ϩⲟ
ⲛ̄ⲧⲉⲧⲛ̄ⲟⲩⲱϣⲧ ⲛⲁϥ ⲡⲉⲧⲙ̄ⲙⲁⲩ ⲡⲉ
ⲡⲉⲧⲛ̄ⲉⲓⲱⲧ

16 ¹ⲡⲉϫⲉ ⲓ̅ⲥ̅ ϫⲉ ⲧⲁⲭⲁ ⲉⲩⲙⲉⲉⲩⲉ
ⲛ̄ϭⲓ ⲣ̄ⲣⲱⲙⲉ ϫⲉ ⲛ̄ⲧⲁⲉⲓⲉⲓ ⲉⲛⲟⲩϫⲉ
ⲛ̄ⲟⲩⲉⲓⲣⲏⲛⲏ ⲉϫⲙ̄ ⲡⲕⲟⲥⲙⲟⲥ ²ⲁⲩⲱ
ⲥⲉⲥⲟⲟⲩⲛ ⲁⲛ ϫⲉ ⲛ̄ⲧⲁⲉⲓⲉⲓ ⲁⲛⲟⲩϫⲉ
ⲛ̄ϩⲛ̄ⲡⲱⲣϫ ⲉϫⲛ̄ ⲡⲕⲁϩ ⲟⲩⲕⲱϩⲧ
ⲟⲩⲥⲏϥⲉ ⲟⲩⲡⲟⲗⲉⲙⲟⲥ ³ⲟⲩⲛ̄ ϯⲟⲩ
ⲅⲁⲣ ⲛⲁϣⲱⲡⲉ ϩⲛ̄ ⲟⲩⲏⲉⲓ ⲟⲩⲛ̄
ϣⲟⲙⲧ ⲛⲁϣⲱⲡⲉ ⲉϫⲛ̄ ⲥⲛⲁⲩ ⲁⲩⲱ
ⲥⲛⲁⲩ ⲉϫⲛ̄ ϣⲟⲙⲧ ⲡⲉⲓⲱⲧ ⲉϫⲙ̄
ⲡϣⲏⲣⲉ ⲁⲩⲱ ⲡϣⲏⲣⲉ ⲉϫⲙ̄ ⲡⲉⲓⲱⲧ
⁴ⲁⲩⲱ ⲥⲉⲛⲁⲱϩⲉ ⲉⲣⲁⲧⲟⲩ ⲉⲩⲟ
ⲙ̄ⲙⲟⲛⲁⲭⲟⲥ

the rocks and devour you."

14 ¹Jesus said to them, "If you fast, you will bring sin upon yourselves, ²and if you pray, you will be condemned, ³and if you give alms, you will harm your spirits. ⁴When you go into any country and walk from place to place,* when the people receive you, eat what they serve you and heal the sick among them. ⁵For what goes into your mouth will not defile you; rather, it is what comes out of your mouth that will defile you."

Chge in dietary restrictions.

15 Jesus said, "When you see one who was not born of woman, fall on your faces and worship him. That is your Father."

16 ¹Jesus said, "Perhaps people think that I have come to cast peace upon the world. ²They do not know that I have come to cast conflicts upon the earth: fire, sword, war. ³For there will be five in a house: there will be three against two and two against three, father against son and son against father, ⁴and they will stand alone."

17 ⲡⲉⲭⲉ ⲓ̄ⲥ̄ ⲭⲉ ϯⲛⲁϯ ⲛⲏⲧⲛ̄
ⲙ̄ⲡⲉⲧⲉ ⲙ̄ⲡⲉ ⲃⲁⲗ ⲛⲁⲩ ⲉⲣⲟϥ ⲁⲩⲱ
ⲡⲉⲧⲉ ⲙ̄ⲡⲉ ⲙⲁⲁⲭⲉ ⲥⲟⲧⲙⲉϥ ⲁⲩⲱ
ⲡⲉⲧⲉ ⲙ̄ⲡⲉ ϭⲓⲭ ϭⲙ̄ϭⲱⲙϥ ⲁⲩⲱ
ⲙ̄ⲡⲉϥⲉⲓ ⲉϩⲣⲁⲓ̈ ϩⲓ ⲫⲏⲧ ⲣ̄ⲣⲱⲙⲉ

18 ¹ⲡⲉⲭⲉ ⲙ̄ⲙⲁⲑⲏⲧⲏⲥ ⲛ̄ⲓ̄ⲥ̄ ⲭⲉ
ⲭⲟⲟⲥ ⲉⲣⲟⲛ ⲭⲉ ⲧⲛ̄ϩⲁⲏ
ⲉⲥⲛⲁϣⲱⲡⲉ ⲛ̄ⲁϣ ⲛ̄ϩⲉ

²ⲡⲉⲭⲉ ⲓ̄ⲥ̄ ⲁⲧⲉⲧⲛ̄ϭⲱⲗⲡ ⲅⲁⲣ
ⲉⲃⲟⲗ ⲛ̄ⲧⲁⲣⲭⲏ ⲭⲉⲕⲁⲁⲥ
ⲉⲧⲉⲧⲛⲁϣⲓⲛⲉ ⲛ̄ⲥⲁ ⲑⲁϩⲏ ⲭⲉ ϩⲙ̄
ⲡⲙⲁ ⲉⲧⲉ ⲧⲁⲣⲭⲏ ⲙ̄ⲙⲁⲩ ⲉⲑⲁϩ
ⲛⲁϣⲱⲡⲉ ⲙ̄ⲙⲁⲩ ³ⲟⲩⲙⲁⲕⲁⲣⲓⲟⲥ
ⲡⲉⲧⲛⲁⲱϩⲉ ⲉⲣⲁⲧϥ ϩⲛ̄ ⲧⲁⲣⲭⲏ
ⲁⲩⲱ ϥⲛⲁⲥⲟⲩⲱⲛ ⲑⲁⲏ ⲁⲩⲱ
ϥⲛⲁⲭⲓ ϯⲡⲉ ⲁⲛ ⲙ̄ⲙⲟⲩ

19 ¹ⲡⲉⲭⲉ ⲓ̄ⲥ̄ ⲭⲉ ⲟⲩⲙⲁⲕⲁⲣⲓⲟⲥ
ⲡⲉ ⲛ̄ⲧⲁϩϣⲱⲡⲉ ϩⲁ ⲧⲉϩⲏ
ⲉⲙⲡⲁⲧⲉϥϣⲱⲡⲉ
²ⲉⲧⲉⲧⲛ̄ϣⲁⲛϣⲱⲡⲉ ⲛⲁⲉⲓ
ⲙ̄ⲙⲁⲑⲏⲧⲏⲥ ⲛ̄ⲧⲉⲧⲛ̄ⲥⲱⲧⲙ̄
ⲁⲛⲁϣⲁⲭⲉ ⲛⲉⲉⲓⲱⲛⲉ
ⲛⲁⲣ̄ⲇⲓⲁⲕⲟⲛⲉⲓ ⲛⲏⲧⲛ̄ ³ⲟⲩⲛ̄ⲧⲏⲧⲛ̄
ⲅⲁⲣ ⲙ̄ⲙⲁⲩ ⲛ̄ϯⲟⲩ ⲛ̄ϣⲏⲛ ϩⲙ̄
ⲡⲁⲣⲁⲇⲓⲥⲟⲥ ⲉⲥⲉⲕⲓⲙ ⲁⲛ ⲛ̄ϣⲱⲙ
ⲙ̄ⲡⲣⲱ ⲁⲩⲱ ⲙⲁⲣⲉ ⲛⲟⲩϭⲱⲃⲉ ϩⲉ
ⲉⲃⲟⲗ ⁴ⲡⲉⲧⲛⲁⲥⲟⲩⲱⲛⲟⲩ ϥⲛⲁⲭⲓ
ϯⲡⲉ ⲁⲛ ⲙ̄ⲙⲟⲩ

20 ¹ⲡⲉⲭⲉ ⲙ̄ⲙⲁⲑⲏⲧⲏⲥ ⲛ̄ⲓ̄ⲥ̄ ⲭⲉ
ⲭⲟⲟⲥ ⲉⲣⲟⲛ ⲭⲉ ⲧⲙⲛ̄ⲧⲉⲣⲟ ⲛ̄ⲙ̄ⲡⲏⲩⲉ
ⲉⲥⲧⲛ̄ⲧⲱⲛ ⲉⲛⲓⲙ

²ⲡⲉⲭⲁϥ ⲛⲁⲩ ⲭⲉ ⲉⲥⲧⲛ̄ⲧⲱⲛ
ⲁⲩⲃⲗ̄ⲃⲓⲗⲉ ⲛ̄ϣⲗ̄ⲧⲁⲙ ³⟨ⲥ⟩ⲥⲟⲃⲕ̄
ⲡⲁⲣⲁ ⲛ̄ϭⲣⲟϭ ⲧⲏⲣⲟⲩ ⁴ϩⲟⲧⲁⲛ ⲇⲉ
ⲉⲥϣⲁⲛϩⲉ ⲉⲭⲙ̄ ⲡⲕⲁϩ ⲉⲧⲟⲩⲣ̄ ϩⲱⲃ
ⲉⲣⲟϥ ϣⲁϥⲧⲉⲩⲟ ⲉⲃⲟⲗ ⲛ̄ⲟⲩⲛⲟϭ
ⲛ̄ⲧⲁⲣ ⲛ̄ϥϣⲱⲡⲉ ⲛ̄ⲥⲕⲉⲡⲏ ⲛ̄ϩⲁⲗⲁⲧⲉ
ⲛ̄ⲧⲡⲉ

17 Jesus said, "I shall give you what no eye has seen, what no ear has heard, what no hand has touched, what has not arisen in the human heart."

18 ¹The disciples said to Jesus, "Tell us how our end will be."

²Jesus said, "Have you discovered the beginning, then, that you are seeking after the end? For where the beginning is, the end will be. ³Blessed is one who stands at the beginning: that one will know the end and will not taste death."

19 ¹Jesus said, "Blessed is one who came into being before coming into being. ²If you become my disciples and hearken to my sayings, these stones will serve you. ³For there are five trees in Paradise for you; they do not change, summer or winter, and their leaves do not fall. ⁴Whoever knows them will not taste death."

20 ¹The disciples said to Jesus, "Tell us what the kingdom of heaven is like."

²He said to them, "It is like a mustard seed. ³⟨It⟩ is the tiniest of all seeds,* ⁴but when it falls on prepared soil, it produces a large plant and becomes a shelter for birds of heaven."

21 ¹ⲡⲉϫⲉ ⲙⲁⲣⲓϩⲁⲙ ⲛⲓⲥ ϫⲉ
ⲉⲛⲉⲕⲙⲁⲑⲏⲧⲏⲥ ⲉⲓⲛⲉ ⲛ̄ⲛⲓⲙ
²ⲡⲉϫⲁϥ ϫⲉ ⲉⲩⲉⲓⲛⲉ ⲛ̄ϩⲛ̄ϣⲏⲣⲉ
ϣⲏⲙ ⲉⲩϭⲉⲗⲓⲧ ⲁⲩⲥⲱϣⲉ ⲉⲧⲟⲩ
ⲁⲛ ⲧⲉ ³ϩⲟⲧⲁⲛ ⲉⲩϣⲁⲉⲓ ⲛ̄ϭⲓ
ⲛ̄ϫⲟⲉⲓⲥ ⲛ̄ⲧⲥⲱϣⲉ ⲥⲉⲛⲁϫⲟⲟⲥ ϫⲉ
ⲕⲉ ⲧⲛ̄ⲥⲱϣⲉ ⲉⲃⲟⲗ ⲛⲁⲛ ⁴ⲛ̄ⲧⲟⲟⲩ
ⲥⲉⲕⲁⲕⲁϩⲏⲩ ⲙ̄ⲡⲟⲩⲙ̄ⲧⲟ ⲉⲃⲟⲗ
ⲉⲧⲣⲟⲩⲕⲁⲁⲥ ⲉⲃⲟⲗ ⲛⲁⲩ ⲛ̄ⲥⲉϯ
ⲧⲟⲩⲥⲱϣⲉ ⲛⲁⲩ ⁵ⲇⲓⲁ ⲧⲟⲩⲧⲟ ϯϫⲱ
ⲙ̄ⲙⲟⲥ ϫⲉ ⲉϥϣⲁⲉⲓⲙⲉ ⲛ̄ϭⲓ
ⲡϫⲉⲥϩⲛ̄ⲏⲉⲓ ϫⲉ ϥⲛⲏⲩ ⲛ̄ϭⲓ
ⲡⲣⲉϥϫⲓⲟⲩⲉ ϥⲛⲁⲣⲟⲉⲓⲥ
ⲉⲙⲡⲁⲧⲉϥⲉⲓ ⲛ̄ϥⲧⲙ̄ⲕⲁⲁϥ ⲉϣⲟϫⲧ
ⲉϩⲟⲩⲛ ⲉⲡⲉϥⲏⲉⲓ ⲛ̄ⲧⲉ ⲧⲉϥⲙⲛ̄ⲧⲉⲣⲟ
ⲉⲧⲣⲉϥϥⲓ ⲛ̄ⲛⲉϥⲥⲕⲉⲩⲟⲥ ⁶ⲛ̄ⲧⲱⲧⲛ̄
ⲇⲉ ⲣⲟⲉⲓⲥ ϩⲁ ⲧⲉϩ ⲙ̄ⲡⲕⲟⲥⲙⲟⲥ
⁷ⲙⲟⲩⲣ ⲙ̄ⲙⲱⲧⲛ̄ ⲉϫⲛ̄ ⲛⲉⲧⲛ̄ϯⲡⲉ
ϩⲛ̄ⲛⲟⲩⲛⲟϭ ⲛ̄ⲇⲩⲛⲁⲙⲓⲥ ϣⲓⲛⲁ ϫⲉ ⲛⲉ
ⲛⲗⲏⲥⲧⲏⲥ ϩⲉ ⲉϩⲓⲏ ⲉⲉⲓ ϣⲁⲣⲱⲧⲛ̄
ⲉⲡⲉⲓ ⲧⲉⲭⲣⲉⲓⲁ ⲉⲧⲉⲧⲛ̄ϭⲱϣⲧ ⲉⲃⲟⲗ
ϩⲏⲧⲥ̄ ⲥⲉⲛⲁϩⲉ ⲉⲣⲟⲥ
⁸ⲙⲁⲣⲉϥϣⲱⲡⲉ ϩⲛ̄ ⲧⲉⲧⲛ̄ⲙⲏⲧⲉ ⲛ̄ϭⲓ
ⲟⲩⲣⲱⲙⲉ ⲛ̄ⲉⲡⲓⲥⲧⲏⲙⲱⲛ ⁹ⲛ̄ⲧⲁⲣⲉ
ⲡⲕⲁⲣⲡⲟⲥ ⲡⲱϩ ⲁϥⲉⲓ ϩⲛ̄ⲛⲟⲩϭⲉⲡⲏ
ⲉⲡⲉϥⲁⲥϩ ϩⲛ̄ ⲧⲉϥϭⲓϫ ⲁϥϩⲁⲥϥ
¹⁰ⲡⲉⲧⲉ ⲟⲩⲛ̄ ⲙⲁⲁϫⲉ ⲙ̄ⲙⲟϥ ⲉⲥⲱⲧⲙ̄
ⲙⲁⲣⲉϥⲥⲱⲧⲙ̄

22 ¹ⲁⲓⲥ ⲛⲁⲩ ⲁϩⲛ̄ⲕⲟⲩⲉⲓ ⲉⲩϫⲓ
ⲉⲣⲱⲧⲉ ²ⲡⲉϫⲁϥ ⲛ̄ⲛⲉϥⲙⲁⲑⲏⲧⲏⲥ
ϫⲉ ⲛⲉⲉⲓⲕⲟⲩⲉⲓ ⲉⲧϫⲓ ⲉⲣⲱⲧⲉ
ⲉⲩⲧⲛ̄ⲧⲱⲛ ⲁⲛⲉⲧⲃⲏⲕ ⲉϩⲟⲩⲛ
ⲁⲧⲙⲛ̄ⲧⲉⲣⲟ
³ⲡⲉϫⲁⲩ ⲛⲁϥ ϫⲉ ⲉⲉⲓⲉⲛⲟ ⲛ̄ⲕⲟⲩⲉⲓ
ⲧⲛ̄ⲛⲁⲃⲱⲕ ⲉϩⲟⲩⲛ ⲉⲧⲙⲛ̄ⲧⲉⲣⲟ
⁴ⲡⲉϫⲉ ⲓⲏⲥ ⲛⲁⲩ ϫⲉ ϩⲟⲧⲁⲛ
ⲉⲧⲉⲧⲛ̄ϣⲁⲣ ⲡⲥⲛⲁⲩ ⲟⲩⲁ ⲁⲩⲱ
ⲉⲧⲉⲧⲛ̄ϣⲁⲣ ⲡⲥⲁ ⲛϩⲟⲩⲛ ⲛ̄ⲑⲉ ⲙ̄ⲡⲥⲁ

21 ¹Mary said to Jesus, "What
are your disciples like?"

²He said, "They are like little
children living in a field that is
not theirs. ³When the owners of
the field come, they will say,
'Give our field back to us.' ⁴They
take off their clothes in their
presence in order to give it back
to them, and they return their
field to them.* ⁵For this reason I
say, if the owner of a house
knows that a thief is coming, he
will be on guard before the thief
arrives, and will not let the thief
break into his house of his
domain and steal his possessions.
⁶As for you, then, be on guard
against the world. ⁷Gird yourselves with great strength, lest
the robbers find a way to get to
you, for the trouble you expect
will come. ⁸Let there be among
you a person who understands.
⁹When the crop ripened, that one
came quickly with sickle in hand
and harvested it. ¹⁰Whoever has
ears to hear should hear."

22 ¹Jesus saw some babies
nursing. ²He said to his disciples,
"These nursing babies are like
those who enter the kingdom."

³They said to him, "Then shall
we enter the kingdom as babies?"

⁴Jesus said to them, "When you
make the two into one, and when
you make the inner like the outer
and the outer like the inner, and

ⲚⲂⲞⲖ ⲀⲨⲰ ⲠⲤⲀ ⲚⲂⲞⲖ ⲚⲐⲈ ⲘⲠⲤⲀ
Ⲛ2ⲞⲨⲚ ⲀⲨⲰ ⲠⲤⲀ ⲚⲦⲠⲈ ⲚⲐⲈ ⲘⲠⲤⲀ
ⲘⲠⲒⲦⲚ ⁵ⲀⲨⲰ ϢⲒⲚⲀ ⲈⲦⲈⲦⲚⲀⲈⲒⲢⲈ
ⲘⲪⲞⲞⲨⲦ ⲘⲚ ⲦⲤ2ⲒⲘⲈ ⲘⲠⲒⲞⲨⲀ
ⲞⲨⲰⲦ ⲬⲈⲔⲀⲀⲤ ⲚⲈ ⲪⲞⲞⲨⲦ Ⲣ̄
2ⲞⲞⲨⲦ ⲚⲦⲈ ⲦⲤ2ⲒⲘⲈ Ⲣ̄ Ⲥ2ⲒⲘⲈ
⁶2ⲞⲦⲀⲚ ⲈⲦⲈⲦⲚ̄ϢⲀⲈⲒⲢⲈ Ⲛ̄2Ⲛ̄ⲂⲀⲖ
ⲈⲠⲘⲀ ⲚⲞⲨⲂⲀⲖ ⲀⲨⲰ ⲞⲨ6ⲒⲬ ⲈⲠⲘⲀ
ⲚⲚⲞⲨ6ⲒⲬ ⲀⲨⲰ ⲞⲨⲈⲢⲎⲦⲈ ⲈⲠⲘⲀ
ⲚⲞⲨⲈⲢⲎⲦⲈ ⲞⲨ2ⲒⲔⲰⲚ ⲈⲠⲘⲀ
ⲚⲞⲨ2ⲒⲔⲰⲚ ⁷ⲦⲞⲦⲈ ⲦⲈⲦⲚⲀⲂⲰⲔ
Ⲉ2ⲞⲨⲚ Ⲉ[Ⲧ]ⲘⲚ̄[ⲦⲈⲢ]Ⲟ

23 ¹ⲠⲈⲬⲈ Ⲓ̄Ⲥ̄ ⲬⲈ ϮⲚⲀⲤⲈⲦⲠ ⲦⲎⲚⲈ
ⲞⲨⲀ ⲈⲂⲞⲖ 2Ⲛ̄ ϢⲞ ⲀⲨⲰ ⲤⲚⲀⲨ ⲈⲂⲞⲖ
2Ⲛ̄ ⲦⲂⲀ ²ⲀⲨⲰ ⲤⲚⲀⲰ2Ⲉ ⲈⲢⲀⲦⲞⲨ
ⲈⲨⲞ ⲞⲨⲀ ⲞⲨⲰⲦ

24 ¹ⲠⲈⲬⲈ ⲚⲈϤⲘⲀⲐⲎⲦⲎⲤ ⲬⲈ
ⲘⲀⲦⲤⲈⲂⲞⲚ ⲈⲠⲦⲞⲠⲞⲤ ⲈⲦⲔⲘ̄ⲘⲀⲨ
ⲈⲠⲈⲒ ⲦⲀⲚⲀⲄⲔⲎ ⲈⲢⲞⲚ ⲦⲈ ⲈⲦⲢⲚ̄ϢⲒⲚⲈ
Ⲛ̄ⲤⲰϤ

²ⲠⲈⲬⲀϤ ⲚⲀⲨ ⲬⲈ ⲠⲈⲦⲈⲨⲚ̄
ⲘⲀⲀⲬⲈ Ⲙ̄ⲘⲞϤ ⲘⲀⲢⲈϤⲤⲰⲦⲘ̄ ³ⲞⲨⲚ̄
ⲞⲨⲞⲈⲒⲚ ϢⲞⲞⲠ Ⲙ̄ⲪⲞⲨⲚ
Ⲛ̄ⲚⲞⲨⲢⲘ̄ⲞⲨⲞⲈⲒⲚ ⲀⲨⲰ ϤⲢ̄ ⲞⲨⲞⲈⲒⲚ
ⲈⲠⲔⲞⲤⲘⲞⲤ ⲦⲎⲢϤ ⲈϤⲦⲘ̄Ⲣ̄ ⲞⲨⲞⲈⲒⲚ
ⲞⲨⲔⲀⲔⲈ ⲠⲈ

25 ¹ⲠⲈⲬⲈ Ⲓ̄Ⲥ̄ ⲬⲈ ⲘⲈⲢⲈ ⲠⲈⲔⲤⲞⲚ
ⲚⲐⲈ Ⲛ̄ⲦⲈⲔⲮⲨⲬⲎ ²ⲈⲢⲒⲦⲎⲢⲈⲒ ⲘⲘⲞϤ
ⲚⲐⲈ Ⲛ̄ⲦⲈⲖⲞⲨ Ⲙ̄ⲠⲈⲔⲂⲀⲖ

26 ¹ⲠⲈⲬⲈ Ⲓ̄Ⲥ̄ ⲬⲈ ⲠⲬⲎ ⲈⲦ2Ⲙ̄
ⲠⲂⲀⲖ Ⲙ̄ⲠⲈⲔⲤⲞϤ ⲔⲚⲀⲨ ⲈⲢⲞϤ
ⲠⲤⲞⲈⲒ ⲆⲈ ⲈⲦ2Ⲙ̄ ⲠⲈⲔⲂⲀⲖ ⲔⲚⲀⲨ ⲀⲚ
ⲈⲢⲞϤ ²2ⲞⲦⲀⲚ ⲈⲔϢⲀⲚⲚⲞⲨⲬⲈ
Ⲙ̄ⲠⲤⲞⲈⲒ ⲈⲂⲞⲖ 2Ⲙ̄ ⲠⲈⲔⲂⲀⲖ ⲦⲞⲦⲈ
ⲔⲚⲀⲚⲀⲨ ⲈⲂⲞⲖ ⲈⲚⲞⲨⲬⲈ Ⲙ̄ⲠⲬⲎ
ⲈⲂⲞⲖ 2Ⲙ̄ ⲠⲂⲀⲖ Ⲙ̄ⲠⲈⲔⲤⲞⲚ

27 ¹ⲈⲦⲈ⟨ⲦⲚ̄⟩ⲦⲘ̄Ⲣ̄ⲚⲎⲤⲦⲈⲨⲈ

the upper like the lower, ⁵and
when you make male and female
into a single one,* so that the
male will not be male nor the
female be female, ⁶when you
make eyes in place of an eye, a
hand in place of a hand, a foot in
place of a foot, an image in place
of an image, ⁷then you will enter
[the kingdom]."

23 ¹Jesus said, "I shall choose
you, one from a thousand and
two from ten thousand, ²and
they will stand as a single one."

24 ¹His disciples said, "Show
us the place where you are, for
we must seek it."

²He said to them, "Whoever
has ears should hear. ³There is
light within a person of light, and
it shines on the whole world. If it
does not shine, it is dark."*

25 ¹Jesus said, "Love your
brother like your soul, ²protect
that one like the pupil of your
eye."

26 ¹Jesus said, "You see the
speck that is in your brother's
eye, but you do not see the beam
that is in your own eye. ²When
you take the beam out of your
own eye, then you will see
clearly to take the speck out of
your brother's eye.

27 ¹"If you do not fast from the

ⲉⲡⲕⲟⲥⲙⲟⲥ ⲧⲉⲧⲛⲁϩⲉ ⲁⲛ
ⲉⲧⲙⲛ̄ⲧⲉⲣⲟ ²ⲉⲧⲉⲧⲛ̄ⲧⲙ̄ⲉⲓⲣⲉ
ⲙ̄ⲡⲥⲁⲙⲃⲁⲧⲟⲛ ⲛ̄ⲥⲁⲃⲃⲁⲧⲟⲛ
ⲛ̄ⲧⲉⲧⲛⲁⲛⲁⲩ ⲁⲛ ⲉⲡⲉⲓⲱⲧ

28 ¹ⲡⲉⲝⲉ ⲓ̄ⲥ̄ ⲝⲉ ⲁⲉⲓⲱϩⲉ ⲉⲣⲁⲧ
ϩⲛ̄ ⲧⲙⲏⲧⲉ ⲙ̄ⲡⲕⲟⲥⲙⲟⲥ ⲁⲩⲱ
ⲁⲉⲓⲟⲩⲱⲛϩ ⲉⲃⲟⲗ ⲛⲁⲩ ϩⲛ̄ ⲥⲁⲣⲝ
²ⲁⲉⲓϩⲉ ⲉⲣⲟⲟⲩ ⲧⲏⲣⲟⲩ ⲉⲩⲧⲁϩⲉ
ⲙ̄ⲡⲓϩⲉ ⲉⲗⲁⲁⲩ ⲛ̄ϩⲏⲧⲟⲩ ⲉϥⲟⲃⲉ
³ⲁⲩⲱ ⲁⲧⲁⲯⲩⲭⲏ ϯ ⲧⲕⲁⲥ ⲉⲝⲛ̄
ⲛ̄ϣⲏⲣⲉ ⲛ̄ⲣ̄ⲣⲱⲙⲉ ⲝⲉ ϩⲛ̄ⲃⲗⲉⲉⲩⲉ
ⲛⲉ ϩⲙ̄ ⲡⲟⲩϩⲏⲧ ⲁⲩⲱ ⲥⲉⲛⲁⲩ ⲉⲃⲟⲗ
ⲁⲛ ⲝⲉ ⲛ̄ⲧⲁⲩⲉⲓ ⲉⲡⲕⲟⲥⲙⲟⲥ
ⲉⲩϣⲟⲩⲉⲓⲧ ⲉⲩϣⲓⲛⲉ ⲟⲛ ⲉⲧⲣⲟⲩⲉⲓ
ⲉⲃⲟⲗ ϩⲙ̄ ⲡⲕⲟⲥⲙⲟⲥ ⲉⲩϣⲟⲩⲉⲓⲧ
⁴ⲡⲗⲏⲛ ⲧⲉⲛⲟⲩ ⲥⲉⲧⲟϩⲉ ϩⲟⲧⲁⲛ
ⲉⲩϣⲁⲛⲛⲉϩ ⲡⲟⲩⲏⲣⲡ ⲧⲟⲧⲉ
ⲥⲉⲛⲁⲣ̄ⲙⲉⲧⲁⲛⲟⲉⲓ

29 ¹ⲡⲉⲝⲉ ⲓ̄ⲥ̄ ⲉϣⲝⲉ ⲛ̄ⲧⲁ ⲧⲥⲁⲣⲝ
ϣⲱⲡⲉ ⲉⲧⲃⲉ ⲡⲛ̄ⲁ̄ ⲟⲩϣⲡⲏⲣⲉ ⲧⲉ
²ⲉϣⲝⲉ ⲡⲛ̄ⲁ̄ ⲁⲉ ⲉⲧⲃⲉ ⲡⲥⲱⲙⲁ
ⲟⲩϣⲡⲏⲣⲉ ⲛ̄ϣⲡⲏⲣⲉ ⲡⲉ ³ⲁⲗⲗⲁ
ⲁⲛⲟⲕ ϯⲣ̄ ϣⲡⲏⲣⲉ ⲙ̄ⲡⲁⲉⲓ ⲝⲉ ⲡⲱⲥ
ⲁⲧⲉⲉⲓⲛⲟϭ ⲙ̄ⲙⲛ̄ⲧⲣⲙ̄ⲙⲁⲟ ⲁⲥⲟⲩⲱϩ
ϩⲛ̄ ⲧⲉⲉⲓⲙⲛ̄ⲧϩⲏⲕⲉ

30 ¹ⲡⲉⲝⲉ ⲓ̄ⲥ̄ ⲝⲉ ⲡⲙⲁ ⲉⲩⲛ̄ ϣⲟⲙⲧ
ⲛ̄ⲛⲟⲩⲧⲉ ⲙ̄ⲙⲁⲩ ϩⲛ̄ⲛⲟⲩⲧⲉ ⲛⲉ ²ⲡⲙⲁ
ⲉⲩⲛ̄ ⲥⲛⲁⲩ ⲏ ⲟⲩⲁ ⲁⲛⲟⲕ ϯϣⲟⲟⲡ
ⲛⲙⲙⲁϥ

31 ¹ⲡⲉⲝⲉ ⲓ̄ⲥ̄ ⲙⲛ̄ ⲡⲣⲟⲫⲏⲧⲏⲥ
ϣⲏⲡ ϩⲙ̄ ⲡⲉϥϯⲙⲉ ²ⲙⲁⲣⲉ ⲥⲟⲉⲓⲛ
ⲣ̄ⲑⲉⲣⲁⲡⲉⲩⲉ ⲛ̄ⲛⲉⲧⲥⲟⲟⲩⲛ ⲙ̄ⲙⲟϥ

32 ⲡⲉⲝⲉ ⲓ̄ⲥ̄ ⲝⲉ ⲟⲩⲡⲟⲗⲓⲥ
ⲉⲩⲕⲱⲧ ⲙ̄ⲙⲟⲥ ϩⲓⲝⲛ̄ ⲟⲩⲧⲟⲟⲩ
ⲉϥⲝⲟⲥⲉ ⲉⲥⲧⲁⲝⲣⲏⲩ ⲙⲛ̄ ϭⲟⲙ
ⲛ̄ⲥϩⲉ ⲟⲩⲁⲉ ⲥⲛⲁϣϩⲱⲡ ⲁⲛ

world, you will not find the kingdom. ²If you do not keep the sabbath a sabbath, you will not see the Father."

28 ¹Jesus said, "I took my stand in the midst of the world, and in flesh I appeared to them. ²I found them all drunk, and I did not find any of them thirsty. ³My soul ached for the children of humanity, because they are blind in their hearts and do not see, for they came into the world empty, and they also seek to depart from the world empty. ⁴But now they are drunk. When they shake off their wine, then they will repent."

29 ¹Jesus said, "If the flesh came into being because of spirit, it is a marvel, ²but if spirit came into being because of the body, it is a marvel of marvels. ³Yet I marvel at how this great wealth has come to dwell in this poverty."

30 ¹Jesus said, "Where there are three deities, they are divine. ²Where there are two or one, I am with that one."

31 ¹Jesus said, "A prophet is not acceptable in the prophet's own town; ²a doctor does not heal those who know the doctor."

32 Jesus said, "A city built upon a high hill and fortified cannot fall, nor can it be hidden."

33 ¹ⲡⲉⲝⲉ ⲓ̅ⲥ̅ ⲡⲉⲧⲕⲛⲁⲥⲱⲧⲙ̅
ⲉⲣⲟϥ ϩ̅ⲙ ⲡⲉⲕⲙⲁⲁⲝⲉ ϩ̅ⲙ
ⲡⲕⲉⲙⲁⲁⲝⲉ ⲧⲁ ⲟⲉⲓ ⲙ̅ⲙⲟϥ
ϩⲓⲝ̅ⲛ ⲛⲉⲧⲛ̅ⲝⲉⲛⲉⲡⲱⲣ ²ⲙⲁⲣⲉ
ⲗⲁⲁⲩ ⲅⲁⲣ ⲝⲉⲣⲉ ϩⲏ̅ⲃ̅ⲥ̅ ⲛ̅ϥⲕⲁⲁϥ ϩⲁ
ⲙⲁⲁⲝⲉ ⲟⲩⲇⲉ ⲙⲁϥⲕⲁⲁϥ ϩ̅ⲙ ⲙⲁ
ⲉϥϩⲏⲡ ³ⲁⲗⲗⲁ ⲉ ⲁⲣⲉϥⲕⲁⲁϥ ϩⲓⲝ̅ⲛ
ⲧⲗⲩⲭⲛⲓⲁ ⲝⲉⲕⲁⲁⲥ ⲟⲩⲟⲛ ⲛⲓⲙ
ⲉⲧⲃⲏⲕ ⲉϩⲟⲩⲛ ⲁⲩⲱ ⲉⲧⲛ̅ⲛⲏⲩ ⲉⲃⲟⲗ
ⲉⲩⲛⲁⲛⲁⲩ ⲁⲡⲉϥⲟⲩⲟⲉⲓⲛ

34 ⲡⲉⲝⲉ ⲓ̅ⲥ̅ ⲝⲉ ⲟⲩⲃⲗ̅ⲗⲉ
ⲉϥ ⲁⲛⲥⲱⲕ ϩⲏⲧϥ̅ ⲛ̅ⲛⲟⲩⲃⲗ̅ⲗⲉ
ⲱⲁⲩϩⲉ ⲙ̅ⲡⲉⲥⲛⲁⲩ ⲉⲡⲉⲥⲏⲧ
ⲉⲩϩⲓⲉⲓⲧ

35 ¹ⲡⲉⲝⲉ ⲓ̅ⲥ̅ ⲙ̅ⲛ ϭⲟⲙ ⲛ̅ⲧⲉ ⲟⲩⲁ
ⲃⲱⲕ ⲉϩⲟⲩⲛ ⲉⲡⲏⲉⲓ ⲙ̅ⲡⲭⲱⲱⲣⲥ
ⲛ̅ϥⲝⲓⲧϥ̅ ⲛ̅ϫⲛⲁϩ ⲉⲓ ⲙⲏⲧⲓ ⲛ̅ϥⲙⲟⲩⲣ
ⲛ̅ⲛⲉϥϭⲓⲝ ²ⲧⲟⲧⲉ ϥⲛⲁⲡⲱⲛⲉ
ⲉⲃⲟⲗ ⲙ̅ⲡⲉϥⲏⲉⲓ

36 ⲡⲉⲝⲉ ⲓ̅ⲥ̅ ⲙ̅ⲛ̅ϥⲓ ⲣⲟⲟⲩ ⲝⲓⲛ
ϩⲧⲟⲟⲩⲉ ⲱⲁ ⲣⲟⲩϩⲉ ⲁⲩⲱ ⲝⲓⲛ
ϩⲓⲣⲟⲩϩⲉ ⲱⲁ ϩⲧⲟⲟⲩⲉ ⲝⲉ ⲟⲩ
ⲡⲉ⟨ⲧ⟩ⲉⲧⲛⲁⲧⲁⲁϥ ϩⲓⲱⲧ ⲧⲏⲩⲧⲛ̅

37 ¹ⲡⲉⲝⲉ ⲛⲉϥⲙⲁⲑⲏⲧⲏⲥ ⲝⲉ ⲁⲱ
ⲛ̅ϩⲟⲟⲩ ⲉⲕⲛⲁⲟⲩⲱⲛϩ ⲉⲃⲟⲗ ⲛⲁⲛ
ⲁⲩⲱ ⲁⲱ ⲛ̅ϩⲟⲟⲩ ⲉⲛⲁⲛⲁⲩ ⲉⲣⲟⲕ
²ⲡⲉⲝⲉ ⲓ̅ⲥ̅ ⲝⲉ ϩⲟⲧⲁⲛ
ⲉⲧⲉⲧⲛ̅ⲱⲁⲕⲉⲕ ⲧⲏⲩⲧⲛ̅ ⲉϩⲏⲩ
ⲙ̅ⲡⲉⲧⲛ̅ⲱⲓⲡⲉ ⲁⲩⲱ ⲛ̅ⲧⲉⲧⲛ̅ϥⲓ
ⲛ̅ⲛⲉⲧⲛ̅ⲱⲧⲏⲛ ⲛ̅ⲧⲉⲧⲛ̅ⲕⲁⲁⲩ ϩⲁ
ⲡⲉⲥⲏⲧ ⲛ̅ⲛⲉⲧⲛ̅ⲟⲩⲉⲣⲏⲧⲉ ⲛ̅ⲑⲉ
ⲛ̅ⲛⲓⲕⲟⲩⲉⲓ ⲛ̅ⲱⲏⲣⲉ ⲱⲏⲙ
ⲛ̅ⲧⲉⲧⲛ̅ϫⲟⲡⲝ̅ⲛ̅ ⲙ̅ⲙⲟⲟⲩ ³ⲧⲟⲧⲉ
[ⲧⲉⲧ]ⲛⲁⲛⲁⲩ ⲉⲡⲱⲏⲣⲉ ⲙ̅ⲡⲉⲧⲟⲛϩ
ⲁⲩⲱ ⲧⲉⲧⲛⲁⲣ̅ ϩⲟⲧⲉ ⲁⲛ

38 ¹ⲡⲉⲝⲉ ⲓ̅ⲥ̅ ⲝⲉ ϩⲁϩ ⲛ̅ⲥⲟⲡ
ⲁⲧⲉⲧⲛ̅ⲣ̅ⲉⲡⲓⲑⲩⲙⲉⲓ ⲉⲥⲱⲧⲙ̅
ⲁⲛⲉⲉⲓⲱⲁⲝⲉ ⲛⲁⲉⲓ ⲉⲧϯⲝⲱ ⲙ̅ⲙⲟⲟⲩ

33 ¹Jesus said, "What you will
hear in your ear, in the other ear*
proclaim from your rooftops.
²For no one lights a lamp and
puts it under a basket, nor does
one put it in a hidden place.
³Rather, one puts it on a stand so
that all who come and go will see
its light."

34 Jesus said, "If a blind person
leads a blind person, both of
them will fall into a hole."

35 ¹Jesus said, "One cannot
enter the house of the strong and
take it by force without tying the
person's hands. ²Then one will
loot the person's house."

36 Jesus said, "Do not worry,
from morning to evening and
from evening to morning, about
what you will wear."

37 ¹His disciples said, "When
will you appear to us, and when
shall we see you?"
²Jesus said, "When you strip
without being ashamed, and you
take your clothes and put them
under your feet like little children and trample them, ³then
[you] will see the son of the living
one and you will not be afraid."

38 ¹Jesus said, "Often you have
desired to hear these sayings that
I am speaking to you, and you

ΝΗΤΝ ΑΥω ΜΝΤΗΤΝ ΚΕΟΥΑ
ΕСΟΤΜΟΥ ΝΤΟΟΤϤ ²ΟΥΝ ΖΝΖΟΟΥ
ΝΑϢωΠΕ ΝΤΕΤΝϢΙΝΕ ΝСωΕΙ
ΤΕΤΝΑΖΕ ΑΝ ΕΡΟΕΙ

39 ¹ΠΕΧΕ ΙС ΧΕ ΜϤΑΡΙСΑΙΟС ΜΝ
ΝΓΡΑΜΜΑΤΕΥС ΑΥΧΙ ΝϢΑϢΤ
ΝΤΓΝωСΙС ΑΥΖΟΠΟΥ ²ΟΥΤΕ
ΜΠΟΥΒωΚ ΕΖΟΥΝ ΑΥω
ΝΕΤΟΥωϢ ΕΒωΚ ΕΖΟΥΝ
ΜΠΟΥΚΑΑΥ ³ΝΤωΤΝ ΔΕ ϢωΠΕ
ΜϤΡΟΝΙΜΟС ΝΘΕ ΝΝΖΟϤ ΑΥω
ΝΑΚΕΡΑΙΟС ΝΘΕ ΝΝϬΡΟΜΠΕ

40 ¹ΠΕΧΕ ΙС ΟΥΒΕΝΕΛΟΟΛΕ
ΑΥΤΟϬС ΜΠСΑ ΝΒΟΛ ΜΠΕΙωΤ
²ΑΥω ΕСΤΑΧΡΗΥ ΑΝ СΕΝΑΠΟΡΚϹ
ΖΑ ΤΕСΝΟΥΝΕ ΝСΤΑΚΟ

41 ¹ΠΕΧΕ ΙС ΧΕ ΠΕΤΕΥΝΤΑϤ ΖΝ
ΤΕϤϬΙΧ СΕΝΑϮ ΝΑϤ ²ΑΥω ΠΕΤΕ
ΜΝΤΑϤ ΠΚΕϢΗΜ ΕΤΟΥΝΤΑϤ
СΕΝΑϤΙΤϤ ΝΤΟΟΤϤ

42 ΠΕΧΕ ΙС ΧΕ ϢωΠΕ
ΕΤΕΤΝΡΠΑΡΑΓΕ

43 ¹ΠΕΧΑΥ ΝΑϤ ΝϬΙ
ΝΕϤΜΑΘΗΤΗС ΧΕ ΝΤΑΚ ΝΙΜ ΕΚΧω
ΝΝΑΪ ΝΑΝ

²ΖΝ ΝΕϮΧω ΜΜΟΟΥ ΝΗΤΝ
ΝΤΕΤΝΕΙΜΕ ΑΝ ΧΕ ΑΝΟΚ ΝΙΜ
³ΑΛΛΑ ΝΤωΤΝ ΑΤΕΤΝϢωΠΕ ΝΘΕ
ΝΝΙΪΟΥΔΑΙΟС ΧΕ СΕΜΕ ΜΠϢΗΝ
СΕΜΟСΤΕ ΜΠΕϤΚΑΡΠΟС ΑΥω
СΕΜΕ ΜΠΚΑΡΠΟС СΕΜΟСΤΕ
ΜΠϢΗΝ

44 ¹ΠΕΧΕ ΙС ΧΕ ΠΕΤΑΧΕ ΟΥΑ
ΑΠΕΙωΤ СΕΝΑΚω ΕΒΟΛ ΝΑϤ
²ΑΥω ΠΕΤΑΧΕ ΟΥΑ ΕΠϢΗΡΕ

have no one else from whom to
hear them. ²There will be days
when you will seek me and you
will not find me."

39 ¹Jesus said, "The Pharisees
and the scribes have taken the
keys of knowledge and have
hidden them. ²They have not
entered, nor have they allowed
those who want to enter to do so.
³As for you, be as shrewd as
snakes and as innocent as
doves."

40 ¹Jesus said, "A grapevine
has been planted apart from the
Father. ²Since it is not strong, it
will be pulled up by its root and
will perish."

41 ¹Jesus said, "Whoever has
something in hand will be given
more, ²and whoever has nothing
will be deprived of even the little
that person has."

42 Jesus said, "Be passersby."

43 ¹His disciples said to him,
"Who are you to say these things
to us?"

²"You do not understand who
I am from what I say to you.
³Rather, you have become like
the Jews, for they love the tree
but hate its fruit, or they love the
fruit but hate the tree."

44 ¹Jesus said, "Whoever
blasphemes against the Father
will be forgiven, ²and whoever

сєнакω євоλ наq ³пєтахє
оуа дє апп̄н̄а̄ єтоуаав
сєнакω ан євоλ наq оутє 2м̄
пка2 оутє 2н̄ тпє

45 ¹пєхє ῑс̄ мауХєλє
єλооλє євоλ 2н̄ шонтє оутє
маукωтq кн̄тє євоλ 2н̄
ср̄бамоуλ мау† карпос гар
²оугаθос р̄рωмє шаqєінє
н̄оугаθон євоλ 2м̄ пєqє2о
³оукак[ос] р̄рωмє шаqєінє
н̄2н̄понηρον євоλ 2м̄ пєqє2о
єθооу єт2н̄ пєq2ητ ауω н̄qхω
н̄2н̄понηρον ⁴євоλ гар 2м̄ фоуо
м̄фητ шаqєінє євоλ
н̄2н̄понηρον

46 ¹пєхє ῑс̄ хє хін ааам ша
їω2аннηс пваптістηс 2н̄ н̄хпо
н̄н̄2іомє мн̄ пєтхосє
аїω2аннηс пваптістηс шіна
хє ноушбп̄ н̄6і нєqваλ
²аєіхоос дє хє пєтнашωпє
2н̄ тηутн̄ єqо н̄коуєі qнасоуωн
тмн̄тєро ауω qнахісє
аїω2аннηс

47 ¹пєхє ῑс̄ хє мн̄ 6ом н̄тє
оур̄рωмє тєλо а2то снау
н̄qхωλк м̄пітє сн̄тє ²ауω мн̄
6ом н̄тє оу2м2аλ шм̄шє хоєіс
снау η qнар̄тіма м̄поуа ауω
пкєоуа qнар̄2увρіζє м̄моq
³марє рωмє сє р̄пас ауω
н̄тєуноу н̄qєпіθумєі асω нρп
б̄вр̄рє ⁴ауω мауноух нρп б̄вр̄рє
єаскос н̄ас хєкаас н̄ноупω2
ауω маунєх нρп н̄ас єаскос

blasphemes against the son will
be forgiven, ³but whoever
blasphemes against the holy
spirit will not be forgiven, either
on earth or in heaven."

45 ¹Jesus said, "Grapes are not
harvested from thorn trees, nor
are figs gathered from thistles,
for they yield no fruit. ²A good
person brings forth good from
the storehouse; ³a bad person
brings forth evil things from the
corrupt storehouse in the heart,
and says evil things. ⁴For from
the abundance of the heart this
person brings forth evil things."

46 ¹Jesus said, "From Adam to
John the Baptist, among those
born of women, no one is so
much greater than John the
Baptist that the person's eyes
should not be averted.* ²But I
have said that whoever among
you becomes a child will know
the kingdom, and will become
greater than John."

47 ¹Jesus said, "A person cannot mount two horses or bend
two bows. ²And a servant cannot
serve two masters, or that
servant will honor the one and
offend the other. ³No person
drinks aged wine and immediately desires to drink new wine.
⁴New wine is not poured into
aged wineskins, lest they break,
and aged wine is not poured into

ⲃⲃⲣ̄ⲣⲉ ϣⲓⲛⲁ ϫⲉ ⲛⲉϥⲧⲉⲕⲁϥ
⁵ⲙⲁⲩϫⲗ̄ϭ ⲧⲟⲉⲓⲥ ⲛ̄ⲁⲥ ⲁϣⲧⲏⲛ
ⲛ̄ϣⲁⲉⲓ ⲉⲡⲉⲓ ⲟⲩⲛ ⲟⲩⲡⲱϩ
ⲛⲁϣⲱⲡⲉ

48 ⲡⲉϫⲉ ⲓ̄ⲥ̄ ϫⲉ ⲉⲣϣⲁ ⲥⲛⲁⲩ ⲣ̄
ⲉⲓⲣⲏⲛⲏ ⲙⲛ̄ ⲛⲟⲩⲉⲣⲏⲩ ϩⲙ̄ ⲡⲉⲓⲏⲉⲓ
ⲟⲩⲱⲧ ⲥⲉⲛⲁϫⲟⲟⲥ ⲙ̄ⲡⲧⲁⲩ ϫⲉ
ⲡⲱⲱⲛⲉ ⲉⲃⲟⲗ ⲁⲩⲱ ϥⲛⲁⲡⲱⲱⲛⲉ

49 ¹ⲡⲉϫⲉ ⲓ̄ⲥ̄ ϫⲉ ϩⲉⲛⲙⲁⲕⲁⲣⲓⲟⲥ
ⲛⲉ ⲛⲙⲟⲛⲁⲭⲟⲥ ⲁⲩⲱ ⲉⲧⲥⲟⲧⲡ ²ϫⲉ
ⲧⲉⲧⲛⲁϩⲉ ⲁⲧⲙⲛ̄ⲧⲉⲣⲟ ϫⲉ ⲛ̄ⲧⲱⲧⲛ̄
ϩⲛ̄ⲉⲃⲟⲗ ⲛ̄ϩⲏⲧⲥ̄ ⲡⲁⲗⲓⲛ
ⲉⲧⲉⲧⲛⲁⲃⲱⲕ ⲉⲙⲁⲩ

50 ¹ⲡⲉϫⲉ ⲓ̄ⲥ̄ ϫⲉ ⲉⲩϣⲁⲛϫⲟⲟⲥ
ⲛⲏⲧⲛ̄ ϫⲉ ⲛ̄ⲧⲁⲧⲉⲧⲛ̄ϣⲱⲡⲉ ⲉⲃⲟⲗ
ⲧⲱⲛ ϫⲟⲟⲥ ⲛⲁⲩ ϫⲉ ⲛ̄ⲧⲁⲛⲉⲓ ⲉⲃⲟⲗ
ϩⲙ̄ ⲡⲟⲩⲟⲉⲓⲛ ⲡⲙⲁ ⲉⲛⲧⲁ ⲡⲟⲩⲟⲉⲓⲛ
ϣⲱⲡⲉ ⲙ̄ⲙⲁⲩ ⲉⲃⲟⲗ ϩⲓⲧⲟⲟⲧϥ
ⲟⲩⲁⲁⲧϥ ⲁϥⲱϩ[ⲉ ⲉⲣⲁⲧϥ] ⲁⲩⲱ
ⲁϥⲟⲩⲱⲛϩ ⲉ[ⲃ]ⲟⲗ ϩⲛ̄ ⲧⲟⲩϩⲓⲕⲱⲛ
²ⲉⲩϣⲁϫⲟⲟⲥ ⲛⲏⲧⲛ̄ ϫⲉ ⲛ̄ⲧⲱⲧⲛ̄ ⲡⲉ
ϫⲟⲟⲥ ϫⲉ ⲁⲛⲟⲛ ⲛⲉϥϣⲏⲣⲉ ⲁⲩⲱ
ⲁⲛⲟⲛ ⲛ̄ⲥⲱⲧⲡ ⲙ̄ⲡⲉⲓⲱⲧ ⲉⲧⲟⲛϩ
³ⲉⲩϣⲁⲛϫⲛⲉ ⲑⲏⲧⲛ̄ ϫⲉ ⲟⲩ ⲡⲉ
ⲡⲙⲁⲉⲓⲛ ⲙ̄ⲡⲉⲧⲛ̄ⲉⲓⲱⲧ ⲉⲧϩⲛ̄ ⲑⲏⲧⲛ̄
ϫⲟⲟⲥ ⲉⲣⲟⲟⲩ ϫⲉ ⲟⲩⲕⲓⲙ ⲡⲉ ⲙⲛ̄
ⲟⲩⲁⲛⲁⲡⲁⲩⲥⲓⲥ

51 ¹ⲡⲉϫⲁⲩ ⲛⲁϥ ⲛ̄ϭⲓ
ⲛⲉϥⲙⲁⲑⲏⲧⲏⲥ ϫⲉ ⲁϣ ⲛ̄ϩⲟⲟⲩ
ⲉⲧⲁⲛⲁⲡⲁⲩⲥⲓⲥ ⲛ̄ⲛⲉⲧⲙⲟⲟⲩⲧ
ⲛⲁϣⲱⲡⲉ ⲁⲩⲱ ⲁϣ ⲛ̄ϩⲟⲟⲩ
ⲉⲡⲕⲟⲥⲙⲟⲥ ⲃⲃⲣ̄ⲣⲉ ⲛⲏⲩ
²ⲡⲉϫⲁϥ ⲛⲁⲩ ϫⲉ ⲧⲏ
ⲉⲧⲉⲧⲛ̄ϭⲱϣⲧ ⲉⲃⲟⲗ ϩⲏⲧⲥ̄ ⲁⲥⲉⲓ
ⲁⲗⲗⲁ ⲛ̄ⲧⲱⲧⲛ̄ ⲧⲉⲧⲛ̄ⲥⲟⲟⲩⲛ ⲁⲛ
ⲙ̄ⲙⲟⲥ

52 ¹ⲡⲉϫⲁⲩ ⲛⲁϥ ⲛ̄ϭⲓ

a new wineskin, lest it spoil. ⁵An old patch is not sewn onto a new garment, for there would be a tear."

48 Jesus said, "If two make peace with each other in a single house, they will say to the mountain, 'Move from here!' and it will move."

49 ¹Jesus said, "Blessed are those who are alone and chosen, for you will find the kingdom. ²For you have come from it, and you will return there again."

50 ¹Jesus said, "If they say to you, 'Where have you come from?' say to them, 'We have come from the light, from the place where the light came into being by itself, established [itself], and appeared in their image.' ²If they say to you, 'Is it you?' say, 'We are its children, and we are the chosen of the living Father.' ³If they ask you, 'What is the evidence of your Father in you?' say to them, 'It is motion and rest.'"

51 ¹His disciples said to him, "When will the rest for the dead take place, and when will the new world come?"

²He said to them, "What you look for has come, but you do not know it."

52 ¹His disciples said to him,

ⲛⲉϥⲙⲁⲑⲏⲧⲏⲥ ϫⲉ ϫⲟⲩⲧⲁϥⲧⲉ
ⲙⲡⲣⲟⲫⲏⲧⲏⲥ ⲁⲩϣⲁϫⲉ ϩⲙ
ⲡⲓⲥⲣⲁⲏⲗ ⲁⲩⲱ ⲁⲩϣⲁϫⲉ ⲧⲏⲣⲟⲩ
ϩⲣⲁⲓ ⲛ̄ϩⲏⲧⲕ

²ⲡⲉϫⲁϥ ⲛⲁⲩ ϫⲉ ⲁⲧⲉⲧⲛ̄ⲕⲱ
ⲙ̄ⲡⲉⲧⲟⲛϩ ⲙ̄ⲡⲉⲧⲛ̄ⲙ̄ⲧⲟ ⲉⲃⲟⲗ ⲁⲩⲱ
ⲁⲧⲉⲧⲛ̄ϣⲁϫⲉ ϩⲁ ⲛⲉⲧⲙⲟⲟⲩⲧ

53 ¹ⲡⲉϫⲁⲩ ⲛⲁϥ ⲛ̄ϭⲓ
ⲛⲉϥⲙⲁⲑⲏⲧⲏⲥ ϫⲉ ⲡⲥⲃ̄ⲃⲉ ⲣ̄ⲱⲫⲉⲗⲉⲓ
ⲏ ⲙ̄ⲙⲟⲛ

²ⲡⲉϫⲁϥ ⲛⲁⲩ ϫⲉ ⲛⲉϥⲣ̄ⲱⲫⲉⲗⲉⲓ
ⲛⲉ ⲡⲟⲩⲉⲓⲱⲧ ⲛⲁϫⲡⲟⲟⲩ ⲉⲃⲟⲗ ϩⲛ̄
ⲧⲟⲩⲙⲁⲁⲩ ⲉⲩⲥⲃ̄ⲃⲏⲩ ³ⲁⲗⲗⲁ
ⲡⲥⲃ̄ⲃⲉ ⲙ̄ⲙⲉ ϩⲙ̄ ⲡⲛ̄ⲁ̄ ⲁϥϭⲛ̄ ϩⲏⲩ
ⲧⲏⲣϥ

54 ⲡⲉϫⲉ ⲓ̄ⲥ̄ ϫⲉ ϩⲛ̄ⲙⲁⲕⲁⲣⲓⲟⲥ ⲛⲉ
ⲛ̄ϩⲏⲕⲉ ϫⲉ ⲧⲱⲧⲛ̄ ⲧⲉ ⲧⲙ̄ⲛ̄ⲧⲉⲣⲟ
ⲛ̄ⲙ̄ⲡⲏⲩⲉ

55 ¹ⲡⲉϫⲉ ⲓ̄ⲥ̄ ϫⲉ ⲡⲉⲧⲁⲙⲉⲥⲧⲉ
ⲡⲉϥⲉⲓⲱⲧ ⲁⲛ ⲙⲛ̄ ⲧⲉϥⲙⲁⲁⲩ ϥⲛⲁϣ̄
ⲙⲁⲑⲏⲧⲏⲥ ⲁⲛ ⲛⲁⲉⲓ ²ⲁⲩⲱ ⲛ̄ϥⲙⲉⲥⲧⲉ
ⲛⲉϥⲥⲛⲏⲩ ⲙⲛ̄ ⲛⲉϥⲥⲱⲛⲉ ⲛ̄ϥϥⲓ
ⲙ̄ⲡⲉϥⲥⳁⲟⲥ ⲛ̄ⲧⲁϩⲉ ϥⲛⲁϣⲱⲡⲉ ⲁⲛ
ⲉϥⲟ ⲛ̄ⲁϩⲓⲟⲥ ⲛⲁⲉⲓ

56 ¹ⲡⲉϫⲉ ⲓ̄ⲥ̄ ϫⲉ ⲡⲉⲧⲁϩⲥⲟⲩⲱⲛ
ⲡⲕⲟⲥⲙⲟⲥ ⲁϥϩⲉ ⲉⲩⲡⲧⲱⲙⲁ ²ⲁⲩⲱ
ⲡⲉⲛⲧⲁϩϩⲉⲉ ⲁⲡⲧⲱⲙⲁ ⲡⲕⲟⲥⲙⲟⲥ
ⲙ̄ⲡϣⲁ ⲙ̄ⲙⲟϥ ⲁⲛ

57 ¹ⲡⲉϫⲉ ⲓ̄ⲥ̄ ϫⲉ ⲧⲙ̄ⲛ̄ⲧⲉⲣⲟ
ⲙ̄ⲡⲉⲓⲱⲧ ⲉⲥⲧⲛ̄ⲧⲱⲛ ⲁⲩⲣⲱⲙⲉ
ⲉⲩⲛ̄ⲧⲁϥ ⲙ̄ⲙⲁⲩ ⲛ̄ⲛⲟⲩϭⲣⲟϭ
ⲉⲛ[ⲁⲛⲟ]ⲩϥ ²ⲁⲡⲉϥϫⲁϫⲉ ⲉⲓ
ⲛ̄ⲧⲟⲩϣⲏ ⲁϥⲥⲓⲧⲉ ⲛ̄ⲟⲩⲍⲓⲍⲁⲛⲓ[ⲟ]ⲛ
ⲉϫⲛ̄ ⲡⲉⲃⲣⲟ[ϭ ⲉ]ⲧⲛⲁⲛⲟⲩϥ ³ⲙ̄ⲡⲉ
ⲡⲣⲱⲙⲉ ⲕⲟⲟⲩ ⲉϩⲱⲗⲉ
ⲙ̄ⲡⲍⲓⲍⲁⲛⲓⲟⲛ ⲡⲉϫⲁϥ ⲛⲁⲩ ϫⲉ

"Twenty-four prophets have spoken in Israel, and they all spoke of you."*

²He said to them, "You have disregarded the living one who is in your presence, and have spoken of the dead."

53 ¹His disciples said to him, "Is circumcision useful or not?"

²He said to them, "If it were useful, their father would produce children* already circumcised from their mother. ³Rather, the true circumcision in spirit has become profitable in every respect."

54 Jesus said, "Blessed are the poor, for yours is the kingdom of heaven."

55 ¹Jesus said, "Whoever does not hate father and mother cannot be a disciple of me, ²and whoever does not hate brothers and sisters and bear the cross as I do, will not be worthy of me."

56 ¹Jesus said, "Whoever has come to know the world has discovered a carcass, ²and whoever has discovered a carcass, of that person the world is not worthy."

57 ¹Jesus said, "The kingdom of the Father is like a person who had [good] seed. ²His enemy came at night and sowed weeds among the good seed. ³The person did not let the workers* pull up the weeds, but said to them, 'No, lest you go to pull up

мнпшс ᾶтєтᾶвшк хє єнагшлє
ᾶпzizanion ᾶтєтᾶгшлє
ᾶпсоуо нᾶмаq ⁴гᾶ фооу гар
ᾶпшᾱᾱ ᾶzizanion наоушнг
євол сєголоу ᾶсєрокгоу

58 пєхє ᾱᾱ хє оумакаріос пє
пршмє ᾶтаггісє аqгє апшнг

59 пєхє ᾱᾱ хє бшшт ᾶса
пєтонг гшс єтєтᾶонг гіна хє
нєтᾶмоу ауш ᾶтєтᾶшінє єнау
єроq ауш тєтнашбᾱ бом ан
єнау

60 ¹⟨аqнау⟩ аусамарєітнс
єqqі ᾶноугієів єqвнк єгоун
єᵗоудаіа ²пєхаq
ᾶнєqмаθнтнс хє пн ᾶпкштє
ᾶпєгієів

³пєхау наq хєкаас
єqнамооутq ᾶqоуомq

⁴пєхаq нау гшс єqонг
qнаоуомq ан алла
єqшамооутq ᾶqшшпє
ᾶоуптшма

⁵пєхау хє ᾶкєсмот qнашас
ан

⁶пєхаq нау хє ᾶтштᾱ
гшттнутᾱ шінє ᾶса оутопос
ннтᾱ єгоун єуанапаусіс
хєкаас ᾶнєтᾶшшпє ᾶптшма
ᾶсєоушм тнутᾱ

61 ¹пєхє ᾱᾱ оуᾱ снау намтон
ᾶмау гі оублоб поуа намоу
поуа нашнг

²пєхє салшмн ᾶтак нім
пршмє гшс євол гᾱ оуа
актєло єхᾱ паблоб ауш
акоушм євол гᾱ татрапєza

³пєхє ᾱᾱ нас хє анок пє

the weeds and pull up the wheat along with them.' ⁴For on the day of the harvest the weeds will be conspicuous, and will be pulled up and burned."

58 Jesus said, "Blessed is the person who has toiled* and has found life."

59 Jesus said, "Look to the living one as long as you live, lest you die and then try to see the living one, and you will be unable to see."

60 ¹⟨He saw⟩* a Samaritan carrying a lamb and going to Judea. ²He said to his disciples, "⟨ … ⟩ that person ⟨ … ⟩ around the lamb."*

³They said to him, "So that he may kill it and eat it."

⁴He said to them, "He will not eat it while it is alive, but only after he has killed it and it has become a carcass."

⁵They said, "Otherwise he cannot do it."

⁶He said to them, "So also with you, seek for yourselves a place for rest, lest you become a carcass and be eaten."

61 ¹Jesus said, "Two will rest on a couch; one will die, one will live."

²Salome said, "Who are you, sir? You have climbed on my couch and eaten from my table as if you are from someone."*

³Jesus said to her, "I am the one

ⲡⲉⲧϣⲟⲟⲡ ⲉⲃⲟⲗ ϩⲙ ⲡⲉⲧϣⲏϣ
ⲁⲩϯ ⲛⲁⲉⲓ ⲉⲃⲟⲗ ϩⲛ ⲛⲁ ⲡⲁⲉⲓⲱⲧ
    ⁴ⲁⲛⲟⲕ ⲧⲉⲕⲙⲁⲑⲏⲧⲏⲥ
    ⁵ⲉⲧⲃⲉ ⲡⲁⲉⲓ ϯϫⲱ ⲙⲙⲟⲥ ϫⲉ
ϩⲟⲧⲁⲛ ⲉϥϣⲁϣⲱⲡⲉ ⲉϥϣⲏⲟ⟨ϣ⟩
ϥⲛⲁⲙⲟⲩϩ ⲟⲩⲟⲉⲓⲛ ϩⲟⲧⲁⲛ ⲇⲉ
ⲉϥϣⲁⲛϣⲱⲡⲉ ⲉϥⲡⲏϣ ϥⲛⲁⲙⲟⲩϩ
ⲛⲕⲁⲕⲉ
    62 ¹ⲡⲉϫⲉ ⲓⲥ ϫⲉ ⲉⲓϫⲱ
ⲛⲛⲁⲙⲩⲥⲧⲏⲣⲓⲟⲛ ⲛⲛⲉ[ⲧⲙⲡϣⲁ]
ⲛ[ⲛⲁ]ⲙⲩⲥⲧⲏⲣⲓⲟⲛ ²ⲡⲉ[ⲧ]ⲉ
ⲧⲉⲕⲟⲩⲛⲁⲙ ⲛⲁⲁϥ ⲙⲛⲧⲣⲉ
ⲧⲉⲕϩⲃⲟⲩⲣ ⲉⲓⲙⲉ ϫⲉ ⲉⲥⲣ ⲟⲩ
    63 ¹ⲡⲉϫⲉ ⲓⲥ ϫⲉ ⲛⲉⲩⲛ ⲟⲩⲣⲱⲙⲉ
ⲙⲡⲗⲟⲩⲥⲓⲟⲥ ⲉⲩⲛⲧⲁϥ ⲙⲙⲁⲩ ⲛϩⲁϩ
ⲛⲭⲣⲏⲙⲁ ²ⲡⲉϫⲁϥ ϫⲉ ϯⲛⲁⲣⲭⲣⲱ
ⲛⲛⲁⲭⲣⲏⲙⲁ ϫⲉⲕⲁⲁⲥ ⲉⲉⲓⲛⲁϫⲟ
ⲛⲧⲁⲱⲥϩ ⲛⲧⲁⲧⲱϭⲉ ⲛⲧⲁⲙⲟⲩϩ
ⲛⲛⲁⲉϩⲱⲣ ⲛⲕⲁⲣⲡⲟⲥ ϣⲓⲛⲁ ϫⲉ ⲛⲓⲣ
ϭⲣⲱϩ ⲗⲗⲁⲁⲩ ³ⲛⲁⲉⲓ ⲛⲉⲛⲉϥⲙⲉⲉⲩⲉ
ⲉⲣⲟⲟⲩ ϩⲙ ⲡⲉϥϩⲏⲧ ⲁⲩⲱ ϩⲛ
ⲧⲟⲩϣⲏ ⲉⲧⲙⲙⲁⲩ ⲁϥⲙⲟⲩ
    ⁴ⲡⲉⲧⲉⲩⲙ ⲙⲁϫⲉ ⲙⲙⲟϥ
ⲙⲁⲣⲉϥⲥⲱⲧⲙ
    64 ¹ⲡⲉϫⲉ ⲓⲥ ϫⲉ ⲟⲩⲣⲱⲙⲉ
ⲛⲉⲩⲛⲧⲁϥ ϩⲛϣⲙⲙⲟ ⲁⲩⲱ
ⲛⲧⲁⲣⲉϥⲥⲟⲃⲧⲉ ⲙⲡⲇⲓⲡⲛⲟⲛ
ⲁϥϫⲟⲟⲩ ⲙⲡⲉϥϩⲙϩⲁⲗ ϣⲓⲛⲁ
ⲉϥⲛⲁⲧⲱϩⲙ ⲛⲛϣⲙⲙⲟⲉⲓ ²ⲁϥⲃⲱⲕ
ⲙⲡϣⲟⲣⲡ ⲡⲉϫⲁϥ ⲛⲁϥ ϫⲉ
ⲡⲁϫⲟⲉⲓⲥ ⲧⲱϩⲙ ⲙⲙⲟⲕ ³ⲡⲉϫⲁϥ
ϫⲉ ⲟⲩⲛⲧⲁⲉⲓ ϩⲛϩⲟⲙⲧ
ⲁϩⲉⲛⲉⲙⲡⲟⲣⲟⲥ ⲥⲉⲛⲛⲏⲩ ϣⲁⲣⲟⲉⲓ
ⲉⲣⲟⲩϩⲉ ϯⲛⲁⲃⲱⲕ ⲛⲧⲁⲟⲩⲉϩ
ⲥⲁϩⲛⲉ ⲛⲁⲩ ϯⲣⲡⲁⲣⲁⲓⲧⲉⲓ
ⲙⲡⲇⲓⲡⲛⲟⲛ ⁴ⲁϥⲃⲱⲕ ϣⲁ ⲕⲉⲟⲩⲁ
ⲡⲉϫⲁϥ ⲛⲁϥ ϫⲉ ⲁⲡⲁϫⲟⲉⲓⲥ ⲧⲱϩⲙ
ⲙⲙⲟⲕ ⁵ⲡⲉϫⲁϥ ⲛⲁϥ ϫⲉ ⲁⲉⲓⲧⲟⲟⲩ
ⲟⲩⲏⲉⲓ ⲁⲩⲱ ⲥⲉⲣⲁⲓⲧⲉⲓ ⲙⲙⲟⲉⲓ

who derives from what is whole.* I was granted from the things of my Father."

⁴"I am your disciple."

⁵"For this reason I say, if one is ⟨whole⟩,* one will be filled with light, but if one is divided, one will be filled with darkness."

62 ¹Jesus said, "I disclose my mysteries to those [who are worthy] of [my] mysteries. ²Do not let your left hand know what your right hand is doing."

63 ¹Jesus said, "There was a rich person who had a great deal of money. ²He said, 'I shall invest my money so that I may sow, reap, plant, and fill my storehouses with produce, that I may lack nothing.' ³These were the things he was thinking in his heart, but that very night he died. ⁴Whoever has ears should hear."

64 ¹Jesus said, "A person was receiving guests. When he had prepared the dinner, he sent his servant to invite the guests. ²The servant went to the first and said to that one, 'My master invites you.' ³That one said, 'Some merchants owe me money; they are coming to me tonight. I must go and give instructions to them. Please excuse me from dinner.' ⁴The servant went to another and said to that one, 'My master has invited you.' ⁵That one said to the servant, 'I have bought a house,

ⲛⲟⲩϩⲏⲙⲉⲣⲁ ϯⲛⲁⲥⲣ̅ϥⲉ ⲁⲛ ⁶ⲁϥⲉⲓ
ϣⲁ ⲕⲉⲟⲩⲁ ⲡⲉⲭⲁϥ ⲛⲁϥ ϫⲉ
ⲡⲁϫⲟⲉⲓⲥ ⲧⲱϩⲙ̅ ⲙ̅ⲙⲟⲕ ⁷ⲡⲉⲭⲁϥ
ⲛⲁϥ ϫⲉ ⲡⲁϣⲃⲏⲣ ⲛⲁⲣ̅ ϣⲉⲗⲉⲉⲧ
ⲁⲩⲱ ⲁⲛⲟⲕ ⲉⲧⲛⲁⲣ̅ ⲇⲓⲡⲛⲟⲛ ϯⲛⲁϣⲓ
ⲁⲛ ϯⲣ̅ⲡⲁⲣⲁⲓⲧⲉⲓ ⲙ̅ⲡⲇⲓⲡⲛⲟⲛ
⁸ⲁϥⲃⲱⲕ ϣⲁ ⲕⲉⲟⲩⲁ ⲡⲉⲭⲁϥ ⲛⲁϥ
ϫⲉ ⲡⲁϫⲟⲉⲓⲥ ⲧⲱϩⲙ ⲙ̅ⲙⲟⲕ
⁹ⲡⲉⲭⲁϥ ⲛⲁϥ ϫⲉ ⲁⲉⲓⲧⲟⲟⲩ
ⲛ̅ⲟⲩⲕⲱⲙⲏ ⲉⲉⲓⲃⲏⲕ ⲁϫⲓ ⲛ̅ϣⲱⲙ
ϯⲛⲁϣⲓ ⲁⲛ ϯⲣ̅ⲡⲁⲣⲁⲓⲧⲉⲓ ¹⁰ⲁϥⲉⲓ ⲛ̅ϭⲓ
ⲡϩⲙ̅ϩⲁⲗ ⲁϥϫⲟⲟⲥ ⲁⲡⲉϥϫⲟⲉⲓⲥ ϫⲉ
ⲛⲉⲛⲧⲁⲕⲧⲁϩⲙⲟⲩ ⲁⲡⲇⲓⲡⲛⲟⲛ
ⲁⲩⲡⲁⲣⲁⲓⲧⲉⲓ ¹¹ⲡⲉϫⲉ ⲡϫⲟⲉⲓⲥ
ⲙ̅ⲡⲉϥϩⲙ̅ϩⲁⲗ ϫⲉ ⲃⲱⲕ ⲉⲡⲥⲁ ⲛⲃⲟⲗ
ⲁⲛϩⲓⲟⲟⲩⲉ ⲛⲉⲧⲕⲛⲁϩⲉ ⲉⲣⲟⲟⲩ
ⲉⲛⲓⲟⲩ ϫⲉⲕⲁⲁⲥ ⲉⲩⲛⲁⲣ̅ⲇⲓⲡⲛⲉⲓ

¹²ⲛ̅ⲣⲉϥⲧⲟⲟⲩ ⲙ̅ⲛ ⲛⲉϣⲟⲧ[ⲉ
ⲥⲉⲛⲁⲃ]ⲱⲕ ⲁⲛ ⲉϩⲟⲩⲛ ⲉⲛⲧⲟⲡⲟⲥ
ⲙ̅ⲡⲁⲓⲱⲧ

65 ¹ⲡⲉⲭⲁϥ ϫⲉ ⲟⲩⲣⲱⲙⲉ
ⲛ̅ⲭⲣⲏ[...]ⲥ ⲛⲉⲩⲛ̅ⲧ[ⲁϥ] ⲛ̅ⲟⲩⲙⲁ
ⲛ̅ⲉⲗⲟⲟⲗⲉ ⲁϥⲧⲁⲁϥ ⲛ̅ϩ̅ⲛⲟⲩⲟⲉⲓⲉ
ϣⲓⲛⲁ ⲉⲩⲛⲁⲣ̅ ϩⲱⲃ ⲉⲣⲟϥ ⲛ̅ϥϫⲓ
ⲙ̅ⲡⲉϥⲕⲁⲣⲡⲟⲥ ⲛ̅ⲧⲟⲟⲧⲟⲩ
²ⲁϥϫⲟⲟⲩ ⲙ̅ⲡⲉϥϩⲙ̅ϩⲁⲗ ϫⲉⲕⲁⲁⲥ
ⲉⲛⲟⲩⲟⲉⲓⲉ ⲛⲁϯ ⲛⲁϥ ⲙ̅ⲡⲕⲁⲣⲡⲟⲥ
ⲙ̅ⲡⲙⲁ ⲛ̅ⲉⲗⲟⲟⲗⲉ ³ⲁⲩⲉⲙⲁϩⲧⲉ
ⲙ̅ⲡⲉϥϩⲙ̅ϩⲁⲗ ⲁⲩϩⲓⲟⲩⲉ ⲉⲣⲟϥ ⲛⲉ
ⲕⲉⲕⲟⲩⲉⲓ ⲡⲉ ⲛ̅ⲥⲉⲙⲟⲟⲩⲧϥ
ⲁⲡϩⲙ̅ϩⲁⲗ ⲃⲱⲕ ⲁϥϫⲟⲟⲥ
ⲉⲡⲉϥϫⲟⲉⲓⲥ ⁴ⲡⲉϫⲉ ⲡⲉϥϫⲟⲉⲓⲥ
ϫⲉ ⲙⲉϣⲁⲕ ⲙ̅ⲡⲉϥⲥⲟⲩⲱⲛⲟⲩ

and I have been called away for a day. I shall have no time.' ⁶The servant went to another and said to that one, 'My master invites you.' ⁷That one said to the servant, 'My friend is to be married, and I am to arrange the dinner. I shall not be able to come. Please excuse me from dinner.' ⁸The servant went to another and said to that one, 'My master invites you.' ⁹That one said to the servant, 'I have bought an estate, and I am going to collect the rent. I shall not be able to come. Please excuse me.' ¹⁰The servant returned and said to his master, 'Those whom you invited to dinner have asked to be excused.' ¹¹The master said to his servant, 'Go out on the streets, and bring back whomever you find to have dinner.' ¹²"Buyers and merchants [will] not enter the places of my Father."

65 ¹He said, "A [...]* person owned a vineyard and rented it to some farmers, that they might work it and he might collect its produce from them. ²He sent his servant that the farmers might give the servant the produce of the vineyard. ³They seized, beat, and almost killed his servant, and the servant returned and told his master. ⁴His master said, 'Perhaps the servant did not know them.'* ⁵He sent another

⁵ⲁϥⲭⲟⲟⲩ ⲛ̄ⲕⲉϩⲙϩⲁⲗ ⲁⲛⲟⲩⲟⲉⲓⲉ
ϩⲓⲟⲩⲉ ⲉⲡⲕⲉⲟⲩⲁ ⁶ⲧⲟⲧⲉ ⲁⲡⲭⲟⲉⲓⲥ
ⲭⲟⲟⲩ ⲙ̄ⲡⲉϥϣⲏⲣⲉ ⲡⲉⲭⲁϥ ⲭⲉ
ⲙⲉϣⲁⲕ ⲥⲉⲛⲁϣⲓⲡⲉ ϩⲏⲧϥ
ⲙ̄ⲡⲁϣⲏⲣⲉ ⁷ⲁⲛⲟⲩⲟⲉⲓⲉ ⲉⲧⲙ̄ⲙⲁⲩ
ⲉⲡⲉⲓ ⲥⲉⲥⲟⲟⲩⲛ ⲭⲉ ⲛ̄ⲧⲟϥ ⲡⲉ
ⲡⲉⲕⲗⲏⲣⲟⲛⲟⲙⲟⲥ ⲙ̄ⲡⲙⲁ ⲛ̄ⲉⲗⲟⲟⲗⲉ
ⲁⲩϭⲟⲡϥ ⲁⲩⲙⲟⲟⲩⲧϥ ⁸ⲡⲉⲧⲉⲩⲙ̄
ⲙⲁⲁⲭⲉ ⲙ̄ⲙⲟϥ ⲙⲁⲣⲉϥⲥⲱⲧⲙ̄

66 ⲡⲉⲭⲉ ⲓ̅ⲥ̅ ⲭⲉ ⲙⲁⲧⲥⲉⲃⲟⲉⲓ
ⲉⲡⲱⲛⲉ ⲡⲁⲉⲓ ⲛ̄ⲧⲁⲩⲥⲧⲟϥ ⲉⲃⲟⲗ ⲛ̄ϭⲓ
ⲛⲉⲧⲕⲱⲧ ⲛ̄ⲧⲟϥ ⲡⲉ ⲡⲱⲛⲉ ⲛ̄ⲕⲱϩ

67 ⲡⲉⲭⲉ ⲓ̅ⲥ̅ ⲭⲉ ⲡⲉⲧⲥⲟⲟⲩⲛ
ⲙ̄ⲡⲧⲏⲣϥ ⲉϥⲡ̄ ϭⲣⲱϩ ⲟⲩⲁⲁϥ ⟨ϥ⟩ⲡ̄
ϭⲣⲱϩ ⲙ̄ⲡⲙⲁ ⲧⲏⲣϥ

68 ¹ⲡⲉⲭⲉ ⲓ̅ⲥ̅ ⲭⲉ ⲛ̄ⲧⲱⲧⲛ̄
ϩⲙ̄ⲙⲁⲕⲁⲣⲓⲟⲥ ϩⲟⲧⲁⲛ
ⲉⲩϣⲁⲛⲙⲉⲥⲧⲉ ⲧⲏⲩⲧⲛ̄ ⲛ̄ⲥⲉⲡ̄ⲇⲓⲱⲕⲉ
ⲙ̄ⲙⲱⲧⲛ̄ ²ⲁⲩⲱ ⲥⲉⲛⲁϩⲉ ⲁⲛ
ⲉⲧⲟⲡⲟⲥ ϩⲙ̄ ⲡⲙⲁ ⲉⲛⲧⲁⲩⲇⲓⲱⲕⲉ
ⲙ̄ⲙⲱⲧⲛ̄ ϩⲣⲁⲓ̈ ⲛ̄ϩⲏⲧϥ

69 ¹ⲡⲉⲭⲉ ⲓ̅ⲥ̅ ϩⲙ̄ⲙⲁⲕⲁⲣⲓⲟⲥ ⲛⲉ
ⲛⲁⲉⲓ ⲛ̄ⲧⲁⲩⲇⲓⲱⲕⲉ ⲙ̄ⲙⲟⲟⲩ ϩⲣⲁⲓ̈ ϩⲙ̄
ⲡⲟⲩϩⲏⲧ ⲛⲉⲧⲙ̄ⲙⲁⲩ
ⲛⲉⲛⲧⲁϩⲥⲟⲩⲱⲛ ⲡⲉⲓⲱⲧ ϩⲛ̄ ⲟⲩⲙⲉ
²ϩⲙ̄ⲙⲁⲕⲁⲣⲓⲟⲥ ⲛⲉⲧϩⲕⲁⲉⲓⲧ ϣⲓⲛⲁ
ⲉⲩⲛⲁⲧⲥⲓⲟ ⲛ̄ⲑ̄ϩ ⲙ̄ⲡⲉⲧⲟⲩⲱϣ

70 ¹ⲡⲉⲭⲉ ⲓ̅ⲥ̅ ϩⲟⲧⲁⲛ
ⲉⲧⲉⲧⲛ̄ϣⲁⲭⲡⲉ ⲡⲏ ϩⲛ̄ ⲧⲏⲩⲧⲛ̄ ⲡⲁⲓ̈
ⲉⲧⲉⲩⲛ̄ⲧⲏⲧⲛ̄ϥ ϥⲛⲁⲧⲟⲩⲭⲉ ⲧⲏⲩⲧⲛ̄
²ⲉϣⲱⲡⲉ ⲙⲛ̄ⲧⲏⲧⲛ̄ ⲡⲏ ϩⲛ̄ ⲧ[ⲏ]ⲩⲧⲛ̄
ⲡⲁⲉⲓ ⲉⲧⲉ ⲙⲛ̄ⲧⲏⲧⲛ̄ϥ ϩⲛ̄ ⲑⲏⲛⲉ
ϥ[ⲛⲁ]ⲙⲟⲩⲧ ⲑⲏⲛⲉ

71 ⲡⲉⲭⲉ ⲓ̅ⲥ̅ ⲭⲉ ϯⲛⲁϣⲟⲣ[ϣⲣ̄]
ⲙ̄ⲡⲉⲉ]ⲓⲏⲉⲓ ⲁⲩⲱ ⲙⲛ̄ ⲗⲁⲁⲩ
ⲛⲁϣⲕⲟⲧϥ [........]

72 ¹[ⲡⲉ]ⲭⲉ ⲟⲩⲣ[ⲱⲙ]ⲉ ⲛⲁϥ ⲭⲉ
ⲭⲟⲟⲥ ⲛ̄ⲛⲁⲥⲛⲏⲩ ϣⲓⲛⲁ

---

servant, and the farmers beat
that one as well. ⁶Then the
master sent his son and said,
'Perhaps they will show my son
some respect.' ⁷Because the
farmers knew that he was the
heir to the vineyard, they seized
him and killed him. ⁸Whoever
has ears should hear."

66 Jesus said, "Show me the
stone that the builders rejected:
that is the cornerstone."

67 Jesus said, "One who knows
all, but is lacking in oneself, is
utterly lacking."

68 ¹Jesus said, "Blessed are you
when you are hated and persecuted; ²and no place will be
found, wherever you have been
persecuted."

69 ¹Jesus said, "Blessed are
those who have been persecuted
in their hearts: they are the ones
who have truly come to know
the Father. ²Blessed are they who
are hungry, that the stomach of
the one in want may be filled."

70 ¹Jesus said, "If you bring
forth what is within you, what
you have will save you. ²If you
do not have that within you,
what you do not have within you
[will] kill you."

71 Jesus said, "I shall destroy
[this] house, and no one will be
able to build it [. . .]."

72 ¹A [person said] to him,
"Tell my brothers to divide my

ⲉⲩⲛⲁⲡⲱϣⲉ ⲛ̄ⲛ̄ϩⲛⲁⲁⲩ ⲙ̄ⲡⲁⲉⲓⲱⲧ
ⲛⲙ̄ⲙⲁⲉⲓ
²ⲡⲉⲝⲁϥ ⲛⲁϥ ⲝⲉ ⲱ ⲡⲣⲱⲙⲉ ⲛⲓⲙ
ⲡⲉ ⲛ̄ⲧⲁϩⲁⲁⲧ ⲛ̄ⲣⲉϥⲡⲱϣⲉ
³ⲁϥⲕⲟⲧϥ̄ ⲁⲛⲉϥⲙⲁⲑⲏⲧⲏⲥ
ⲡⲉⲝⲁϥ ⲛⲁⲩ ⲝⲉ ⲙⲏ ⲉⲉⲓϣⲟⲟⲡ
ⲛ̄ⲣⲉϥⲡⲱϣⲉ

73 ⲡⲉⲝⲉ ⲓ̅ⲥ̅ ⲝⲉ ⲡⲱϩⲥ ⲙⲉⲛ
ⲛⲁϣⲱϥ ⲛ̄ⲉⲣⲅⲁⲧⲏⲥ ⲇⲉ ⲥⲟⲃⲕ
ⲥⲟⲡⲥ̅ ⲇⲉ ⲙ̄ⲡⲝⲟⲉⲓⲥ ϣⲓⲛⲁ
ⲉϥⲛⲁⲛⲉⲝ ⲉⲣⲅⲁⲧⲏⲥ ⲉⲃⲟⲗ ⲉⲡⲱϩⲥ̅

74 ⲡⲉⲝⲁϥ ⲝⲉ ⲡⲝⲟⲉⲓⲥ ⲟⲩⲛ̄ ϩⲁϩ
ⲙ̄ⲡⲕⲱⲧⲉ ⲛ̄ⲧⲝⲱⲧⲉ ⲙⲛ̄ ⲗⲁⲁⲩ ⲇⲉ
ϩⲛ̄ ⲧϣⲱ⟨ⲧ⟩ⲉ

75 ⲡⲉⲝⲉ ⲓ̅ⲥ̅ ⲟⲩⲛ̄ ϩⲁϩ
ⲁϩⲉⲣⲁⲧⲟⲩ ϩⲓⲣⲙ̄ ⲡⲣⲟ ⲁⲗⲗⲁ
ⲙ̄ⲙⲟⲛⲁⲭⲟⲥ ⲛⲉⲧⲛⲁⲃⲱⲕ ⲉϩⲟⲩⲛ
ⲉⲡⲙⲁ ⲛ̄ϣⲉⲗⲉⲉⲧ

76 ¹ⲡⲉⲝⲉ ⲓ̅ⲥ̅ ⲝⲉ ⲧⲙⲛ̄ⲧⲉⲣⲟ
ⲙ̄ⲡⲉⲓⲱⲧ ⲉⲥⲛ̄ⲧⲱⲛ ⲁⲩⲣⲱⲙⲉ
ⲛ̄ⲉϣⲱⲱⲧ ⲉⲩⲛ̄ⲧⲁϥ ⲙ̄ⲙⲁⲩ
ⲛ̄ⲟⲩⲫⲟⲣⲧⲓⲟⲛ ⲉⲁϥϩⲉ
ⲁⲩⲙⲁⲣⲅⲁⲣⲓⲧⲏⲥ ²ⲡⲉϣⲱⲧ ⲉⲧⲙ̄ⲙⲁⲩ
ⲟⲩⲥⲁⲃⲉ ⲡⲉ ⲁϥϯ ⲡⲉⲫⲟⲣⲧⲓⲟⲛ
ⲉⲃⲟⲗ ⲁϥⲧⲟⲟⲩ ⲛⲁϥ
ⲙ̄ⲡⲓⲙⲁⲣⲅⲁⲣⲓⲧⲏⲥ ⲟⲩⲱⲧ ³ⲛ̄ⲧⲱⲧⲛ̄
ϩⲱⲧⲧⲏⲩⲧⲛ̄ ϣⲓⲛⲉ ⲛ̄ⲥⲁ ⲡⲉϥⲉϩⲟ
ⲉⲙⲁϥϣⲱⲛ̄ ⲉϥⲙⲏⲛ ⲉⲃⲟⲗ ⲡⲙⲁ
ⲉⲙⲁⲣⲉ ⲝⲟⲟⲗⲉⲥ ⲧϩⲛⲟ ⲉϩⲟⲩⲛ
ⲉⲙⲁⲩ ⲉⲟⲩⲱⲙ ⲟⲩⲇⲉ ⲙⲁⲣⲉ ϥϥⲛ̄ⲧ
ⲧⲁⲕⲟ

77 ¹ⲡⲉⲝⲉ ⲓ̅ⲥ̅ ⲝⲉ ⲁⲛⲟⲕ ⲡⲉ
ⲡⲟⲩⲟⲉⲓⲛ ⲡⲁⲉⲓ ⲉⲧϩⲓⲝⲱⲟⲩ ⲧⲏⲣⲟⲩ
ⲁⲛⲟⲕ ⲡⲉ ⲡⲧⲏⲣϥ ⲛ̄ⲧⲁ ⲡⲧⲏⲣϥ ⲉⲓ
ⲉⲃⲟⲗ ⲛ̄ϩⲏⲧ ⲁⲩⲱ ⲛ̄ⲧⲁ ⲡⲧⲏⲣϥ ⲡⲱϩ
ϣⲁⲣⲟⲉⲓ ²ⲡⲱϩ ⲛ̄ⲟⲩϣⲉ ⲁⲛⲟⲕ
ϯⲙ̄ⲙⲁⲩ ³ϥⲓ ⲙ̄ⲡⲱⲛⲉ ⲉϩⲣⲁⲓ̈ ⲁⲩⲱ
ⲧⲉⲧⲛⲁϩⲉ ⲉⲣⲟⲉⲓ ⲙ̄ⲙⲁⲩ

father's possessions with me."

²He said to the person, "Sir,
who made me a divider?"

³He turned to his disciples and
said to them, "I am not a divider,
am I?"

73 Jesus said, "The harvest is
large but the workers are few, so
beg the lord to send out workers
to the harvest."

74 He said,* "Lord, there are
many around the drinking
trough,* but there is nothing* in
the well."

75 Jesus said, "There are many ⎫
standing at the door, but those ⎬ *Alone?*
who are alone will enter the ⎭
wedding chamber."

76 ¹Jesus said, "The kingdom
of the Father is like a merchant
who had a supply of merchandise, and then found a pearl.
²That merchant was prudent; he
sold the merchandise and bought
the single pearl for himself. ³So
also with you, seek his* treasure
that is unfailing, that is abiding,
where no moth comes to con-
sume and no worm destroys."

77 ¹Jesus said, "I am the light
that is over all things. I am all:
from me all came forth, and to
me all attained. ²Split a piece of
wood; I am there. ³Lift up the
stone, and you will find me
there."

78 ¹ⲡⲉⲭⲉ ⲓ̄ⲥ̄ ⲭⲉ ⲉⲧⲃⲉ ⲟⲩ
ⲁⲧⲉⲧⲛ̄ⲉⲓ ⲉⲃⲟⲗ ⲉⲧⲥⲱϣⲉ ⲉⲛⲁⲩ
ⲉⲩⲕⲁϣ ⲉϥⲕⲓⲙ ⲉ[ⲃⲟⲗ] ϩⲓⲧⲙ̄ ⲡⲧⲏⲩ
²ⲁⲩⲱ ⲉⲛⲁⲩ ⲉⲩⲣⲱⲙ[ⲉ ⲉ]ⲩⲛ̄ϣⲧⲏⲛ
ⲉⲩϭⲏⲛ ϩⲓⲱⲱⲃ ⲛ̄[ⲑⲉ ⲛ̄ⲛⲉⲧ]ⲛ̄ⲣ̄ⲣⲱⲟⲩ
ⲙⲛ̄ ⲛⲉⲧⲙ̄ⲙⲉⲅⲓⲥⲧⲁⲛⲟⲥ ³ⲛⲁⲉⲓ
ⲉⲛ[ⲉ]ϣⲧⲏⲛ ⲉ[ⲧ]ϭⲏⲛ ϩⲓⲱⲟⲩ ⲁⲩⲱ
ⲥⲉⲛ[ⲁ]ϣⲥ̄ⲥⲟⲩⲛ ⲧⲙⲉ ⲁⲛ

79 ¹ⲡⲉⲭⲉ ⲟⲩⲥϩⲓⲙ[ⲉ] ⲛⲁϥ ϩⲙ̄
ⲡⲙⲏϣⲉ ⲭⲉ ⲛⲉⲉⲓⲁⲧⲥ [ⲛ̄]ⲑⲏ
ⲛ̄ⲧⲁϩϥⲓ ϩⲁⲣⲟⲕ ⲁⲩⲱ ⲛ̄ⲕⲓ[ⲃ]ⲉ
ⲉⲛⲧⲁϩⲥⲁⲛⲟⲩϣⲕ

²ⲡⲉⲭⲁϥ ⲛⲁ[ⲥ] ⲭⲉ ⲛⲉⲉⲓⲁⲧⲟⲩ
ⲛ̄ⲛⲉⲛⲧⲁϩⲥⲱⲧⲙ̄ ⲁⲡⲗⲟⲅⲟⲥ
ⲙ̄ⲡⲉⲓⲱⲧ ⲁⲩⲁⲣⲉϩ ⲉⲣⲟϥ ϩⲛ̄ ⲟⲩⲙⲉ
³ⲟⲩⲛ̄ ϩⲛ̄ϩⲟⲟⲩ ⲅⲁⲣ ⲛⲁϣⲱⲡⲉ
ⲛ̄ⲧⲉⲧⲛ̄ⲭⲟⲟⲥ ⲭⲉ ⲛⲉⲉⲓⲁⲧⲉ̄ ⲛ̄ⲑⲏ
ⲧⲁⲉⲓ ⲉⲧⲉ ⲙ̄ⲡⲥⲱ ⲁⲩⲱ ⲛ̄ⲕⲓⲃⲉ ⲛⲁⲉⲓ
ⲉⲙⲡⲟⲩϯ ⲉⲣⲱⲧⲉ

80 ¹ⲡⲉⲭⲉ ⲓ̄ⲥ̄ ⲭⲉ ⲡⲉⲛⲧⲁϩⲥⲟⲩⲱⲛ
ⲡⲕⲟⲥⲙⲟⲥ ⲁϥϩⲉ ⲉⲡⲥⲱⲙⲁ
²ⲡⲉⲛⲧⲁϩϩⲉ ⲇⲉ ⲉⲡⲥⲱⲙⲁ
ⲡⲕⲟⲥⲙⲟⲥ ⲙ̄ⲡϣⲁ ⲙ̄ⲙⲟϥ ⲁⲛ

81 ¹ⲡⲉⲭⲉ ⲓ̄ⲥ̄ ⲭⲉ ⲡⲉⲛⲧⲁϩⲣ̄
ⲣⲙ̄ⲙⲁⲟ ⲙⲁⲣⲉϥⲣ̄ ⲣⲣⲟ ²ⲁⲩⲱ
ⲡⲉⲧⲉⲩⲛ̄ⲧⲁϥ ⲛ̄ⲟⲩⲇⲩⲛⲁⲙⲓⲥ
ⲙⲁⲣⲉϥⲁⲣⲛⲁ

82 ¹ⲡⲉⲭⲉ ⲓ̄ⲥ̄ ⲭⲉ ⲡⲉⲧϩⲏⲛ ⲉⲣⲟⲉⲓ
ⲉϥϩⲏⲛ ⲉⲧⲥⲁⲧⲉ ²ⲁⲩⲱ ⲡⲉⲧⲟⲩⲏⲩ
ⲙ̄ⲙⲟⲉⲓ ϥⲟⲩⲏⲩ ⲛ̄ⲧⲙⲛ̄ⲧⲉⲣⲟ

83 ¹ⲡⲉⲭⲉ ⲓ̄ⲥ̄ ⲭⲉ ⲛ̄ϩⲓⲕⲱⲛ
ⲥⲉⲟⲩⲟⲛϩ ⲉⲃⲟⲗ ⲙ̄ⲡⲣⲱⲙⲉ ⲁⲩⲱ
ⲡⲟⲩⲟⲉⲓⲛ ⲉⲧⲛ̄ϩⲏⲧⲟⲩ ϥϩⲏⲡ ϩⲛ̄
ⲑⲓⲕⲱⲛ ⲙ̄ⲡⲟⲩⲟⲉⲓⲛ ⲙ̄ⲡⲉⲓⲱⲧ

78 ¹Jesus said, "Why have you come out to the countryside? To see a reed shaken by the wind? ²And to see a person dressed in soft clothing, [like your] rulers and your powerful ones? ³They are dressed in soft clothing, and cannot understand truth."*

79 ¹A woman in the crowd said to him, "Blessed are the womb that bore you and the breasts that fed you."

²He said to [her], "Blessed are those who have heard the word of the Father and have truly kept it. ³For there will be days when you will say, 'Blessed are the womb that has not conceived and the breasts that have not given milk.'"

80 ¹Jesus said, "Whoever has come to know the world has discovered the body, ²and whoever has discovered the body, of that person the world is not worthy."

81 ¹Jesus said, "Let one who has become wealthy reign, ²and let one who has power renounce (it)."

82 ¹Jesus said, "Whoever is near me is near the fire, ²and whoever is far from me is far from the kingdom."

83 ¹Jesus said, "Images are visible to people, but the light within them is hidden in the image of the Father's light. ²He*

²ϥⲛⲁϭⲱⲗⲡ ⲉⲃⲟⲗ ⲁⲩⲱ ⲧⲉϥϩⲓⲕⲱⲛ
ϩⲏⲡ ⲉⲃⲟⲗ ϩⲓⲧⲛ̄ ⲡⲉϥⲟⲩⲟⲉⲓⲛ
84 ¹ⲡⲉⲝⲉ ⲓ̅ⲥ̅ ⲛ̄ϩⲟⲟⲩ ⲉⲧⲉⲧⲛ̄ⲛⲁⲩ
ⲉⲡⲉⲧⲛ̄ⲉⲓⲛⲉ ϣⲁⲣⲉⲧⲛ̄ⲣⲁϣⲉ
²ϩⲟⲧⲁⲛ ⲇⲉ ⲉⲧⲉⲧⲛ̄ϣⲁⲛⲛⲁⲩ
ⲁⲛⲉⲧⲛ̄ϩⲓⲕⲱⲛ ⲛ̄ⲧⲁϩϣⲱⲡⲉ ϩⲓ
ⲧⲉⲧⲛⲉϩ ⲟⲩⲧⲉ ⲙⲁⲩⲙⲟⲩ ⲟⲩⲧⲉ
ⲙⲁⲩⲟⲩⲱⲛϩ ⲉⲃⲟⲗ ⲧⲉⲧⲛⲁϥⲓ ϩⲁ
ⲟⲩⲏⲣ
85 ¹ⲡⲉⲝⲉ ⲓ̅ⲥ̅ ⲝⲉ ⲛ̄ⲧⲁ ⲁⲇⲁⲙ
ϣⲱⲡⲉ ⲉⲃⲟⲗ ϩⲛ̄ⲛⲟⲩⲛⲟϭ
ⲛ̄ⲇⲩⲛⲁⲙⲓⲥ ⲙⲛ̄ ⲟⲩⲛⲟϭ
ⲙ̄ⲙⲛ̄ⲧⲣⲙ̄ⲙⲁⲟ ⲁⲩⲱ ⲙ̄ⲡⲉϥϣⲱⲡⲉ
ⲉ[ϥⲙ̄]ⲡϣⲁ ⲙ̄ⲙⲱⲧⲛ̄ ²ⲛⲉⲩⲁϩⲓⲟⲥ
ⲅⲁⲣ ⲡⲉ [ⲛⲉϥⲛⲁϫⲓ] †ⲡ[ⲉ] ⲁⲛ
ⲙ̄ⲡⲙⲟⲩ
86 ¹ⲡⲉⲝⲉ ⲓ̅ⲥ̅ ⲝⲉ [ⲛⲃⲁϣⲟⲣ
ⲟⲩⲛ̄ⲧ]ⲁⲩ ⲛⲟⲩ[ⲃ]ⲏⲃ ⲁⲩⲱ
ⲛ̄ϩⲁⲗⲁⲧⲉ ⲟⲩⲛ̄ⲧⲁⲩ ⲙ̄ⲙⲁⲩ
ⲙ̄ⲡⲉⲩⲙⲁϩ ²ⲡϣⲏⲣⲉ ⲇⲉ ⲙ̄ⲡⲣⲱⲙⲉ
ⲙⲛ̄ⲧⲁϥ ⲛ̄ⲛ[ⲟ]ⲩⲙⲁ ⲉⲣⲓⲕⲉ ⲛ̄ⲧⲉϥⲁⲡⲉ
ⲛ̄ϥⲙ̄ⲧⲟⲛ ⲙ̄ⲙ[ⲟ]ϥ
87 ¹ⲡⲉⲝⲁϥ ⲛ̄ϭⲓ ⲓ̅ⲥ̅ ⲝⲉ
ⲟⲩⲧⲁⲗⲁⲓⲡⲱⲣⲟⲛ ⲡⲉ ⲡⲥⲱⲙⲁ
ⲉⲧⲁϣⲉ ⲛ̄ⲟⲩⲥⲱⲙⲁ ²ⲁⲩⲱ
ⲟⲩⲧⲁⲗⲁⲓⲡⲱⲣⲟⲥ ⲧⲉ ⲧⲯⲩⲭⲏ
ⲉⲧⲁϣⲉ ⲛ̄ⲛⲁⲉⲓ ⲙ̄ⲡⲥⲛⲁⲩ
88 ¹ⲡⲉⲝⲉ ⲓ̅ⲥ̅ ⲝⲉ ⲛ̄ⲁⲅⲅⲉⲗⲟⲥ ⲛⲏⲩ
ϣⲁⲣⲱⲧⲛ̄ ⲙⲛ̄ ⲛ̄ⲡⲣⲟⲫⲏⲧⲏⲥ ⲁⲩⲱ
ⲥⲉⲛⲁ† ⲛⲏⲧⲛ̄ ⲛ̄ⲛⲉⲧⲉⲩⲛ̄ⲧⲏⲧⲛ̄ⲥⲉ
²ⲁⲩⲱ ⲛ̄ⲧⲱⲧⲛ̄ ϩⲱⲧⲧⲏⲩⲧⲛ̄
ⲛⲉⲧⲛ̄ⲧⲟⲧⲧⲏⲛⲉ ⲧⲁⲁⲩ ⲛⲁⲩ
ⲛ̄ⲧⲉⲧⲛ̄ⲝⲟⲟⲥ ⲛⲏⲧⲛ̄ ⲝⲉ ⲁϣ ⲛ̄ϩⲟⲟⲩ
ⲡⲉⲧⲟⲩⲛ̄ⲛⲏⲩ ⲛ̄ⲥⲉⲝⲓ ⲡⲉⲧⲉ ⲡⲱⲟⲩ
89 ¹ⲡⲉⲝⲉ ⲓ̅ⲥ̅ ⲝⲉ ⲉⲧⲃⲉ ⲟⲩ
ⲧⲉⲧⲛ̄ⲉⲓⲱⲉ ⲙ̄ⲡⲥⲁ ⲛⲃⲟⲗ
ⲙ̄ⲡⲡⲟⲧⲏⲣⲓⲟⲛ ²ⲧⲉⲧⲛ̄ⲣ̄ⲛⲟⲉⲓ ⲁⲛ ⲝⲉ
ⲡⲉⲛⲧⲁϩⲧⲁⲙⲓⲟ ⲙ̄ⲡⲥⲁ ⲛϩⲟⲩⲛ ⲛ̄ⲧⲟϥ

will be disclosed, but his image is hidden by his light."

84 ¹Jesus said, "When you see your likeness, you are happy. ²But when you see your images that came into being before you and that neither die nor become visible, how much you will bear!"

85 ¹Jesus said, "Adam came from great power and great wealth, but he was not worthy of you. ²For had he been worthy, [he would] not [have tasted] death."

86 ¹Jesus said, "[Foxes have] their dens and birds have their nests, ²but the child of humankind has no place to lay his head and rest."

87 ¹Jesus said, "Wretched is the body that depends on a body, ²and wretched is the soul that depends on these two."

88 ¹Jesus said, "The messengers* and the prophets will come to you and give you what is yours. ²You, in turn, give them what you have, and say to yourselves, 'When will they come and take what is theirs?'"

89 ¹Jesus said, "Why do you wash the outside of the cup? ²Do you not understand that the one who made the inside is also the

ON ΠΕΝΤΑqΤΑΜΙΟ Μ̄ΠΟΑ ΝΒΟΛ

90 ¹ΠΕΧΕ ῙΗ̄Ϲ̄ ΧΕ ΑΜΗΕΙΤΝ̄
Ϣ̄ΑΡΟΕΙ ΧΕ ΟΥΧΡΗϹΤΟϹ ΠΕ
ΠΑΝΑϨΒ ΑΥΩ ΤΑΜΝ̄ΤΧΟΕΙϹ
ΟΥΡΜ̄ΡΑϢ ΤΕ ²ΑΥΩ ΤΕΤΝΑϨΕ
ΑΥΑΝΑΥΠΑϹΙϹ ΝΗΤΝ̄

91 ¹ΠΕΧΑΥ ΝΑq ΧΕ ΧΟΟϹ ΕΡΟΝ
ΧΕ Ν̄ΤΚ ΝΙΜ ϢΙΝΑ ΕΝΑΡ̄ΠΙϹΤΕΥΕ
ΕΡΟΚ

²ΠΕΧΑq ΝΑΥ ΧΕ ΤΕΤΝ̄Ρ̄ΠΙΡΑϨΕ
Μ̄ΠϨΟ Ν̄ΤΠΕ ΜΝ̄ ΠΚΑϨ ΑΥΩ
ΠΕΤΝ̄ΠΕΤΝ̄ΜΤΟ ΕΒΟΛ
Μ̄ΠΕΤΝ̄ϹΟΥΩΝq ΑΥΩ
ΠΕΕΙΚΑΙΡΟϹ ΤΕΤΝ̄ϹΟΟΥΝ ΑΝ
Ν̄Ρ̄ΠΙΡΑϨΕ Μ̄ΜΟq

92 ¹ΠΕΧΕ ῙϹ̄ ΧΕ ϢΙΝΕ ΑΥΩ
ΤΕΤΝΑ6ΙΝΕ ²ΑΛΛΑ
ΝΕΤΑΤΕΤΝ̄ΧΝΟΥΕΙ ΕΡΟΟΥ
Ν̄ΝΙϨΟΟΥ ΕΜ̄ΠΙΧΟΟΥ ΝΗΤΝ̄ Μ̄ΦΟΟΥ
ΕΤΜ̄ΜΑΥ ΤΕΝΟΥ ΕϨΝΑΪ ΕΧΟΟΥ
ΑΥΩ ΤΕΤΝ̄ϢΙΝΕ ΑΝ Ν̄ϹΩΟΥ

93 ¹Μ̄ΠΡ̄† ΠΕΤΟΥΑΑΒ Ν̄ΝΟΥϨΟΟΡ
ΧΕΚΑϹ ΝΟΥΝΟΧΟΥ ΕΤΚΟΠΡΙΑ
²Μ̄ΠΡ̄ΝΟΥΧΕ Ν̄Μ̄ΜΑΡΓΑΡΙΤΗ[Ϲ
Ν̄]ΝΕϢΑΥ ϢΙΝΑ ΧΕ ΝΟΥΑΑq
Ν̄ΛΑ[...]

94 ¹[ΠΕΧ]Ε ῙϹ̄ ΠΕΤϢΙΝΕ
qΝΑ6ΙΝΕ ²[ΠΕΤΤΩϨΜ̄ Ε]ϨΟΥΝ
ϹΕΝΑΟΥΩΝ ΝΑq

95 ¹[ΠΕΧΕ ῙϹ̄ ΧΕ] ΕϢΩΠΕ
ΟΥΝ̄ΤΗΤΝ̄ ϨΟΜΤ Μ̄ΠΡ̄† ΕΤΜΗϹΕ
²ΑΛΛΑ † [Μ̄ΜΟq]
Μ̄ΠΕΤ[Ε]ΤΝΑΧΙΤΟq ΑΝ Ν̄ΤΟΟΤq

96 ¹Π[ΕΧ]Ε ῙϹ̄ ΧΕ Τ̄ΜΝ̄ΤΕΡΟ
Μ̄ΠΕΙΩΤ ΕϹΤΝ̄ΤΩ[Ν ΑΥ]Ϲ̄ϨΙΜΕ
²ΑϹΧΙ Ν̄ΟΥΚΟΥΕΙ Ν̄ϹΑΕΙΡ
Α[ϹϨ]ΟΠq ϨΝ̄ ΟΥϢΩΤΕ ΑϹΑΑq
Ν̄ϨΝ̄ΝΟ[6 Ν̄]ΝΟΕΙΚ ³ΠΕΤΕΥΜ̄
ΜΑΑΧΕ Μ̄ΜΟq ΜΑ[ΡΕ]qϹΩΤΜ̄

---

one who made the outside?"

90 ¹Jesus said, "Come to me,
for my yoke is easy and my
lordship is gentle, ²and you will
find rest for yourselves."

91 ¹They said to him, "Tell us
who you are so that we may
believe in you."

²He said to them, "You examine the face of heaven and earth,
but you have not come to know
the one who is in your presence,
and you do not know how to
examine this moment."

92 ¹Jesus said, "Seek and you
will find. ²In the past, however, I
did not tell you the things about
which you asked me then. Now I
am willing to tell them, but you
are not seeking them.

93 ¹"Do not give what is holy
to dogs, lest they cast them upon
the dunghill. ²Do not cast pearls
[to] swine, lest they . . . it [. . .]."*

94 ¹Jesus [said], "One who
seeks will find, ²and to [one who
knocks] it will be opened."

95 ¹[Jesus said], "If you have
money, do not lend it at interest.
²Rather, give [it] to someone from
whom you will not get it back."

96 ¹Jesus [said], "The kingdom
of the Father is like [a] woman.
²She took a little yeast, [hid] it in
dough, and made it into large
loaves of bread. ³Whoever has
ears should hear."

97 ¹ⲡⲉϫⲉ ⲓⲥ ϫⲉ ⲧⲙⲛⲧⲉⲣⲟ
ⲙⲡⲉ[ⲓⲱⲧ ⲉ]ⲥⲧⲛⲧⲱⲛ ⲁⲩⲥϩⲓⲙⲉ
ⲉⲥϥⲓ ϩⲁ ⲟⲩϭⲗ[ⲙⲉⲉⲓ] ⲉϥⲙⲉϩ
ⲛⲛⲟⲉⲓⲧ ²ⲉⲥⲙⲟⲟϣⲉ ϩ[ⲓ ⲟⲩ]ϩⲓⲏ
ⲉⲥⲟⲩⲏⲟⲩ ⲁⲡⲙⲁⲁϫⲉ ⲙⲡϭⲗ[ⲉ]ⲉⲓ
ⲟⲩⲱϭⲡ ⲁⲡⲛⲟⲉⲓⲧ ϣⲟⲩⲟ ⲛⲥⲱⲥ [ϩ]ⲓ
ⲧⲉϩⲓⲏ ³ⲛⲉⲥⲥⲟⲟⲩⲛ ⲁⲛ ⲡⲉ ⲛⲉ
ⲙⲡⲉⲥⲉⲓⲙⲉ ⲉϩⲓⲥⲉ ⁴ⲛⲧⲁⲣⲉⲥⲡⲱϩ
ⲉϩⲟⲩⲛ ⲉⲡⲉⲥⲛⲉⲓ ⲁⲥⲕⲁ ⲡϭⲗⲙⲉⲉⲓ
ⲁⲡⲉⲥⲏⲧ ⲁⲥϩⲉ ⲉⲣⲟϥ ⲉϥϣⲟⲩⲉⲓⲧ

98 ¹ⲡⲉϫⲉ ⲓⲥ ⲧⲙⲛⲧⲉⲣⲟ ⲙⲡⲉⲓⲱⲧ
ⲉⲥⲧⲛⲧⲱⲛ ⲉⲩⲣⲱⲙⲉ ⲉϥⲟⲩⲱϣ
ⲉⲙⲟⲩⲧ ⲟⲩⲣⲱⲙⲉ ⲙⲙⲉⲅⲓⲥⲧⲁⲛⲟⲥ
²ⲁϥϣⲱⲗⲙ ⲛⲧⲥⲏϥⲉ ϩⲙ ⲡⲉϥⲏⲉⲓ
ⲁϥϫⲟⲧⲥ ⲛⲧϫⲟ ϫⲉⲕⲁⲁⲥ
ⲉϥⲛⲁⲉⲓⲙⲉ ϫⲉ ⲧⲉϥϭⲓϫ ⲛⲁⲧⲱⲕ
ⲉϩⲟⲩⲛ ³ⲧⲟⲧⲉ ⲁϥϩⲱⲧⲃ
ⲙⲡⲙⲉⲅⲓⲥⲧⲁⲛⲟⲥ

99 ¹ⲡⲉϫⲉ ⲙⲙⲁⲑⲏⲧⲏⲥ ⲛⲁϥ ϫⲉ
ⲛⲉⲕⲥⲛⲏⲩ ⲙⲛ ⲧⲉⲕⲙⲁⲁⲩ
ⲥⲉⲁϩⲉⲣⲁⲧⲟⲩ ϩⲓ ⲡⲥⲁ ⲛⲃⲟⲗ
²ⲡⲉϫⲁϥ ⲛⲁⲩ ϫⲉ ⲛⲉⲧⲛⲛⲉⲉⲓⲙⲁ
ⲉⲧⲣⲉ ⲙⲡⲟⲩⲱϣ ⲙⲡⲁⲉⲓⲱⲧ ⲛⲁⲉⲓ ⲛⲉ
ⲛⲁⲥⲛⲏⲩ ⲙⲛ ⲧⲁⲙⲁⲁⲩ ³ⲛⲧⲟⲟⲩ ⲡⲉ
ⲉⲧⲛⲁⲃⲱⲕ ⲉϩⲟⲩⲛ ⲉⲧⲙⲛⲧⲉⲣⲟ
ⲙⲡⲁⲉⲓⲱⲧ

100 ¹ⲁⲩⲧⲥⲉⲃⲉ ⲓⲥ ⲁⲩⲛⲟⲩⲃ ⲁⲩⲱ
ⲡⲉϫⲁⲩ ⲛⲁϥ ϫⲉ ⲛⲉⲧⲏⲡ ⲁⲕⲁⲓⲥⲁⲣ
ⲥⲉϣⲓⲧⲉ ⲙⲙⲟⲛ ⲛⲛϣⲱⲙ
²ⲡⲉϫⲁϥ ⲛⲁⲩ ϫⲉ ϯ ⲛⲁ ⲕⲁⲓⲥⲁⲣ
ⲛⲕⲁⲓⲥⲁⲣ ³ϯ ⲛⲁ ⲡⲛⲟⲩⲧⲉ
ⲙⲡⲛⲟⲩⲧⲉ ⁴ⲁⲩⲱ ⲡⲉⲧⲉ ⲡⲱⲉⲓ ⲡⲉ
ⲙⲁⲧⲛⲛⲁⲉⲓϥ

101 ¹ⲡⲉⲧⲁⲙⲉⲥⲧⲉ ⲡⲉϥⲉⲓ[ⲱⲧ] ⲁⲛ
ⲙⲛ ⲧⲉϥⲙⲁⲁⲩ ⲛⲧⲁϩⲉ ϥⲛⲁϣⲣ
ⲙ[ⲁⲑⲏⲧ]ⲏⲥ ⲛⲁⲉⲓ ⲁⲛ ²ⲁⲩⲱ
ⲡⲉⲧⲁⲙⲣⲣⲉ ⲡⲉϥ[ⲉⲓⲱⲧ ⲁⲛ ⲙ]ⲛ

---

97 ¹Jesus said, "The kingdom of the [Father] is like a woman who was carrying a [jar] full of meal. ²While she was walking on [a] distant road,* the handle of the jar broke and the meal spilled behind her [on] the road. ³She did not know it; she had not noticed a problem.* ⁴When she reached her house, she put the jar down and discovered that it was empty."

98 ¹Jesus said, "The kingdom of the Father is like a person who wanted to put someone powerful to death. ²He drew his sword at home and thrust it into the wall to find out whether his hand would go in.* ³Then he killed the powerful one."

99 ¹The disciples said to him, "Your brothers and your mother are standing outside."
²He said to them, "Those here who do the will of my Father are my brothers and my mother. ³They are the ones who will enter the kingdom of my Father."

100 ¹They showed Jesus a gold coin and said to him, "Caesar's people demand taxes from us."
²He said to them, "Give Caesar the things that are Caesar's, ³give God the things that are God's, ⁴and give me what is mine.

101 ¹"Whoever does not hate [father] and mother as I do cannot be a [disciple] of me, ²and whoever does [not] love [father

The Gospel of Thomas

ⲣⲁⲍⲉ ϥⲛⲁϣ̅ⲡ̅
.ⲥ ⲛⲁ]ⲉⲓ ⲁⲛ ³ⲧⲁⲙⲁⲁⲩ ⲅⲁⲣ
.[...........]ⲟⲗ ⲧⲁ[ⲙⲁⲁ]ⲩ ⲇⲉ
.ⲉ ⲁⲥϯ ⲛⲁⲉⲓ ⲙ̅ⲡⲱⲛϩ

102 ⲡⲉⲭⲉ ⲓ̅ⲥ̅ [ⲭⲉ ⲟ]ⲩⲟⲉⲓ ⲛⲁⲩ
ⲙ̅ⲫⲁⲣⲓⲥⲁⲓⲟⲥ ⲭⲉ ⲉⲅⲉⲓⲛⲉ
[ⲛ̅ⲛ]ⲟⲩⲟⲩϩⲟⲣ ⲉϥⲛ̅ⲕⲟⲧⲕ ϩⲓⲭⲛ̅
ⲡⲟⲩⲟⲛⲉϥ ⲛ̅ϩ[ⲛ̅]ⲛⲉϩⲟⲟⲩ ⲭⲉ ⲟⲩⲧⲉ
ϥⲟⲩⲱⲙ ⲁⲛ ⲟⲩⲧⲉ ϥⲕ[ⲱ] ⲁⲛ
ⲛ̅ⲛⲉϩⲟⲟⲩ ⲉⲟⲩⲱⲙ

103 ⲡⲉⲭⲉ ⲓ̅ⲥ̅ ⲭⲉ ⲟⲩⲙⲁ[ⲕⲁ]ⲣⲓⲟⲥ
ⲡⲉ ⲡⲣⲱⲙⲉ ⲡⲁⲉⲓ ⲉⲧⲥⲟⲟⲩⲛ ⲭⲉ ϩ[ⲛ̅
ⲁϣ] ⲙ̅ⲙⲉⲣⲟⲥ ⲉⲛⲗⲏⲥⲧⲏⲥ ⲛⲏⲩ
ⲉϩⲟⲩⲛ ϣⲓⲛⲁ [ⲉϥ]ⲛⲁⲧⲱⲟⲩⲛ
ⲛ̅ϥⲥⲱⲟⲩϩ ⲛ̅ⲧⲉϥⲙⲛ̅ⲧⲉ[ⲣⲟ] ⲛ̅ϥⲙⲟⲩⲣ
ⲙ̅ⲙⲟϥ ⲉⲭⲛ̅ ⲧⲉϥϯ̅ⲡⲉ ϩ[ⲁ] ⲧⲉϩⲏ
ⲉⲙⲡⲁⲧⲟⲩⲉⲓ ⲉϩⲟⲩⲛ

104 ¹ⲡⲉⲭⲁⲩ ⲛ̅[ⲓ̅]ⲥ̅ ⲭⲉ ⲁⲙⲟⲩ
ⲛ̅ⲧⲛ̅ϣⲗⲏⲗ ⲙ̅ⲡⲟⲟⲩ ⲁⲩⲱ
ⲛ̅ⲧⲛ̅ⲣ̅ⲛⲏⲥⲧⲉⲩⲉ

²ⲡⲉⲭⲉ ⲓ̅ⲥ̅ ⲭⲉ ⲟⲩ ⲅⲁⲣ ⲡⲉ ⲡⲛⲟⲃⲉ
ⲛ̅ⲧⲁⲉⲓⲁⲁϥ ⲏ ⲛ̅ⲧⲁⲩⲭⲣⲟ ⲉⲣⲟⲉⲓ ϩⲛ̅
ⲟⲩ ³ⲁⲗⲗⲁ ϩⲟⲧⲁⲛ ⲉⲣϣⲁⲛ
ⲡⲛⲩⲙⲫⲓⲟⲥ ⲉⲓ ⲉⲃⲟⲗ ϩⲙ̅ ⲡⲛⲩⲙⲫⲱⲛ
ⲧⲟⲧⲉ ⲙⲁⲣⲟⲩⲛⲏⲥⲧⲉⲩⲉ ⲁⲩⲱ
ⲙⲁⲣⲟⲩϣⲗⲏⲗ

105 ⲡⲉⲭⲉ ⲓ̅ⲥ̅ ⲭⲉ ⲡⲉⲧⲛⲁⲥⲟⲩⲱⲛ
ⲡⲉⲓⲱⲧ ⲙⲛ̅ ⲧⲙⲁⲁⲩ ⲥⲉⲛⲁⲙⲟⲩⲧⲉ
ⲉⲣⲟϥ ⲭⲉ ⲡϣⲏⲣⲉ ⲙ̅ⲡⲟⲣⲛⲏ

106 ¹ⲡⲉⲭⲉ ⲓ̅ⲥ̅ ⲭⲉ ϩⲟⲧⲁⲛ
ⲉⲧⲉⲧⲛ̅ϣⲁⲣ̅ ⲡⲥⲛⲁⲩ ⲟⲩⲁ
ⲧⲉⲧⲛⲁϣⲱⲡⲉ ⲛ̅ϣⲏⲣⲉ ⲙ̅ⲡⲣⲱⲙⲉ
²ⲁⲩⲱ ⲉⲧⲉⲧⲛ̅ϣⲁⲛⲭⲟⲟⲥ ⲭⲉ
ⲡⲧⲟⲟⲩ ⲡⲱⲱⲛⲉ ⲉⲃⲟⲗ ϥⲛⲁⲡⲱⲱⲛⲉ

107 ¹ⲡⲉⲭⲉ ⲓ̅ⲥ̅ ⲭⲉ ⲧⲙⲛ̅ⲧⲉⲣⲟ
ⲉⲥⲧⲛ̅ⲧⲱⲛ ⲉⲩⲣⲱⲙⲉ ⲛ̅ϣⲱⲥ
ⲉⲩⲛ̅ⲧⲁϥ ⲙ̅ⲙⲁⲩ ⲛ̅ϣⲉ ⲛ̅ⲉⲥⲟⲟⲩ
²ⲁⲟⲩⲁ ⲛ̅ϩⲏⲧⲟⲩ ⲥⲱⲣⲙ ⲉⲡⲛⲟϭ ⲡⲉ

---

and] mother as I do cannot be a [disciple of] me. ³For my mother [. . .],* but my true [mother] gave me life."

102 Jesus said, "Woe to the Pharisees, for they are like a dog sleeping in the manger of cattle, for it neither eats nor [lets] the cattle eat."

103 Jesus said, "Blessed is the person who knows where the robbers are going to enter, so that [he] may arise, bring together his domain, and gird himself before they enter."

104 ¹They said to Jesus, "Come, let us pray today, and let us fast."

²Jesus said, "What sin have I committed, or how have I been undone? ³Rather, when the bridegroom leaves the wedding chamber, then let people fast and pray."

105 Jesus said, "Whoever knows the father and the mother will be called the child of a whore."

106 ¹Jesus said, "When you make the two into one, you will become children of humankind, ²and when you say, 'Mountain, move from here!' it will move."

107 ¹Jesus said, "The kingdom is like a shepherd who had a hundred sheep. ²One of them, the largest, went astray. He left

ⲁϥⲕⲱ ⲙ̄ⲡⲥⲧⲉⲯⲓⲧ ⲁϥϣⲓⲛⲉ ⲛ̄ⲥⲁ
ⲡⲓⲟⲩⲁ ϣⲁⲛⲧⲉϥϩⲉ ⲉⲣⲟϥ
³ⲛ̄ⲧⲁⲣⲉϥϩⲓⲥⲉ ⲡⲉⲭⲁϥ ⲙ̄ⲡⲉⲥⲟⲟⲩ
ⲭⲉ ϯⲟⲩⲟϣⲕ ⲡⲁⲣⲁ ⲡⲥⲧⲉⲯⲓⲧ

108 ¹ⲡⲉⲭⲉ ⲓ̄ⲥ̄ ⲭⲉ ⲡⲉⲧⲁⲥⲱ ⲉⲃⲟⲗ
ϩⲛ̄ ⲧⲁⲧⲁⲡⲣⲟ ϥⲛⲁϣⲱⲡⲉ ⲛ̄ⲧⲁϩⲉ
²ⲁⲛⲟⲕ ϩⲱ ϯⲛⲁϣⲱⲡⲉ ⲉⲛⲧⲟϥ ⲡⲉ
³ⲁⲩⲱ ⲛⲉⲑⲏⲡ ⲛⲁⲟⲩⲱⲛϩ ⲉⲣⲟϥ

109 ¹ⲡⲉⲭⲉ ⲓ̄ⲥ̄ ⲭⲉ ⲧⲙ̄ⲛ̄ⲧⲉⲣⲟ
ⲉⲥⲧⲛ̄ⲧⲱⲛ ⲉⲩⲣⲱⲙⲉ ⲉⲩⲛ̄ⲧⲁϥ ⲙ̄ⲙⲁⲩ
ϩⲛ̄ ⲧⲉϥⲥⲱϣⲉ ⲛ̄ⲛⲟⲩⲉϩⲟ ⲉϥϩⲏ[ⲡ
ⲉ]ϥⲟ ⲛ̄ⲁⲧⲥⲟⲟⲩⲛ ⲉⲣⲟϥ ²ⲁⲩⲱ
ⲙ̄[ⲙⲛ̄ⲛⲥⲁ ⲧ]ⲣⲉϥⲙⲟⲩ ⲁϥⲕⲁⲁϥ
ⲙ̄ⲡⲉϥ[ϣⲏⲣⲉ ⲛⲉ] ⲡϣⲏⲣⲉ ⲥⲟⲟⲩⲛ
ⲁⲛ ⲁϥϥⲓ ⲧⲥⲱϣⲉ ⲉⲧⲙ̄ⲙⲁⲩ
ⲁϥⲧⲁⲁⲥ [ⲉⲃⲟ]ⲗ ³ⲁⲩⲱ
ⲡⲉ[ⲛ]ⲧⲁϩⲧⲟⲟⲩⲥ ⲁϥⲉⲓ ⲉϥⲥⲕⲁⲉⲓ
ⲁ[ϥϩ]ⲉ ⲁⲡⲉϩⲟ ⲁϥⲁⲣⲭⲉⲓ ⲛ̄ϯ ϩⲟⲙⲧ
ⲉⲧⲙⲏⲥⲉ ⲛ̄[ⲛⲉ]ⲧϥ̄ⲟⲩⲟϣⲟⲩ

110 ⲡⲉⲭⲉ ⲓ̄ⲥ̄ ⲭⲉ ⲡⲉⲛⲧⲁϩϭⲓⲛⲉ
ⲙ̄ⲡⲕⲟⲥⲙⲟⲥ ⲛ̄ϥⲣ̄ ⲣ̄ⲙⲙⲁⲟ
ⲙⲁⲣⲉϥⲁⲣⲛⲁ ⲙ̄ⲡⲕⲟⲥⲙⲟⲥ

111 ¹ⲡⲉⲭⲉ ⲓ̄ⲥ̄ ⲭⲉ ⲙ̄ⲡⲏⲩⲉ ⲛⲁϭⲱⲗ
ⲁⲩⲱ ⲡⲕⲁϩ ⲙ̄ⲡⲉⲧⲛ̄ⲙ̄ⲧⲟ ⲉⲃⲟⲗ
²ⲁⲩⲱ ⲡⲉⲧⲟⲛϩ ⲉⲃⲟⲗ ϩⲛ̄ ⲡⲉⲧⲟⲛϩ
ϥⲛⲁⲛⲁⲩ ⲁⲛ ⲉⲙⲟⲩ ³ⲟⲩⲭ ϩⲟⲧⲓ ⲉⲓ̄ⲥ̄
ⲭⲱ ⲙ̄ⲙⲟⲥ ⲭⲉ ⲡⲉⲧⲁϩⲉ ⲉⲣⲟϥ
ⲟⲩⲁⲁϥ ⲡⲕⲟⲥⲙⲟⲥ ⲙ̄ⲡϣⲁ ⲙ̄ⲙⲟϥ ⲁⲛ

112 ¹ⲡⲉⲭⲉ ⲓ̄ⲥ̄ ⲭⲉ ⲟⲩⲟⲉⲓ ⲛ̄ⲧⲥⲁⲣⲝ
ⲧⲁⲉⲓ ⲉⲧⲟϣⲉ ⲛ̄ⲧⲯⲩⲭⲏ ²ⲟⲩⲟⲉⲓ
ⲛ̄ⲧⲯⲩⲭⲏ ⲧⲁⲉⲓ ⲉⲧⲟϣⲉ ⲛ̄ⲧⲥⲁⲣⲝ

113 ¹ⲡⲉⲭⲁⲩ ⲛⲁϥ ⲛ̄ϭⲓ

the ninety-nine and sought the one until he found it. ³After he had toiled, he said to the sheep, 'I love you more than the ninety-nine.'"

108 ¹Jesus said, "Whoever drinks from my mouth will become like me; ²I myself shall become that person, ³and the hidden things will be revealed to that one."

Drink words from my mouth?

109 ¹Jesus said, "The kingdom is like a person who had a treasure hidden in his field but did not know it. ²[At] death he left it to his [son]. The son [did] not know (about it). He took over the field and sold it. ³The buyer went plowing, [discovered] the treasure, and began to lend money at interest to whomever he wished."

110 Jesus said, "Let one who has found the world, and has become wealthy, renounce the world."

111 ¹Jesus said, "The heavens and the earth will roll up in your presence, ²and whoever is living from the living one will not see death." ³Does not Jesus say, "Whoever has found oneself, of that person the world is not worthy?"

112 ¹Jesus said, "Woe to the flesh that depends on the soul. ²Woe to the soul that depends on the flesh."

113 ¹His disciples said to him,

The Gospel of Thomas

꜀ ϫⲉ ⲧⲙ̄ⲧⲉⲣⲟ
.ⲁϣ ⲛ̄ϩⲟⲟⲩ
ⲛ̄ⲏⲩ ⲁⲛ ϩⲛ̄ ⲟⲩϭⲱϣⲧ ⲉⲃⲟⲗ
ⲛⲁϫⲟⲟⲥ ⲁⲛ ϫⲉ ⲉⲓⲥϩⲏⲏⲧⲉ
ⲙ̄ⲡⲓⲥⲁ ⲏ ⲉⲓⲥϩⲏⲏⲧⲉ ⲧⲏ ⁴ⲁⲗⲗⲁ
ⲧⲙ̄ⲧⲉⲣⲟ ⲙ̄ⲡⲉⲓⲱⲧ ⲉⲥⲡⲟⲣϣ̄ ⲉⲃⲟⲗ
ϩⲓϫⲙ̄ ⲡⲕⲁϩ ⲁⲩⲱ ⲣ̄ⲣⲱⲙⲉ ⲛⲁⲩ ⲁⲛ
ⲉⲣⲟⲥ

114 ¹ⲡⲉϫⲉ ⲥⲓⲙⲱⲛ ⲡⲉⲧⲣⲟⲥ ⲛⲁⲩ
ϫⲉ ⲙⲁⲣⲉ ⲙⲁⲣⲓϩⲁⲙ ⲉⲓ ⲉⲃⲟⲗ ⲛ̄ϩⲏⲧⲛ̄
ϫⲉ ⲛ̄ⲥϩⲓⲟⲙⲉ ⲙ̄ⲡϣⲁ ⲁⲛ ⲙ̄ⲡⲱⲛϩ
²ⲡⲉϫⲉ ⲓ̄ⲥ̄ ϫⲉ ⲉⲓⲥϩⲏⲏⲧⲉ ⲁⲛⲟⲕ
ϯⲛⲁⲥⲱⲕ ⲙ̄ⲙⲟⲥ ϫⲉⲕⲁⲁⲥ ⲉⲉⲓⲛⲁⲁⲥ
ⲛ̄ϩⲟⲟⲩⲧ ϣⲓⲛⲁ ⲉⲥⲛⲁϣⲱⲡⲉ ϩⲱⲱⲥ
ⲛ̄ⲟⲩⲡⲛ̄ⲁ̄ ⲉϥⲟⲛϩ ⲉϥⲉⲓⲛⲉ ⲙ̄ⲙⲱⲧⲛ̄
ⲛ̄ϩⲟⲟⲩⲧ ³ϫⲉ ⲥϩⲓⲙⲉ ⲛⲓⲙ ⲉⲥⲛⲁⲁⲥ
ⲛ̄ϩⲟⲟⲩⲧ ⲥⲛⲁⲃⲱⲕ ⲉϩⲟⲩⲛ
ⲉⲧⲙⲛ̄ⲧⲉⲣⲟ ⲛⲙ̄ⲡⲏⲩⲉ

"When will the kingdom come?"
²"It will not come by watching for it. ³It will not be said,* 'Behold, here' or 'Behold, there.' ⁴Rather, the kingdom of the Father is spread out upon the earth, and people do not see it."

114 ¹Simon Peter said to them, "Let Mary leave us, for females are not worthy of life."
²Jesus said, "Behold, I shall guide her to make her male, so that she too may become a living spirit resembling you males. ³For every female who makes herself male will enter the kingdom of heaven."

Notes

8:3   or: *without any difficulty*
13:5   or: *I am not your teacher, for you have drunk and have become intoxicated*
14:4   literally: *in the places*
20:2   perhaps: *It is like a mustard seed, the tiniest . . .*
21:4   or: *to give it back to them and return their field to them*
22:5   or: *in order that you may make male and female into a single one,*
24:3   or: *and he shines on the whole world. If he does not shine, he is dark.*
33:1   *in the other ear*; this difficult phrase may well represent an instance of dittography; otherwise the phrase may indicate someone else's ear, or even one's own "inner" ear.
46:1   *averted*; literally: *be broken*
52:1   literally: *in you*
53:2   literally: *them*
57:3   *the workers*; literally: *them*
58   or: *suffered*
60:1   ⟨*He saw*⟩: this restoration is based on a suggested omission due to haplography (an omission occasioned by skipping from one sound to another

similar sound). The restoration ⟨*They saw*⟩ is also possible.
60:2   The text is uncertain and probably corrupt. A possible reading is: ⟨*Why does*⟩ *that person* ⟨*carry*⟩ *around the lamb?* The text may be taken literally to read: *That person is around the lamb.*
61:2   *someone*; literally: *as from one.* The meaning of the text is uncertain. Possibly: *as if you are from someone special.*
61:3   or: *integrated*
61:5   The Coptic word may be translated, without emendation, as *desolate.*
65:1   The text may be restored to read: *A* [*creditor*], or: *A* [*good*] *person.*
65:4   Possibly correct the text to read: ⟨*they*⟩ *did not know* ⟨*him*⟩.
74   *He said*; probably read: *Someone said.* Sayings 73–75 may very well constitute a brief dialogue.
   drinking trough; possibly correct to read: *well.*
   or: *no one*
76:3   *his*; probably read: *the*

78:3 or: *and your powerful ones,* ³*who are dressed in soft clothing, and cannot understand truth?*

83:2 or: *It*

88:1 or: *angels*

93:2 None of the suggested restorations has proved to be convincing. The following may be noted: *lest they make [mud] of it; lest they bring it to [naught]; lest they grind it [to bits].*

97:2 or: *on [the] road, still far off* (restoration proposed by Bentley Layton)

97:3 or: *she had not understood how to toil.*

98:2 *go in;* or: *be strong enough*

101:3 The lacuna cannot be restored with confidence. One proposal: *For my mother [gave me falsehood]*

113:3 or: *They will not say*

The Gospel of Thomas

GREEK FRAGMENTS

Prologue (POxy 654)

These are the [secret] sayings [that] the living Jesus spoke, [and Judas, who is] also (called) Thomas, [recorded].

1 (POxy 654)

1 And he said, "[Whoever finds the interpretation] of these sayings will not taste [death]."

2 (POxy 654)

2 ¹[Jesus says], "Let one who [seeks] not stop [seeking until] one finds. ²When one finds, [one will be astounded, ³and having been] astounded, one will reign, ⁴and [having reigned], one will [rest]."

3 (POxy 654)

3 ¹Jesus says, "[If] your leaders [say to you, 'Behold], the kingdom is in heaven,' the birds of heaven [will precede you. ²If they say] that it is under the earth, the fish of the sea [will enter, preceding] you. ³And the [kingdom of God] is within you [and outside (you). ⁴Whoever] knows [oneself] will find this. [And when you] know yourselves, [you will understand that] you

are [children] of the [living] Father. ⁵[But if] you do [not] know yourselves, [you are] in [poverty], and you are the [poverty]."

4 (POxy 654)

4 ¹[Jesus says], "A [person old in] days will not hesitate to ask a [little child seven days] old about the place of [life, and] that person will [live]. ²For many of the [first] will be [last, and] the last first, ³and they [will become one]."

5 (POxy 654)

5 ¹Jesus says, "[Know what is before] your face, and [what is hidden] from you will be disclosed [to you. ²For there is nothing] hidden that [will] not [become] manifest, ³and (nothing) buried that [will not be raised]."

6 (POxy 654)

6 ¹[His disciples] ask him [and] say, "How [shall we] fast? [How shall] we [pray]? How [shall we give alms]? What [diet] shall [we] observe?"

²Jesus says, "[Do not lie, ³and] do

not do [what] you [hate, ⁴because all things are apparent before] truth. ⁵[For there is nothing] hidden [that will not be manifest]."

7 (POxy 654)

7 ¹[... "Blessed] is [the lion that a human eats, so that* the lion] will be [human. ²And cursed is the human] that [a lion eats . . .]."

24 (POxy 655)

24³"[...] There [is light within a person] of light, [and it shines on the whole] world. [If it does not shine, then] it is [dark]."*

26 (POxy 1)

26²"[...] and then you will see clearly to take out the speck that is in your brother's eye."

27 (POxy 1)

27 ¹Jesus says, "If you do not fast from the world, you will not find the kingdom of God. ²And if you do not keep the sabbath a sabbath, you will not see the Father.

28 (POxy 1)

28 ¹Jesus says, "I took my stand in the midst of the world, and in flesh I appeared to them. ²I found them all drunk, and I found none of them thirsty. ³My soul aches for the children of humanity, because they are blind in their hearts and [do not] see, [for ...]."

29 (POxy 1)

29³"[... comes to dwell in this] poverty."

30 & 77 (POxy 1)

30 ¹[Jesus says], "Where there are [three, they are without] God,* ²and where there is only [one], I say, I am

with that one.

77 ² "Lift up the stone, and you will find me there. ³Split the piece of wood, and I am there."

31 (POxy 1)

31 ¹Jesus says, "A prophet is not acceptable in the prophet's own town,* ²nor does a doctor perform healings on those who know the doctor."

32 (POxy 1)

32 Jesus says, "A city built on top of a high hill and fortified can neither fall nor be hidden."

33 (POxy 1)

33 ¹Jesus says, "⟨What⟩ you hear in one ear of yours [proclaim ...]."

36 (POxy 655)

36¹[Jesus says, "Do not worry], from morning [to evening nor] from [evening to] morning, either [about] your [food], what [you will] eat, [or] about [your clothing], what you [will] wear. ²[You are much] better than the lilies, which do not card nor [spin]. ³As for you, when you have no garment, what [will you put] on? ⁴Who might add to your stature? That very one will give you your garment."

37 (POxy 655)

37 ¹His disciples say to him, "When will you be revealed to us, and when shall we see you?"

²He says, "When you strip and are not ashamed, ³[... and you will not be afraid]."

38 (POxy 655)

38 ¹[Jesus says, "Often you have desired to hear these sayings of mine], and [you have no one else from whom

to hear (them)]. [2]And [there will come days when you will seek me and you will not find me]."

39 (POxy 655)

39 [1][Jesus says, "The Pharisees and the scribes] have [taken the keys] of [knowlege; they themselves have] hidden [them. [2]Neither] have [they] entered, [nor] have they [allowed those who are in the process of] entering [to enter. [3]As for you, be as shrewd] as [snakes and as] innocent [as doves]."

77 (POxy 1)

(see 30)

4 (Hippolytus, Ref. 5.7.20–21)

[20]⟨And⟩ not only the mysteries of the Assyrians and the Phrygians ⟨but also those of the Egyptians⟩, they say, bear witness to their doctrine about the blessed nature, both hidden and revealed, of what has been and is and is yet to be, which, he says, is ⟨the⟩ kingdom of heaven within humanity which is sought, concerning which they explicitly teach in the Gospel entitled According to Thomas, saying thus, *"One who seeks will find me in children from seven years, for there, hidden in the fourteenth age, I am revealed."*

[21]And this is not of Christ, but of Hippocrates, saying, "A child of seven years is half a father." Hence, having placed the generative nature of all in the generative seed, and having heard the Hippocratic (saying) that a child of seven years is half a father, they say that one is revealed at four⟨teen⟩ years according to Thomas. This is the unutterable and mystical doctrine they have.

Notes

7:1	[*so that*]; literally: [*and*]
24:3	*it; it* may be translated *he* throughout this saying.
30:1	[*without*] God; others read: *gods (deities)*.
31:1	or: *country*

Q – Thomas Parallels

	Q	Thomas		Q	Thomas
1.	11:9	2:1	21.	6:45a	45:2
2.	12:2	5:2	22.	6:45b	45:3
3.	[11:1–4]	6:1–2	23.	7:28	46:1
4.	12:2	6:3	24.	16:13	47:2
5.	[16:17]	11:1	25.	6:20b	54
6.	12:51–53	16:1–4	26.	14:26–27	55
7.	[10:23–24]	17	27.	[6:22]	58
8.	12:39	21:3	28.	14:15–24	64:1–12
9.	6:41–42	26:1–2	28.	6:22–23	68:1–2, 69:1
10.	12:3	33:1	30.	6:21a	69:2
11.	11:33	33:2–3	31.	10:2	73
12.	6:39	34	32.	7:24–26	78:1–3
13.	11:21–22	35:1–2	33.	9:58	86:1–2
14.	12:22–30	36	34.	11:39–41	89:1–2
15.	[10:23–24]	38:1	35.	11:9	92:1
16.	11:52	39:1–2	36.	6:34–35a	95:1–2
17.	19:26	41:1–2	37.	13:20–21	96:1–2
18.	6:43–44a	43:3	38.	14:26–27	101:1–3
19.	12:10	44:1–3	39.	12:39	103
20.	6:44b	45:1	40.	15:3–7	107:1–3

The references in square brackets [ ] are rough parallels.

Glossary

Abgar Legend: The account of a legendary correspondence between Jesus and King Abgar V Ukkama of Edessa. The earliest attestation for the legend is in the *Ecclesiastical History* of Eusebius (early fourth century C.E.), who claims to have gotten it from the archives of Edessa.

Aboth: see Pirke Aboth

Acts of Thomas: The legendary accounts of the deeds of the apostle Judas Thomas (probably to be identified with Judas Didymos Thomas of the Gospel of Thomas), written in the style of Hellenistic romance literature. The Acts of Thomas tell of Thomas' missionary journeys east, to Parthia and eventually to India. In these adventuresome tales Thomas preaches the values of asceticicm and gnosis as the path to salvation. It contains, among other things, the well-known *Hymn of the Pearl*, one of the most eloquent poetic rehearsals of the gnostic myth of origins to survive antiquity.

Ahikar: The hero of a folk legend in which he is, successively, advisor to Sennacherib, king of Assyria; betrayed by his adopted son and sentenced to death; saved and hidden by a friendly officer; restored to his original position, after which he "instructs" his unworthy son. The story originated sometime from the fifth to the seventh centuries B.C.E. and became widely known in the Near East. There are several parallels to the wisdom of Ahikar in the New Testament.

Apocalyptic/Apocalypticism: A type of religious thinking characterized by the notion that through an act of divine intervention, the present evil world is about to be destroyed and replaced with a new and better world in which God's justice prevails. Apocalyptic schemes usually involve a moment of judgment, in which persons are called upon to answer for the evil of the world, and are either acquitted to salvation in the new world, or convicted to suffer divine punishment or destruction.

Clement of Alexandria (ca. 150–215 C.E.): The head of a well-known Christian school for catechumens in Alexandria, widely regarded as one of the most learned persons of his time. Among his many works are the *Stromateis*, which deal extensively with the question of the relationship between Christian faith and Greek philosophy. A recently discovered letter of Clement contains excerpts from a secret version of the Gospel of Mark, which presumably circulated in Egypt during the second century C.E.

1 Clement: A letter written from Clement, bishop of Rome (92–101 C.E.), to the church at Corinth. Clusters of sayings are found in 1 Clement 13:1-2, 46:7-8.

chreia (or chria), plural **chreiai** (or chriae): A brief story or anecdote that reaches its climax in a striking saying or action. The chreia is often called a pronouncement story by New Testament scholars following a convention adopted by form critics.

deuteronomistic: The theological framework within which the principal historical books of the Old Testament were conceived: Israel disobeys God; Israel is punished, usually by one of her enemies; Israel cries out for help; Israel receives forgiveness and is restored. The prophets played a role in this cycle of events: they condemned Israel for her apostasy; they were crushed by opponents; they led Israel in repenting; they held out fresh hope to a redeemed people.

Cyril of Jerusalem (ca. 315–386 C.E.): Bishop of Jerusalem from 348 until his death. In the fourth century conflicts over Arianism he was expelled from his See three times, but eventually restored each time. Among his writings, twenty-four catechetical lectures and one homily (on John 5:5) have survived.

Dead Sea Scrolls: The writings of a sectarian Jewish community (possibly Essene), which lived in a fortified community atop the cliffs overlooking the Dead Sea. The collection of scrolls was discovered in 1947 in a series of caves near the site of the ancient community. The collection contains a variety of writings, including biblical texts, commentaries, and tractates of the sect.

Didache: A Greek term meaning "teaching." It is also the name of an early Christian tractate or compendium of instruction, an incipient catechism, now included in the collection of early Christian works called the Apostolic Fathers. The final form of the Didache, which was discovered in 1875, dates from at least the early second century C.E., but its main sections go back to the first century C.E.

Didymos Judas Thomas: The author to whom the Gospel of Thomas is attributed in its incipit. Didymos and Thomas are the Greek and Syriac words for "twin," so the name probably means something like Judas the Twin.

Epiphanius (ca. 315–403 C.E.): Bishop of Salamis (Cyprus), noted defender of orthodoxy in the fourth century. His best known work is the *Panarion* (or "Medicine Chest"), which aims to diagnose and offer the antidote for a host of ancient Christian heresies.

Ephraem of Syria (ca. 306–373 C.E.): Perhaps the most influential teacher of the Syrian church, first as a monk and deacon in Nisibis, then as the founder of the "Persian School" in Edessa. He wrote widely, including many commentaries and published sermons.

form criticism: A method of studying the oral traditions that were collected into the writings of early Christianity, especially the gospels. Developed originally to study the folklore and stories belonging to the Hebrew Bible, form criticism focuses on the typical forms various types of orally transmitted material tends to take, and correlates each of these typical forms with a particular type of situation in the life of the community which used the tradition—e.g., worship, preaching/recruitment, instruction, etc. Rudolph

Bultmann and Martin Dibelius adapted the method to deal with the oral traditions which have been incorporated into the canonical gospels, Matthew, Mark, and Luke.

genre: A composition of any kind characterized by a particular style, form, or content, or a combination of these features. A genre is thus a class or species of literature, painting, musical composition, etc. The novel, epic, gospel are examples of literary genres (German: *Gattung*).

gnosticism/gnosic/gnosis: Gnosticism is a religious movement widespread in antiquity, which in general terms focused on the world as a place of fallenness and evil, the illegitimate creation of a rebellious demi-god. Gnostics believed that their origin is not this world of evil, but a higher realm wherein dwells the one true God, who, through a messenger or redeemer, has seen fit to send forth to them the knowledge (*gnosis*) of their true heavenly home. Armed with this *gnosis*, the Gnostic seeks to break free from the world and its rebellious creator, to be reunited with the godhead in the heavenly realm above. Gnosticism was characteristically very adaptable and manifested itself in numerous forms, attaching to and transforming older traditional religious systems, such as Judaism or Christianity. The second century C.E. saw the greatest flowering of Christian Gnostic groups, among them Valentinians, Naasenes, and the like. In the east Gnosticism in the form of Manichaeism spread throughout Persia, Central Asia, and eventually as far as China.

Gospel of the Ebionites: A second-century C.E. gospel used by a Greek-speaking, Jewish-Christian group known as the Ebionites, who flourished in the second and third centuries C.E. No copy of this gospel survived antiquity, but several quotations from it in the work of Epiphanius indicate that it was a narrative gospel, much like the canonical gospels, Matthew, Mark, Luke, and John.

Gospel of the Hebrews: A gospel written sometime in the late first or early second century C.E. in Egypt. A copy of this gospel did not survive antiquity, but several quotations from it in the works of various church fathers provide some indication of its contents. Among other things, it was concerned with Jesus' pre-existence, and narrated at least one post-resurrection appearance to James.

Gospel of Mary: A second-century C.E. Gnostic tractate in which the resurrected Jesus encounters the disciples and answers their questions. The motif of resurrection appearances in which the risen Lord reveals new and marvelous information to the disciples is the basis of a popular genre of literature, used primarily in Gnostic circles. In the second half of the tractate the focus is on Mary, who tells the disciples of the special revelation Jesus has imparted to her.

Gospel of Thomas: A sayings gospel, or collection of Jesus sayings, written originally in Greek, and dating from the second half of the first century C.E. In form it is similar to Q, but its content differs substantially from that of Q. In addition to providing independent attestation for a number of Jesus' sayings already known from the canonical gospels, it also preserves many previously unknown sayings attributed to Jesus. It survived antiquity in one complete copy, a Coptic version found among the tractates in the Nag Hammadi library, and in three Greek fragments known as POxy 1, POxy 654, and POxy 655.

Hippolytus (d. 235 C.E.): A learned theologian of Rome. He opposed Pope Callistus when the latter appeared to be too lax on the issue of penance for fornication, and was elected bishop of Rome by a small but powerful group of dissidents in the Roman church, thus becoming the first anti-Pope. The schism was not resolved until shortly before his death. He wrote extensively, including a book against heresies (*Refutation of all Heresies*), in which he quotes a version of Thom 4.

incipit: The first line of an ancient text, which in ancient times was used to identify the text. As such, it functioned as a kind of title.

James the Just: The name given by tradition to James the brother of Jesus (Mark 6:3; Matt 13:55). After the death of Jesus he became a leader in the Jerusalem-based Jesus movement and met with Paul on his first visit to Jerusalem (Gal. 1:19). He was probably martyred under the High Priest Ananus shortly before the fall of Jerusalem in 70 C.E. It is probably this James who is referred to in Jude 1:1 and regarded by the tradition as the author of the Epistle of James.

Jerome (ca. 347–420 C.E.): The famed translator of the Vulgate. In addition to this well-known legacy, he also wrote a number of commentaries, a tract against Pelagius, and a work called *De viris illustribus*, from which come many fragments of ancient gospels now lost.

Josephus (b. ca. 37 C.E.): An officer in the Jewish resistance forces which led the Jewish rebellion against Rome in 66–70 C.E. After the war, Josephus made his peace with the Romans, moved to Rome, and took up writing history. His two principal works, the *Jewish War* and the *Jewish Antiquities*, are the most important ancient historical sources for Jewish history during the period 200 B.C.E.–100 C.E.

Judas (the brother of Jesus): Judas is named as a brother of Jesus in Mark 6:3 and Matt 13:55 along with James, Joses and Simon. Judas (=Jude), "a servant of Jesus and brother of James" is named as the author of the Epistle of Jude. It is possible that these two figures are one and the same Judas, even though the Epistle of Jude demures from claiming the status of "brother" with respect to Jesus, opting instead for the deprecatory term "servant."

kerygma: A technical term of New Testament scholarship deriving from the Greek word for "preaching." It is used to refer to the earliest Christian preaching about Jesus. Most New Testament scholars agree that the gospels were profoundly influenced by the early Christian kerygma, and thus are more the product of early Christian preaching rather than a desire to preserve history.

logoi sophon: A Greek phrase meaning "sayings of the sages" or "words of the wise." The term also refers to a literary genre: a collection of wise words or wisdom sayings. Both Q and the Gospel of Thomas are collections of the "words of the wise," *logoi sophōn*.

Mani (ca. 216–276): The founder of Manichaeism, a Persian form of Gnosticism which flourished during Mani's lifetime and spread in succeeding years throughout the east, extending its influence as far as China by the seventh century C.E. Mani believed that the secrets of the universe had been revealed to him in a vision, and that he was called to share this knowledge as God's prophet.

Naasenes: A group of Gnostic Christians described by Hippolytus in *Ref.* 5.6.3–11.1 and 10.9.1–3. Their name derives from the Hebrew word for serpent, *nahash*, which is transliterated in Greek as *naas*.

Origen (ca. 185–253 C.E.): The successor to Clement of Alexandria as head of the famous school for catechumens in Alexandria, and later the founder of his own school in Caesarea in Palestine. He was the premier Christian scholar of the third century C.E. He wrote volumes, within which one finds many quotations of ancient documents now lost.

Oxyrhynchus: The site of an ancient village in upper Egypt (approximately 125 miles south of Cairo), which has been the source of numerous papyrological finds since the turn of the century. Among its most important treasures are POxy 1, 654, and 655, the three witnesses to the Greek version of the Gospel of Thomas.

paraenesis, also **parenesis**: A form of speech or composition the aim of which is to admonish, exhort, give advice or counsel.

parousia: Literally, "presence"; in the New Testament parousia refers to the arrival or coming of the expected one, the Son of Man, or the messiah (Jesus), who will sit in cosmic judgment at the end of history. It is thus commonly understood to mean "second coming," as distinguished from the first coming or advent of the messianic figure.

Philo (b. ca. 20 B.C.E.): A Jewish philosopher of Alexandria. His writings typically bring together Jewish traditions (especially Wisdom) with Hellenistic philosophy, employing an allegorical method of interpretation.

Pirke Aboth: A collection of wise sayings or maxims attributed to sixty-five named and other anonymous Jewish teachers (rabbis) who lived between about 300 B.C.E. and 200 C.E. *Aboth*, as it is sometimes also called, is one of sixty-three tractates of the Mishnah, which is itself a codification of the traditions of the Jewish elders. The title means "Chapters of the Fathers," but it is customarily referred to as "Sayings of the Fathers."

Pistis Sophia: A third-century C.E. Gnostic tractate in which the resurrected Jesus encounters the disciples and answers their questions. The motif of resurrection appearances, in which the risen Lord reveals new and marvelous information to the disciples is the basis of a popular genre of literature, the revelation discourse, used primarily in Gnostic circles.

POxy 1: Papyrus Oxyrhynchus 1, a fragment from a papyrus codex (or book), written in Greek, and to be dated at about 200 C.E. It is a single papyrus leaf inscribed on both sides. On one side fragments of Thomas 26, 27, 28, 29 and 30 are found, on the other side fragments of Thomas 77, 31, 32, and 33. It is from a copy of the Greek Gospel of Thomas that is distinct from POxy 654 or 655.

POxy 654: Papyrus Oxyrhynchus 654, a Greek papyrus fragment to be dated to the third century C.E. On one side is a land survey list, on the other are the Prologue and the first five sayings of the Gospel of Thomas. It was common for ancients to make use of the uninscribed side of an old document. The original document would have been a copy of the Greek Gospel of Thomas that is distinct from POxy 1 or 655.

POxy 655: Papyrus Oxyrhynchus 655, a series of eight small scraps from a Greek papyrus scroll to be dated to the mid-third century C.E. On these scraps are fragments of Thom 36, 37, 38, 39, and 40. Presumably the original scroll would have contained a copy of the Gospel of Thomas that is distinct from POxy 1 and 654.

pseudo-Clementine writings: A series of writings which purport to tell of the life and spiritual development of Clement of Rome, to whom tradition assigns the third position in the Petrine succession. They recount Clement's early life, and his eventual pilgrimage east to Judea, where he encounters Peter and is converted to Christianity by his preaching. In their present form, which probably derives from fourth-century C.E. Syria, they are organized into a series of "Recognitions" and "Homilies." But these are based on two earlier writings from out of the Petrine tradition: the Kerygmata Petrou and the Acts of Peter.

Q: The collection of Jesus' sayings used in the composition of Matthew and Luke. The authors of Matthew and Luke used this common source to fill out the basic outline provided to them by the Gospel of Mark. This early Christian sayings source did not survive antiquity, and thus must be reconstructed using the texts shared by Matthew and Luke. The designation Q does not derive from the document's original title, which is lost, but from the German word *Quelle*, which means simply "source."

redaction criticism: A method of investigation that seeks to isolate an evangelist's purpose and perspective by analyzing the way he handles material derived from sources. It is called redaction criticism because it focuses on an author's editorial or redactional techniques or proclivities as clues to his/her point of view.

sapiential: From Latin *sapientia*, "wisdom." Proverbs, Ecclesiastes, Sirach, Q are sapiential books.

Sirach: Ecclesiasticus or the Wisdom of Jesus son of Sirach is a book belonging to the so-called Old Testament apocrypha. It belongs, together with Proverbs, Ecclesiastes, and the Wisdom of Solomon, to the wisdom literature of the Hebrews. The book contains a large compendium of maxims and counsels related to virtually every aspect of life. Sirach originated in the second century B.C.E. It has been preserved in Greek, Syriac, and Hebrew versions.

Thomas the Contender: A book recounting a post-resurrection dialogue between Jesus and Judas Thomas. It is generally considered to be the work of Gnostic Christianity from the third century C.E. A copy of it survived antiquity in the Nag Hammadi library.

Index

Attridge, Harry, 121 nn. 1, 3
Augustine, 8
Bacon, B. W., 16, 26 n. 20
Bauer, Johannes, 118
Boring, M. Eugene, 22, 27 n. 44; 28
Bultmann, Rudolf, 14–15, 18–19, 20, 26 nn. 14, 31, 32, 33; 115, 116, 117
Bundy, W. E., 16, 26 n. 21
Burkitt, F. C., 16, 26 n. 21
Cameron, Ron, 124
Clement of Alexandria, 77, 89
Corley, Bruce, 122 n. 16
Crossan, J. Dominic, 28, 124
Cyril of Jerusalem, 77, 78
Davies, Stevan, 124
Dibelius, M., 13, 14, 18, 19, 26 n. 13
Dodd, C. H., 102, 122 n. 20
Doresse, Jean, 81
Eichorn, J. G., 9
Epiphanius, 77
Eusebius, 8, 12, 92
Fallon, F. T., 124
Freedman, David N., 125
Funk, Robert W., 124
Gieseler, J. K. L., 9
Grant, Robert M., 125
Grenfell, Bernard, 84, 121 n. 8, 125
Griessbach, J. J., 8
Grobel, Kendrick, 125
Guillaumont, A., 121 n. 7, 125
von Harnack, Adolf, 17, 18, 23, 26 n. 22, 27 n. 46
Haenchen, Ernst, 125
Havener, Ivan, 25 nn. 1, 2; 29
Hedrick, C. W., 122 n. 15, 123 n. 25
von Herder, J. G., 9
Hippocrates, 15
Hippolytus, 78, 121 n. 2
Hirsch, Emanuel, 16, 26 n. 21

Hodgson, Jr., R., 122 n. 15, 123 n. 25
Holtzmann, H. J., 9–10, 11–12, 15, 26 n. 16
Horman, J., 122 n. 13
Hunt, Arthur S., l84, 121 n. 8, 125
Jacobson, Arland, 24, 27 nn. 49, 52
Jeremias, Joachim, 118, 123 n. 28
Jerome, 77, 78
Josephus, 92
Jülicher, Adolf, 17, 26 n. 23
Kee, Howard C., 25 n. 3
Kelber, Werner, 22, 27 n. 45
Kloppenborg, John S., 23, 24, 25 n. 10; 26 nn. 18, 24, 25, 30, 34; 27 nn. 43, 48, 50; 28, 29, 105
Koester, Helmut, 21–22, 27 nn. 40, 42; 29, 88, 89–90, 91, 108, 121 n. 15, 122 n. 16, 125–26
Kümmel, W. G., 25 n. 3
Labib, Pahor, 82, 115
Lambdin, T. O., 126
Lantero, Erminie Huntress, 123 n. l26
Layton, Bentley, 121 n. 1, 122 n. 17, 126
Leipoldt, Johannes, 82
Lessing, G. E., 9
Lührmann, Dieter, 27 n. 51
Mack, Burton L., 29
Mani, 78
Manson, T. W., 17, 19, 23, 26 n. 27; 27 n. 46
al Masih, Yassah 'Abd, 121 n. 7, 125
McArthur, Harvey K., 126
Meyer, Marvin W., 126
Meyer, Paul, 27 n. 53
Montefiore, H. W., 126
Origen, 77, 78, 92, 121 n. 1
Overbeck, Franz, 14, 26 n. 12

Papias, 12–13
Patterson, Stephen J., 122 n. 14
Philo of Alexandria, 112
Piper, Ronald A., 29–30
Plato, 81
Polag, Athanasius, 23, 27 n. 47
Puech, Henri-Ch., 84–85, 121 n. 7, 121 n. 7, 125
Quispel, G., 121 n. 7, 125
Rehkopf, F., 12, 25 n. 5
Robinson, James M., 20–21, 27 n. 40; 30, 88, 104, 121 n. 4, 122 nn. 15, 19; 125–26
Rudolph, Kurt, 126
Schleiermacher, F., 9, 15, 26 n. 15
Schmid, Josef, 23, 27 n. 46
Schmidt, Karl Ludwig, 14, 25 n. 11
Schrage, Wolfgang, 86, 127
Schulz, Siegfried, 20, 26 nn. 38, 39; 27 n. 53
Schürmann, Heinz, 12, 25 n. 5
Smith, Louise P., 123 n. 26
Steck, O. H., 27 n. 52
Streeter, B. H., 12, 13, 17–18, 19, 25 n. 6; 26 nn. 26, 28, 29, 35
Taylor, V., 12, 25 nn. 4, 6
Theissen, Gerd, 106
Till, W. C., l125
Tödt, H. E., 19–20, 26 nn. 36, 37
Tyson, J. B., 12, 25 n. 5
van Unnik, W. C., 123 n. 29
Vaganay, L., 25 n. 8
Weiss, Bernard, 16, 26 nn. 17, 19
Weiss, Johannes, 3, 25 n.1
Wernle, Paul, 17
Wellhausen, Julius, 3, 17
Wikenhauser, Alfred, 25 n. 9
Wilson, R. McL., 118, 127

166